This book reassesses the love poetry of Maurice Scève from a phenomenological viewpoint. It calls into question the traditional critical view of Scève as a poet who laments the anguish and darkness of unrequited love, and whose poetic and erotic quests lead him nowhere, and argues instead that the conflicting forces in Scève's poetic expression of love (light and dark, night and day, heaven and hell) do ultimately lead him to a sense of equilibrium and a transcendent paradisal state. Contemplation and portrayal of the ineffable are shown to constitute the central and unifying concern of this compelling body of Renaissance love poetry.

Cambridge Studies in French

THE LOVE AESTHETICS
OF MAURICE SCEVE

Cambridge Studies in French

General editor: MALCOLM BOWIE

Recent titles in this series include

MICHAEL MORIARTY
Taste and Ideology in Seventeenth-Century France

JOHN FORRESTER
*The Seductions of Psychoanalysis: Freud,
Lacan and Derrida*

JEROME SCHWARTZ
*Irony and Ideology in Rabelais: Structures
of Subversion*

DAVID BAGULEY
Naturalist Fiction: The Entropic Vision

LESLIE HILL
Beckett's Fiction: In Different Words

F. W. LEAKEY
Baudelaire: Collected Essays, 1953–1988

SARAH KAY
Subjectivity in Troubadour Poetry

GILLIAN JONDORF
French Renaissance Tragedy: The Dramatic Word

LAWRENCE D. KRITZMAN
*The Rhetoric of Sexuality and the Literature
of the French Renaissance*

A complete list of books in the series will be found at the end of this volume.

THE LOVE AESTHETICS
OF MAURICE SCEVE

POETRY AND STRUGGLE

JERRY C. NASH

The right of the
University of Cambridge
to print and sell
all manner of books
was granted by
Henry VIII in 1534.
The University has printed
and published continuously
since 1584.

CAMBRIDGE UNIVERSITY PRESS

CAMBRIDGE

NEW YORK   PORT CHESTER

MELBOURNE   SYDNEY

Published by the Press Syndicate of the University of Cambridge
The Pitt Building, Trumpington Street, Cambridge CB2 1RP
40 West 20th Street, New York, NY 10011, USA
10 Stamford Road, Oakleigh, Melbourne 3166, Australia

First published 1991

Printed in Great Britain
at the University Press, Cambridge

British Library cataloguing in publication data
Nash, Jerry C.
The love aesthetics of Maurice Scève: poetry and
struggle. – (Cambridge studies in French).
1. Poetry in French. Scève, Maurice, ca. 1510–ca. 1560
2. Poetry in French.
1. Title
841.3

Library of Congress cataloguing in publication data
Nash, Jerry C.
The love aesthetics of Maurice Scève: poetry and struggle – Jerry
C. Nash
p.   cm. – (Cambridge studies in French)
Includes bibliographical references.
ISBN 0 521 39412 0
1. Scève, Maurice, 16th cent. – Criticism and interpretation.
2. Love poetry. French – History and criticism. I. Title.
II. Series.
PQ1705 S5Z84   1991
841′.3 – dc20   90–32228   CIP

ISBN 0 521 39412 0 hardback

GG

For Ian McFarlane,
who introduced so many of us to Scève,
and to the memory of Enzo Giudici.
Also, for J and B.

Love is the magician, the enchanter . . .
with it, earth is heaven.

Robert Ingersoll

To see a World in a Grain of Sand
And a Heaven in a Wild Flower,
Hold Infinity in the palm of your hand
And Eternity in an hour.
. . .
God appears and God is Light
To those poor Souls who dwell in Night
But does a Human Form Display
To those who Dwell in Realms of Day.

William Blake

Apperceuant cest Ange en forme humaine,
Qui aux plus fortz rauit le dur courage
Pour le porter au gracieux domaine
Du Paradis terrestre en son visage,
Ses beaulx yeulx clers par leur priué vsage
Me dorent tout de leurs rayz espanduz.

Maurice Scève

CONTENTS

PREFACE

My largely phenomenological approach to poetry and paradise as presented in this book has been molded, on the one hand, by an epistemological tradition concerned with the problem of expressing the ineffable in literature, a tradition to which, I believe, Maurice Scève rightfully belongs and that includes Aquinas, Artaud, Augustine, Baudelaire, Blake, Boccaccio, Dante, Donne, Flaubert, Mallarmé, Pascal, Petrarch, Plotinus, Proust, Shakespeare, Speroni, Valéry, as well as other writers; and, on the other hand, by a long tradition in critical reading which attempts to come to terms with the ineffable in literature and that includes, among others, such diverse critics as Yvonne Bellenger, Maud Bodkin, Wolfgang Iser, Julia Kristeva, and Philip Wheelwright. It is a pleasure to acknowledge my special debt not only to the above writers and critics but also to many others in this distinguished tradition as invaluable guides in my own pursuit of an ineffable meaning in Scève's poetic love masterpiece. These authors and critics will receive fuller mention in the pages that follow.

This book also owes much to the advice and encouragement of friends and colleagues. Most notably, I wish to thank Professor Donald Stone, Jr., Harvard University, and Professor John R. Williams, University of New Orleans, who took of their own time to read the text of this study at an early stage and to offer me many sound and helpful suggestions, and Professor Hope H. Glidden, Tulane University, who read the Epilogue. I also wish to acknowledge with gratitude the long-term encouragement and generosity of Professor Emeritus I. D. McFarlane, University of Oxford, who has always provided me needed clarification on Scève and on other Renaissance writers when I have turned to him over the past ten years. It is only fitting that I should, with pleasure, dedicate this book on Scève to him, as well as to the memory of another devoted and generous 'scéviste' without whose seminal work on Scève we would not be where we are today in Scève studies, the late Enzo

Giudici. In their dealings with me and the present book, Professor Malcolm Bowie and Dr. Katharina Brett, of Cambridge Studies in French/Cambridge University Press, have exhibited an exemplary level of professionalism and patience, and I am most grateful to them for their help and understanding.

I also wish to thank the University of New Orleans, through its faculty research funds, for providing me the released time that was necessary to research and write this study. A special word of thanks is also due my typist, Debra Berthelot, without whose cheerful and expert attention to detail this book would have been greatly delayed. Finally, I wish to acknowledge several earlier published pieces on Scève by me whose ideas have been greatly expanded in this book: "Stoicism and the Stoic Theme of *Honestum* in Early French Renaissance Literature," *Studies in Philology*, 76 (1979); "The Notion and Meaning of Art in the *Délie*," *The Romanic Review*, 71 (1980); "Logic and Lyric: Poetic Closure in Scève's *Délie*," *French Studies*, 38 (1984); "Maurice Scève, poète de l'ineffable," in *Lire Maurice Scève*, ed. Françoise Charpentier and Simone Perrier, 1987; and "Maurice Scève et la poésie paradisiaque," in *Il Rinascimento a Lione*, ed. Giulia Mastrangelo Latini and Antonio Possenti, 1988.

1

THE PROBLEM OF THE DARK SIDE OF A LOVE POET: AN INTRODUCTION AND REASSESSMENT

Ever since the publication of the *Délie* in 1544, Maurice Scève has been considered by many readers and critics to be the most difficult, anguished, and perplexing love poet of the French Renaissance. The purpose of this book is to question our understanding of this long-standing critical view, one that has always been for me problematic and unsatisfying, and to offer another interpretive possibility which has to do with poetry, struggle, and the pursuit of love's paradise. I intend to explore how Scève's love lyrics, largely perceived as dark and anguished, can be associated with a more positive poetic tradition whose primary feature of struggle always accompanies intense, diaphoric poetic creations of light and life so essential to a transcendent paradisal perspective. I shall argue that it is Scève's primary quest to come to terms with and portray the ineffable that constitutes the central and unifying concern of his love lyrics. This study runs counter to the prevailing critical view of Scève as a poet painfully preoccupied with the lamentation of unrequited love. It offers instead the view of Scève as a remarkable and persevering and successful poet of the ineffable intent on giving a more positive, higher meaning to the love experience and its expression. In the final analysis, this phenomenologically oriented reading of the *Délie* will seek to demonstrate that Scève's greater achievement is ultimately to be found in his poetics of ineffable love, not of lamented love.

These notions may appear at the outset perverse to some readers, since indeed, as I have indicated, posterity has quite often found it difficult if not impossible to give a favorable interpretation to the *Délie*, as we see especially in the more recent criticism of this work. If we continue to accept the current and prevailing interpretation

1

of Scève and his engaging body of Renaissance love poetry, then we would indeed have to continue to view him as the opposite of a paradisal poet: as the dark poet-lover exhibiting psychological confusion and even torment which translate in his lyrics into textual obscurity. This negative view has existed from Scève's own day to the present and has in large part conditioned the reader's response to the *Délie*. One of the earliest critics of Scève's poetry, the humanist Estienne Pasquier, helped to set the tone. He disliked the "obscure," "dark" symbolism of the *Délie* which, according to him, was written "avec un sens si *ténébreux* que, le lisant, je disois estre très content de ne l'entendre, puisqu'il ne vouloit estre entendu."[1] This early assessment of Scève's willful quest for darkness was carried over into contemporary criticism at the turn of this century by Ferdinand Brunetière and Gustave Lanson. Brunetière considered Scève just as "unreadable" as he thought the symbolist poets were of his day: "C'est un curieux poète que ce Scève *obscur* et prétentieux d'ailleurs, à peu près illisible aujourd'hui, et que pour ce motif je m'étonne que nos symbolistes et nos décadens n'aient pas essayé de le remettre un peu en honneur. . . . Ni M. Paul Verlaine, ni M. Stéphane Mallarmé n'ont rien écrit de plus difficile à interpréter, sinon précisément à comprendre, car j'ai peur de les avoir quelquefois compris."[2] Lanson's often-quoted assessment of Scève is similar: "Maurice Scève, compliqué, savant, singulier, *obscur* . . .".[3]

An impressive number of critics working today on the *Délie* have responded to it in the same terms: they see there primary thematic and structural patterns of overt complexity and obscurity which they in turn have tried to associate, unsuccessfully in my view, with a modernist aesthetic whose purpose it is to highlight psychological anguish and artistic crisis. Furthermore, they stress the tortured uncertainty and general hermetic strain underlying Scève's dark vision of love as well as its disorienting and disoriented articulation in his poetry. Among others, Michael J. Giordano speaks of *Délie*'s "ambiguous language, tortuous and involuted syntax and the poet-lover's fragmented perception" and also of "the narrator's own admission of verbal paralysis and his tendency to obfuscate the realities of painful dissonance."[4] In another very recent piece ("The Curing Text: Maurice Scève's Délie as the *Délie*"), Gregory de Rocher recognizes the fact that "the [*Délie*] holds fast to its reputation of proving difficult if not impenetrable to hosts of readers" (p. 10), and carries Scève's so-called verbal paralysis and painful dissonance to the point of mental neurosis and textual chaos in need of Lacanian–Freudian psychoanalysis, which he attempts to provide. He sets out to study "the concept of free-floating signifiers in the unconscious" (p. 10) and "the generation of meaning in terms of *the subject's 'neurotic tendencies'* " (p. 11).[5] The conclusion of yet another recent article seeking to uncover the "obscure" meaning of the *Délie* suggests that it has something to do with the mathematical solution of the double of the cubical altar of Apollo – that is, the cube root of two![6] And another reader of Scève reduces the meaning of the *Délie* to "le baratin d'amour": the obscure, incomprehensible, and in fact meaningless babble of a lover: "Ceci revient à dire . . . qu'il n'y a ni sens ni message à proprement parler (ni contenu ni forme, etc.) par ce baratin d'amour."[7] Finally, to conclude for now this overview of the critically perceived dark side of Scève, of his poetic obscurity and anguished experience in love, I wish to quote the following passage from such a devoted contemporary critic of Scève as Dorothy Gabe Coleman: "To Scève the important things are Délie and himself. There is only one theme, constantly renewed and contradictory and made up of approximations – love: the continual presence of Délie within the poet and more particularly in his memory (which is a leitmotif of the whole cycle), *the permanence of the torment* assured by her occupation of his whole being."[8] For Coleman too, the eternal suffering of human love, and especially of the existential condition of unrequited love, is what best defines the experience of Scève's poet in love.

In this introductory chapter, I propose to look further into the complicated matter of Scève's poetic anguish and obscurity. I wish to suggest that, far from representing the dark, final picture of psychological and artistic crisis which some have come to associate with a modernist aesthetic, these poetic qualities are purposefully and strategically and productively involved in the poet's ongoing struggle towards creating a different kind of love aesthetic that actually seeks to reconstruct order and harmony out of chaos. Scève's poetic undertaking in the *Délie* is a reconstructive one, not deconstructive. *Délie*'s poetic of struggle culminates in the triumph of *difficulté vaincue*. We shall analyze this difficult aesthetic progression by looking closely at the artistic meaning which Scève gives to the all-important revelatory concept of "virtue," one of the most frequently used words and concepts in the *Délie*. Our ultimate goal will be a reassessment of Scève's "dark" side and a better understanding and appreciation of what I see to be his other concern with defining and moving towards a transcendent paradisal state. The main points of the interpretive revision presented in this chapter will be developed more extensively in subsequent chapters of this book.

Clearly, this dark legacy and anguished side of Scève surveyed above are a formidable obstacle in the interpretive dilemma confronting students and readers of the *Délie*. As France's major Renaissance "metaphysical" poet,[9] Scève's reputation, like that of John Donne, has acquired a certain notoriety, and the poems of the *Délie* are often thought of and responded to as primarily and (in my view) as unnecessarily complicated and anguished. Stressing Scève's dark side in and of itself represents an inadequate and unfair reading of him. As his readers, we should keep in mind certain notions involved in Renaissance views of obscurity prevalent when Scève was composing his dizains. During the Renaissance, obscurity was thought of as a necessary artistic means to an end, not as the poetic end itself of artistic failure or crisis. Poetic obscurity was considered by many humanists an essential condition and prerequisite for literary creativity and excellence. In addition to having a writerly (creative) usefulness, obscurity was also viewed as having a readerly (interpretive) usefulness. Renaissance writers inclined towards obscurantism held that a reader who misunderstood their works had only himself to blame, or, as Du Bellay put it metaphorically, the latter preferred to eat acorns after the invention of wheat:

Quand à ceulx qui ne vouldroient recevoir ce genre d'escripre, qu'ilz appellent *obscur*, pource qu'il excede leur jugement, je les laisse avecq' ceulx qui, après l'invention du bled, vouloient encores vivre de glan. Je ne cherche point les applaudissemens populaires. Il me suffit pour tous lecteurs avoir un S. Gelays, un Heroët, un de Ronsart, un Carles, un Sceve . . .[10]

Du Bellay is echoing here the notion on obscurity as developed by Horace in *Carmina* (Book III, Ode 1) of the *odi profanum vulgus et arceo*. Scève will likewise support this view. As he tells us in D414 when he speaks of the solitary environment in which he must compose his "durs Epygrammes," he is more interested in pursuing the demanding and fulfilling potential of poetry and its "bien inuentif" than the "vil gaing" sought by the rest of the world: "Ce lieu sans paour, & sans sedition / S'escarte a soy, & son bien inuentif. / Aussi i'y vis loing de l'Ambition, / Et du sot Peuple au vil gaing intentif."[11]

Of much more importance to Renaissance poets, however, is

their belief that obscurity can play an even more useful role in the creation of a certain kind of poetry, as both classical and modern advocates of this view throughout time have recognized. What I have in mind can be seen by turning to the notion of obscurity as poetic principle so clearly and so fervently expounded by such seemingly diverse writers and theorists of poetry as Boccaccio and Valéry. In spite of their distance in time and literary canon, both of these geniuses share common ground on the crucial role of obscurity in poetry and they can enlighten us on this same problem in Scève.

In his widely read and extremely influential defense of poetry entitled *Genealogia deorum gentilium*, and especially in its Chapter 12 of Book XIV, "The Obscurity of Poetry is not Just Cause for Condemning It," Boccaccio shows readers how to understand better, and appreciate, poetic obscurity as used by a poet like Scève. In defense of obscurity in poetry, Boccaccio begins his essay:

These cavillers further object that poetry is often obscure, and that poets are to blame for it, since their end is to make an incomprehensible statement appear to be wrought with exquisite artistry. Perverse notion! . . . They should have realized that when things perfectly clear seem obscure, it is the beholder's fault. To a half-blind man, even when the sun is shining its brightest, the sky looks cloudy. Some things are naturally so profound that not without difficulty can the most exceptional keennesses in intellect sound their depths; like the sun's globe, by which before they can clearly discern it, strong eyes are sometimes repelled. . . . Yet not by this token is it fair to condemn them; for surely it is not one of the poet's various functions to rip up and lay bare the meaning which lies hidden in his inventions. Rather where matters truly solemn and memorable are too much exposed, it is his office by every effort to protect as well as he can and remove them from the gaze of the irreverent, that they cheapen not by too common familiarity.[12]

Boccaccio helps pave the way for Du Bellay's view of obscurity in poetry stated above. It is quite often the "irreverent" reader of this poetry who falls short of full and satisfying interpretation; the "profound" nature of some poetry requires its elaboration through an obscure poetic; truly "solemn and memorable" poetry must be protected and preserved through obscurity. There is, in other words, according to Boccaccio, a very legitimate and positive value in poetic obscurity which must be discerned and appreciated. This value must be sought after and properly understood by both poet and reader. As Boccaccio continues his discussion, we soon realize that this value really involves the reader-response as well as writerly process of *difficulté vaincue*, the creative and interpretive effort and struggle required for the proper response to the problematics of poetic obscurity. For Boccaccio, poetic truths can best be revealed only through the ongoing interpretive struggle in coming to terms with poetic obscurities:

Surely no one can believe that poets invidiously veil the truth with fiction, either to deprive the reader of the hidden sense, or to appear the more clever; but rather to make truths which would otherwise cheapen by exposure the object of strong intellectual effort and various interpretation, *that in ultimate discovery they shall be more precious*.   (p. 60)

Turning to quote Augustine in the *City of God* and his view on the obscurity of Holy Writ, Boccaccio elaborates on the purpose of this challenging principle of *difficulté vaincue*:

"The obscurity of the divine word has certainly this advantage, that it causes many opinions about the truth to be started and discussed, each reader seeing some fresh meaning in it. . . . There is nothing in it contradictory: somewhat there is which is obscure, not in order that it may be denied thee, but that it may exercise him that shall afterward receive it."
                                                                        (pp. 60–61)

And turning to Petrarch to support further his notion of the potential strategic value of obscurity in hermeneutics, Boccaccio similarly cites from the Third Book of his *Invectives*:

"Such majesty and dignity [found in poetic obscurities] are not intended to hinder those who wish to understand, but rather propose a delightful task, and are designed to enhance the reader's pleasure and support his memory. What we acquire with difficulty and keep with care is always the dearer to us."
                                                                        (pp. 61–62)

Surely these views of Boccaccio, and those of Augustine and Petrarch provided by Boccaccio, on poetic obscurity can enlighten us on this same question which is raised so acutely by Scève's poetry. These writers begin by deploring the ease and facility demanded by the reading public. For their part, they require a power of *resistance* in a body of great poetry, and the capacity in the reader to match the unique presence and firm design of this poetic resistance with corresponding virtues of patience, deliberate attention, and above all critical endurance. The very efficacy of such poetry depends on its challenge of obscurity and the positive process of interpretation and unraveling by the reader. Rather than being viewed negatively as the failure to attain a state of perfect clarity, obscurity in poetry should be likened to the fundamental obscurity found in the actual thought and creative process itself striving for intellectual and emotional unity in any complex experience, especially love. This unity quite often cannot be adequately measured or appreciated by the instruments of reason and logic. But if it seems to have no clear and rational meaning, this kind of poetic understanding derived from obscurity has the indescribable power to suggest *thought and feeling* working together towards the discovery, triumph, and insight of sustained, *unified* experience, of what Boccaccio calls quite simply the poetic triumph of "higher truth" (p. 62). One of the premises of this book is that Scève's own reader can attain some understanding of this higher truth Boccaccio speaks of if he is willing to pursue the difficult yet rewarding progression undertaken by our own poet in coming to successful terms with *Délie, obiect de plus haulte vertu*. As we shall see, Scève's ultimate triumph is to be found in this poet coming to an understanding and portrayal of the transcendent meaning implied especially in the second part of his work's title: both Délie the beloved object and *Délie* the love text viewed as *obiect de plus haulte vertu*.

Later on, does not Valéry also defend the "obscure" poetry of his symbolist colleague Mallarmé by praising the same notion of obscurity and its challenge of *difficulté vaincue*, which he specifically calls "résistances vaincues"? For Valéry, the most powerful quality of the poetry of Mallarmé, its magical formula of incantation, is derived precisely from what he considers its poetic of obscurity, its pursuit of a *via negativa*, as he believes all great poetry is. The "true glory" of Mallarmé's poetry is, as Valéry puts it,

plus fondée sur des différences et des *résistances vaincues* [Valéry's italics] que sur le consentement immédiat à quelque merveille et jouissance commune. . . . Cependant que cette œuvre sans pareille surprenait, à peine entr'ouverte . . . tout de suite elle embarrassait l'esprit, l'intriguait, le défiait parfois de comprendre. . . . Quant à moi, je le confesse, je ne saisis à peu près rien d'un livre qui ne me *résiste* pas.

Thus, for Valéry too, as for Boccaccio, a poetic of obscurity can have a positive, meaning-acquiring value for both poet and reader-interpreter. Textual resistance is what makes possible the triumph of *difficulté vaincue*; it is inseparable from the creative process and from critical reading. In a meaningful way, both poet and reader are involved in the same "diaphoric" challenge and struggle posed by textual resistance.[13]

Scève too shares these ideas on obscurity as poetic resistance and practices them to a high degree in his love lyrics. As with the "obscurity" of Mallarmé's poetry, that of the *Délie* should function, not negatively to thwart meaning, but positively to mobilize the reader and to effect in him a state of suspended judgment in his ongoing search for purpose and design, as it obviously did for Scève's poet: "Je me complais en si doulce bataille, / Qui sans resoudre, en *suspend* m'entretient" (D78). In fact, it can be said of Scève's love poetry in general that its poetic worth and power can be fully experienced and appreciated only through the intensity of its obscurity and anguish which challenges the reader to respond to the poet's own *résistances vaincues*. This highly resistant and challenging process of interpretation, as with the creation of the poetry it is devoted to explicating, is largely based on the diaphoric principle of the *via negativa* – often presented metaphorically and structurally in the *Délie* as having to go down in order to find one's way back up. This principle connecting the activity of the reader to that of the writer is ingeniously described for us in what I consider to be one of *Délie*'s most important and suggestive poems – D94. The "fall," struggle, and recovery of Love presented in D94 I see as emblematic of and pointing to the greater meaning of the *Délie* as a whole, of the struggle of great love poetry (and of its interpretation) to overcome the obscurity and obstacles standing in its way to higher definition and meaning:

> Si treslas fut d'enuironner le Monde
> Le Dieu volant, qu'en Mer il s'abysma:
> Mais retournant a chef de temps sur l'vnde,
> Sa Trousse print, & en fuste l'arma:
> De ses deux traictz deligemment rama,
> De l'arc fit l'arbre, & son bendeau tendit
> Aux ventz pour voille, & en Port descendit
> Tresioyeux d'estre arriué seurement.
> Ainsi Amour, perdu a nous, rendit
> *Vexation*, qui donne *entendement*.

As in so many of Scève's perplexing lyrics, this skillful narrative posits meaning only after it has worked its way through obscurity. Scève's concept of love and of love poetry involves the pursuit of an obscure, negative, and difficult path requiring the fullest exercise of the powers of the poet and the reader; furthermore, this undertaking has the potential of bringing about a far-reaching transformation of those powers. The creative tension resulting in the difficult yet successful poetic portrayal of D94, its process of *difficulté vaincue*, is what provides both an emotional and an intellectual enhancement. It occasions, in other words, a restructuring of the inner self – a poetically felt need which is both the source of the difficulty and the measure of the reward when the difficulty is finally surmounted. The paradox which Scève is developing in D94, and one which he will develop in other narratives and images in other poems, is the positive affirmation that insight and understanding can and often must come from a negative and seemingly hopeless perspective. Scève is also telling us here that life and art require some power of resistance, some opposition, some incomprehensibility which can serve as an impetus to call forth our energies and save us from boredom and a life of routine existence. Scève's poet is the creator of a world in which what eludes and even baffles us in the real world is seized and bent to his creative will. One does not ordinarily live in the diaphoric realization (as presented in D94) that life comes out of death, joy out of sorrow, light out of dark, up out of down, or the recovery of Love out of the loss of Love. But to envision in the narrative and imagery of a poem the dissolution that is the prelude to new and greater life, indeed to welcome and bring it about through the individual, strenuous effort requiring ingenuity, development, and fulfillment (which is what I take to be the meaning of the first stanza above culminating in Love's safe and joyful arrival at Port), is to rise above our common level of feeling and understanding and to pursue the diaphoric direction of difficult beauty and art. In the conclusion of D94 ("Ainsi Amour, perdu a nous, rendit / Vexation, qui donne entendement"), the poet is telling us that some experiences in life and in art, such as love, often require us to confront and respond to complexities not wholly familiar and easy for us to assimilate and comprehend. In the end, however, the triumph of insight and understanding can be had from an aesthetic response which develops enlargement of mind, change of habits and perspective, and travail of spirit. It is the spiritual euphoria and enlightenment that can arise out of "vexation" and culminate in "entendement" that Scève is clearly alluding to in D94. This poem enacts Love's recovery from the sea, which is highly charged with symbolic significance involving cleansing, restructuring, struggle, and renewal. The down-and-out direction Love is forced to take in D94 becomes part of an allegory of spiritual quest for a transcendent state, an idea this study intends to develop more fully in its interpretation of the *Délie*. This poem forcefully and dramatically presents a difficult situation translated through reconstructive language and meaning,

9

with a premium being placed on human action and struggle; the result is the poetic triumph over difficulty. The affective quality of a futile world and existence is being invoked as descent and death ("Si treslas fut d'enuironner le Monde / Le Dieu volant, qu'en Mer il s'abysma"), but, through struggle ("Mais retournant a chef de temps sur l'vnde, / Sa Trousse print, & en fuste l'arma: / De ses deux traictz deligemment rama, / De l'arc fit l'arbre, & son bendeau tendit / Aux ventz pour voille . . ."), recovery and insight are what are brought forth ("& en Port descendit / Tresioyeux d'estre arriué seurement. / Ainsi Amour, perdu a nous, rendit / Vexation, qui donne entendement"). Dualism or tension is being resolved in language and imagery. The poet's definition of reality as a challenge or struggle requiring a restructuring of self and world in the present and luminous – in *entendement* – is a sure and ultimate denial to obscurity and anguish as having a final role to play in the poet's quest. These resistances do, of course, function meaningfully in a metaphoric way to propel the poet towards that very "entendement."

One could indeed argue that the higher emotive quality and illumination which Scève sought and achieved in his lyrics, the poet's pursuit of an intense *entendement*, could only spring from an initially obscure and anguished poetic impulse. In wishing to distance himself aesthetically from other love poets, Scève attempts to rid his poetic treatment of love of what he calls the "veue coustumiere" – of superficiality, facility, the ordinary. He scrupulously avoids a language that might trivialize intellectual and emotive content. Rather he seeks to dignify his poetry by making it capable of expressing a higher and more exclusive meaning and purpose. To this end, poetic discourse through "tensive ambiguities" (Wheelwright, *Metaphor and Reality*, p. 46) such as the resistant constructs of obscurity and anguish can serve a very useful purpose. Thematically and artistically, the most heightened emotive sense of poetic and psychological luminosity in Scève's poems (of *entendement*) is often best achieved when he constructs this luminosity through the tensive, aesthetic ambiguity afforded by chiaroscuro: light which is made more visible, more radiant, more meaningful by darkness and obscurity setting it off. The poet's perception of this central paradox of light in darkness – of the possibility of obtaining clarity from darkness and thus of light triumphant over darkness – goes to the very heart of Scève's poetic endeavor, as we shall see more fully in Chapters 4 and 5 of this book. This aesthetic paradox is beautifully modulated in his apostrophe to Light in D24 and is another good indication of Scève's continual concern with developing the art of *difficulté vaincue*. The darkness and obscurity of the poet's blurred vision presented in this poem play a very meaningful role. Developing Boccaccio's linking of profoundness of subject matter with an *initial* obscurity of vision, a notion Boccaccio presented imagistically as human eyes which are first repelled by the brightness of light before they can clearly discern it, Scève similarly begins D24:

> Quand l'œil aux champs est d'esclairs esblouy,
> Luy semble nuict quelque part, qu'il regarde:
> Puis peu a peu de clarté resiouy,
> Des soubdains feuz du Ciel se contregarde.
> Mais moy conduict dessoubs la sauuegarde
> De ceste tienne, & *vnique lumiere*,
> Qui m'offusca ma lyesse premiere
> Par tes doulx rayz aiguement suyuiz,
> Ne me pers plus en veue coustumiere.
> Car seulement pour t'adorer ie vis.

The poet's initial condition of painful and obscured vision clearly represents for him an *interim* state, both psychological and artistic, through which he must often progress ("Qui m'offusca ma lyesse *premiere* / Par tes doulx rayz *aiguement* suyuiz") in order to reach a higher and more secure state of privileged clarity and lucidity afforded by Délie. And having had access to this "exceptional light," the poet will settle for nothing less. That is, Scève's obscurity, from which his thought and images rise, is but the foundation or starting point of a poetic ambition which seeks understanding and expression of the ineffable and the uncommon ("De ceste tienne, & vnique lumiere") in and *through* the obscure, and thus the importance of diaphoric portrayal in his poetry. The subjectivity and exclusivity of this highly refined and quintessential art are bound to be associated with darkness and obscurity. One may rightly say that Scève is "obscure," "difficult," "impenetrable," and so forth, but with a highly metaphorical purpose: he desired to go (and to take the reader) beyond the "veue coustumiere" to seek a higher and more original, emotionally and intellectually an intensely more luminous, level of meaning: "Ne me pers plus en veue coustumiere."

Coming early in the sequence, D24 reveals to us this higher implication of obscurity and also something significant about the higher meaning of darkness in Scève's poetic world, a meaning we will see him expand throughout this study. This poem does give the reader

11

a clue to the purpose of gloom (of *vexation*) in Scève's work. Given his desire to pursue the complexities of human love, the poet can afford to wander in safety along the dark paths of human confusion and anguish because he has a fixed and unique light – that provided by Délie – to guide him. In the end, the psychological and aesthetic balance will be righted. Délie as "vnique lumiere" and "obiect de plus haulte vertu" will, in the final analysis, exert upon the poet a correcting influence. Délie will bring forth in him a clarity not only of mind but also of art. Early in his poetic sequence in this D24, Scève is also showing us something that will become even more apparent to the reader as he progresses in the *Délie*: namely, that as a great love poet Scève does not present a commonly understood view of love instantly accessible to the reader, but rather is consumed by and intent on relating a *unique* experience of love – a love transformed into a kind of religion in which a genuinely individual and personal grasp of things is expressed. For me, there is no other adequate way of explaining the uniquely felt, religious intensity and adoration evoked in this poem ("Car seulement pour t'adorer ie vis"), as in so many others we will be looking at.

To be sure, Scève is not completely unique in his diaphoric search for higher meaning gained through poetic obscurity. Certain poets in any period may feel the need to adjust their art to the changing depths of poetic thought, feeling, and intensity. Later the symbolists saw that the essence of their art lay in making poetry still more individualized, metaphorical, and suggestive of new moods. And the same has to be said for Scève, up to a reasonable point, as has been said for Mallarmé and other symbolist poets: difficulty is indeed a general critical problem.[14] However, no real purpose is served in our efforts to advance the intelligibility and aesthetics of Scève's love poetry by continuing to identify and to stress imaginary difficulties, both textual and psychological. To continue to view Scève's poetic obscurity and anguish as primary features in themselves and, in modernist terms, especially as representative of the crisis of representation itself will not take us, or Scève's poetry, very far. If, as some critics still believe today, we accept the twofold principle that the purpose of literary criticism is to make some positive sense out of a literary text and that one of the primary purposes of Renaissance writing is to strive for certainty and reassurance even amid the literary perception and portrayal of uncertainty and chaos, then it is obvious that Scève studies have not gone far enough.[15] Far enough, that is, in identifying and fully appreciating the very real positive note – textually the sense of poetic certainty and illumination, and psychologically the sense of positive and satisfying awareness – which Scève strove for and ultimately achieved in his love lyrics.

I do not wish to be misunderstood on this point. It is not my intention to underemphasize the fact that difficulty and anguish not only surface in Scève's poetry, but at times appear to be its primary characteristics. *Délie* is indeed full of chaos, of the thematic, resistant presence of obscurity and anguish, as D45 painfully shows us:

> Ma face, angoisse a quiconques la voit,
> Eust a pitié esmeue la Scythie:
> Ou la tendresse, en soy que celle auoit,
> S'est soubz le froit de durté amortie.
> Quelle du mal sera donc la sortie,
> Si ainsi foible est d'elle l'asseurance?
> Auec le front serenant l'esperance,
> l'asseure l'Ame, & le Cœur obligez,
> Me promettant, au moins, pour deliurance
> La Mort, seul bien des tristes affligez.

But of much greater significance and prominence than the picture of chaos, obscurity, and anguish in the *Délie* is this love poet's response to chaos. As Scève's readers, we should not continue to overlook the fact that our poet is continually looking for a way out of his "mal," for satisfying answers to the very agonizing questions raised by the love experience, as he does in this most anguished of all his poems: "Quelle du mal sera donc la *sortie*?" This study will concentrate on some of the poet's "exits," his responses to anguish and obscurity. It will attempt to place the perplexing intricacies of the *Délie* in a new and fresh perspective, to show how the darker side of Scève, his "moments d'angoisse" which have attracted so much critical attention lately, ultimately yields aesthetically, through intense poetic struggle and perseverance, to more significant, privileged moments of amorous certainty and even ecstasy. For my part, this other side of Scève, which has far too long been underrated, is by far the more meaningful of the two sides of this love poet.

Stated in paradisal terms, D157 forms a stark and welcome contrast to the despair and anguish displayed above in D45 and is a good indication of the side of Scève this study is interested in pursuing:

> Me rauissant ta *diuine harmonie*
> Souuentesfois iusques aux Cieulx me tire:

Dont transporté de si doulce manye,
Le Corps tressue en si plaisant martyre,
Que plus i'escoute, & plus a soy m'attire
D'vn tel concent la *delectation*.

Here the poet, I believe, provides us an answer to the agonizing question he raises above in D45. It is Délie's (and also *Délie*'s) "diuine harmonie," or at least the poet ever working towards understanding and portraying it, that will provide him the "exit" from anguish and obscurity – and not only the way out, but also the way up, the way towards "d'vn tel concent la *delectation*." (Chapter 3 will develop these claims.) While a number of critics have been forced to conclude that certain difficult and frustrating dizains of the *Délie* provide them no satisfying answers to the questions they raise, that is not really the point. Scève's poems did provide the poet satisfying answers. Scève did not view textual obscurity and psychological anguish as final stops or ends in themselves, and neither should we as his readers. D256 and D423, among many others, clearly support and justify this position of not viewing obscurity and anguish as primary and final features of Scève's poetic intention and execution. Scève desired above all else the enlightenment and euphoria of *entendement*, and struggled to progress towards it from the obscurity and anguish of *vexation*. In my view, he succeeded admirably.

In D256, the reader is confidently told by the poet that in spite of the seemingly endless nature of his sorrow and despair, there is the possibility of a change and reversal. That is, perhaps every sadness is but a prelude to a new-found joy:

> Poure de ioye, & riche de douleur
> On me peult veoir tous les iours augmentant:
> Augmentant, dy ie, en cest heureux malheur,
> Qui va tousiours mon espoir alentant.
> Et de mon pire ainsi me contentant,
> Que l'esperance a l'heure plus me fasche,
> Quand plus au but de mon bien elle tasche.
> Dont n'est plaisir, ny doulx concent, que i'oye,
> Qui ne m'ennuye, encores que ie sache
> *Toute tristesse estre veille de ioye*.

And in D423, the poet reassures the reader as well as himself that his inner struggle and debate between sorrow and joy *will* be resolved in favor of the latter, that coming to terms with despair and sorrow in his poetry will produce the therapeutic reward for him of being led from despair to joy:

> Respect du lieu, soulacieux esbat,
> A toute vie austerement humaine,
> Nourrit en moy l'intrinseque debat,
> *Qui de douleur a ioye me pourmeine.*

In other poems concerned with finding an "exit" from his "mal," as the poet first presented his intention back in D45 ("Quelle du mal sera donc la sortie?"), he is even more determined and confident of finding this release: "Ie *sortiray* de l'obscure nuisance, / Ou me tient clos cest enfant inhumain" (D169). To achieve this poetic triumph over difficulty, over obscurity and anguish, the poet often shows us, through a dramatic handling of imagery, that he will escape, as he sees it, from "the night of [his] dark thought": "De mon cler iour ie sens l'Aulbe approcher, / Fuyant la nuict de ma pensée obscure" (D266). He will break through and triumph over the troubling bondage of his anguished condition colored by obscurity and uncertainty. This longed-for triumph is beautifully and confidently revealed to the reader once again in the little drama and narrative being unfolded imagistically in D365:

> La Lune au plein par sa clarté puissante
> Rompt l'espaisseur de l'obscurité trouble,
> Qui de la nuict, & l'horreur herissante,
> Et la paour pasle ensemble nous redouble:
> Les desuoyez alors met hors de trouble,
> Ou l'incertain des tenebres les guide.

The poet's depiction of the struggle for release and recovery in this poem is further illustration of a central and simple theme in Scève which we first saw in his portrayal of Love's recovery from the sea in D94: the regaining of meaning and luminosity ("entendement") from darkness and obscurity ("vexation"). All the above poems show concretely that the poet's seemingly inescapable condition of anguish and obscurity is not only his structure but, more important, his possibility. Human as well as poetic potential, meaning, and insight come only by going through the thickness of finite existence (through "l'espaisseur de l'obscurité trouble" as the poet says above in D365) and never by escaping from it. For both Scève's love and his art, this drama *is* the meaning of *difficulté vaincue*. It is also the hermeneutic principle the serious reader must keep in mind in his own struggle to come to terms with Scève's love poetry.

Boccaccio's conclusion to the chapter which we considered earlier at some length makes it clear that an initial stage of poetic obscurity is important and even essential not only to the writing of great poetry, but also to our interpretation of it. Obscurity does have the potential of generating higher understanding and meaning in both author and reader – that is, if both are willing to confront the difficult yet always rewarding and illuminating challenge of a higher kind of poetic intention and art:

But I repeat my advice to those who would appreciate poetry, and unwind its difficult involutions. You must read, you must persevere, you must sit up nights, you must inquire, and exert the utmost power of your mind. If one way does not lead to the desired meaning, take another; if obstacles arise, then still another; until, if your strength holds out, you will find that *clear* which at first looked dark. (p. 62)[16]

Those instances of textual resistance, of seemingly unresolved and unresolvable tension in Scève's poems – fully recognized by Scève, as we saw in D78 when the poet says: "Je me complais en si *doulce bataille*, / Qui sans resouldre, *en suspend* m'entretient" – should function as a stratagem to mobilize the reader and engage him in an ongoing search for the unity and harmony of certain privileged moments, as I submit they did for Scève the poet. These moments beyond the problematics of obscurity and anguish will bear the marks of sacred and transcendent invention; they will fulfill the role of imaginative enhancement and the probing of reality associated with it. If nothing else, D256 and D423, as well as the other poems just looked at concerned with finding a release from obscurity and anguish, make it clear that there is a process or pattern of development being unfolded in the *Délie*, if not always from the problem to the answer, then at least from the testing of a hypothesis to its results, and then on to yet another hypothesis. For Scève knew, or thought he knew, what the ineffable or sacred is, and where it is to be found. His problem became that of all inspired writers: how adequately and truly to portray this "vertu" and "infinité" of Délie, as the poet tells us in D23 and D166:

> Seule raison, de la Nature loy,
> T'à de chascun l'affection acquise.
> Car ta *vertu* de trop meilleur alloy,
> Qu'Or monnoyé, ny aultre chose exquise,
> Te veult du Ciel (Ô tard) estre requise,
> Tant approchante est des Dieux ta coustume.
> Doncques en vain trauailleroit ma plume

Pour t'entailler a perpetuité. (D23)

Tout jugement de celle *infinité*,
Ou tout concept se trouue superflus,
Et tout aigu de perspicuité
Ne pourroyent ioindre au sommet de son plus. (D166)

In the poet's intense struggle towards capturing the sacred and ineffable meaning of love, and the supreme contentment and feeling of paradise that come with it, the drama of poetic creation (and of critical reading) is enacted and acquires a strong aesthetic function. Along the way, the poet is forced to come to terms with difficulty and ambiguities which he (and the reader) must puzzle over. Hence the presence of paradoxically strained metaphors, non sequiturs, no-exit situations, multiple semantic possibilities, and so forth. Though they seem to have a primarily disordering and disillusioning purpose or effect, these textual resistances are actually being used to move the poet and the reader towards the processing and affirmation of higher meaning. Scève does construct a dialectic of love, but one which is always reaching towards completion and synthesis, towards the poetic triumph over difficulty. To be sure, this completion and synthesis cannot be achieved without the consideration of an obscure poetic – of contrast, opposition, negation. Negativity is the gap and the tension between the poet and his higher goal, and the reason for their relation and reconciliation. Negativity is the motivating force of differentiation and integration. In this display of polarity, of antithesis and synthesis, negativity, chaos, and death eventually become a symbolization of the genesis of life itself, poetic as well as spiritual. Scève's treatment of chaos, disorder, and death points to the possibility of reversal; his vision of development is obstinately forward – onward and upward. This whole strategy of moving strenuously through obscurity towards a sacred and ineffable understanding of Délie's "vertu" and "infinité" cannot have been less than deliberate.

Since it is method or process, I believe, and not the ultimate revelation of the ineffable that is always in question in Scève's poems, there is indeed a dialectic in these poems between form and fragmentation, between self-satisfying order and chaos. This dialectic is, paradoxically, the necessary condition for the establishment of order and the ultimate capturing of the ineffable:

Suyuant celuy, qui pour l'honneur se iecte,
Ou pour le gaing, au peril dangereux,
Ie te rendy ma liberté subiecte,

Pour l'affranchir en viure plus heureux.
Apres le sault ie m'estonnay paoureux
Du grand *Chaos* de si haulte entreprise.   (D103)

Scève's desire to experience sacred and ineffable meaning does
have its origins in chaos and its undeniable unity with love and
poetry. Finding that "viure plus heureux" the poet longs for
requires that he come to some satisfying, acceptable terms with the
"grand Chaos" or disorder of such a high undertaking. That chaos
is the beginning of being and of art is a paradox as ancient as the
universe: the foundation of all order is disorder. It must be empha-
sized that chaos as Scève construed it is not finally something nega-
tive; rather it is the source of all form and substance, containing a
potential harmony of its own, perceptible to a poet like Scève who
contemplates it creatively. Quite often, in pondering this chaos, this
beautiful confusion at the heart of the poet's "heureux malheur"
(D256) and which is always the initial stage in his ineffable quest,
Scève is forced to cancel the progression and laws of rational
thought and accept the fact that contradictions and paradoxes are
often useful for the understanding and creation of higher truths.
This does, of course, make at times for difficult unity:

> D'elle puis dire, & ce sans rien mentir,
> Qu'ell' à en soy, ie ne scay quoy de beau,
> Qui remplit l'œil, & qui se fait sentir
> Au fond du cœur par vn desir noueau,
> Troublant a tous le sens, & le cerueau,
> Voire & *qui l'ordre a la raison efface.*
> Et tant plus plaict, que si attrayant face
> Pour esmouuoir ce grand Censeur Romain,
> Nuyre ne peult a chose qu'elle face,
> Seure viuant de tout oultrage humain.   (D410)

Délie's ineffable beauty, as the poet puts it her "ie ne scay quoy de
beau," appears to go beyond the rational powers of the poet to
contemplate and understand. It "troubles" his mind and intelli-
gence. This beauty even removes "order" from the poet's faculty
of "reason." Yet, for all these negative aspects depicted in D410,
Délie's beauty, the poet concludes, does not truly intend him any
harm. Indeed, it may just become his protection or therapy against
human injury and sorrow ("Nuyre ne peult a chose qu'elle face, /
Seure viuant de tout oultrage humain").

From the interpreter's side, this dialectic of the ineffable – its
having a negative yet potentially positive effect on the poet, this "ie

ne scay quoy de beau" of Délie that baffles and frustrates the poet
yet compels him to keep searching for its higher meaning – or at
least the reader's own attempts at working it out, greatly accounts
for the drama of reading Scève. Apart from its aesthetic effective-
ness, the dialectical discourse Scève is forced to create and think
through, the poet's recommencing of thought and interpretive per-
severance, pervades and orders the *Délie* as a whole by giving it a
definite sense of direction and by putting a premium on ongoing
interpretation. This discourse of dialectical resistance entices and
compels the reader to keep searching, along with the poet, for an
ultimately higher insight and meaning to love:

> A mon instinct ie laisse conceuoir
> Vn doulx souhait, qui, non encor bien né,
> Est de plaisirs nourry, & gouuerné,
> Se paissant puis *de chose plus haultaine*.   (D33)

> Quiconques fut ce Dieu, qui m'enseigna
> Celle raison, qui d'elle me reuoque,
> D'un trop grand bien, certes, il me daingna:
> Pource qu'*a mieulx* ma voulenté prouoque.   (D40)

> La roue en fin le fer assubtilie,
> Et le rend apte a trancher la durté.
> Aduersité qui l'orgueil humilie,
> Au cœur gentil de passion hurté
> Fait mespriser fortune, & malheurté,
> Le reseruant *a plus seconde chose*.   (D402)

These references by the poet to "chose plus haultaine," "mieulx,"
and "plus seconde chose" (like the very sub-title of his poetic
sequence: "obiect de plus haulte vertu"), reaffirm Scève's belief in
the ability of thought and of art to come to meaningful terms with
disorder and ultimately to reveal the sacred order of the ineffable.
This higher illumination of experience which these references point
to becomes the real objective of our love poet's "loyal persister" in
his "tant saincte amytie" (D346). They also point to his awareness
of the human need to give to the soul a higher principle that will
enable him to transcend his psychological dilemma of despair and
anguish. These references indicate direction; they announce
Scève's greater attempt at translating and processing personal
experience, including anguish and obscurity, through the virtue of
poetic art into universal terms and releasing into his poetry the
permanent and perfected essence of that experience. Scève is, fi-
nally, a poet who finds vision by asking questions and surmounting

obstacles. His mind inquires and his imagination answers. His imagination supplies his poems with images and metaphors through which these poems begin to reveal order. In the next chapter, we will look more closely at this dialectical discourse which concerns itself with discovering order and withstanding chaos, an aesthetic order which Scève's poems both create and impose. In this chapter, I have been more interested in exploring Scève's desire for purpose, for a reassurance without which a poet's quest of the ineffable cannot continue. I have been attempting to highlight Scève's steadfast determination to come to terms with the poetic ineffable, the object of his love art. Scève's desire or purpose is both serious and severe; it is disciplined and obstinate – "si *durs* Epygrammes" as the poet calls his work in *Délie*'s introductory poem. Given the high objective the poet sets for himself, there can be no easy answers for him in attaining it. Scève's difficult artistic process involves asking and defining, reasking and redefining, which at times does seem to lead only to emotional and mental confusion, and even anguish. However, without the tentative formulations and provisional answers, even the inconclusive or negative ones, there would be no movement towards final insight into the poetic ineffable, into "chose plus haultaine."[17]

What this initial discussion and reassessment of Scève's "dark" side can lead us to is a new understanding of the important concept of virtue, of the primary meaning and role of *poetic* virtue as it emerges in the *Délie*. Though Scève has received a lot of critical attention in the past few decades, none of his readers has paid much attention to that quality which I consider to be *Délie*'s most obvious and most powerful as well as most endearing: Scève's preoccupation with virtue, *Délie*'s *poetic* virtue that is. Metaphorically, Scève's unresolved "sweet battle" with both himself and his text, as specifically presented above in D78: "Ie me complais en si doulce bataille, / Qui sans resouldre, en suspend m'entretient" and which is implied in all the other poems we have considered thus far in this chapter, is a prerequisite state of mind and art for higher accomplishment and satisfaction, for ultimately defining Délie the beloved and *Délie* the love text as "obiect de plus haulte *vertu*." And for Scève, as for other Renaissance love poets and emblematists, virtue is as much a difficult and challenging intellectual, pyschological, and aesthetic concept and process as it is a moral one – the persistent and glorious struggle of *difficulté vaincue*. A closer look at and reassessment of the important meaning of "vertu" in the *Délie* can shed additional light on Scève's "dark" side as well as further demonstrate his aesthetic commitment to *difficulté vaincue*. Indeed, in the *Délie*, virtue can be viewed as a metaphor for the artistic struggle and process of *difficulté/résistance vaincues*. The latter's meaning is encapsulated in *vertu*. Virtue's specific role in poetic production is summed up succinctly and nicely by the English contemporary of Scève, Alexander Barclay:

> I man confirme, augment and edefy
> With honor, laude, and knowledge of science,
> And to express my might in briefe sentence,
> None may here win but by my succour,
> Laude, fame ne health, riches nor honour.[18]

In spite of his momentary dark detours, Scève too is confident of the ultimate benefits, both psychological and literary, to be enjoyed from his sustained efforts at representing this poetic virtue. The uplifting expansion and higher definition of mind, soul, and poetic art which the "virtue" of Délie/*Délie* brings about for the poet are a continual source of pleasure and creative renewal for him. The pursuit of this virtue is what will shape and enlarge his mental faculties ("Agrandissant mes espritz faictz petitz") and what will ultimately bestow poetic immortality ("la renommée") upon both Délie and the poet:

> Par ce hault bien, qui des Cieulx plut sur toy,
> Tu m'excitas du sommeil de paresse:
> Et par celuy qu'ores ie ramentoy,
> Tu m'endormis en mortelle destresse.
> Luy seul a viure euidemment m'adresse,
> Et toy ma vie a mort as consommée.
> Mais (si tu veulx) *vertu* en toy nommée,
> *Agrandissant mes espritz faictz petitz*,
> De toy, & moy fera la renommée
> Oultrepasser & Ganges, & Bethys.   (D90)

In fact, I believe it can be rightly claimed that Scève's principal preoccupation and truly his poetic obsession are to be found in his coming to successful terms with virtue, another indication of the great importance he places on the aesthetic process of *difficulté vaincue*.[19] As a *mot-révélateur* appearing forty-seven times in the sequence and highlighted in its sub-title, "vertu" is obviously a key concept on which the overall interpretation of Scève's poetry depends. Its aesthetic and artistic implications have generally been overlooked or at least slighted in favor of a Neoplatonic or moral thesis.[20] However, the aesthetic meaning of virtue which posits the vigorous mental power of the poet and the sustained creative force and activity of that power can no longer be underestimated. This power and force of *vertu* not only pervade and bestow always a higher meaning upon Scève's love poems, but also connect the *Délie* to Scève's other major poetic work, the *Microcosme*. The affinity between these two works is much greater than has been allowed by critics in that both deal with Scève's attempt, through *vertu*, to come to terms with the difficult Renaissance concept of *dignitas hominis*.[21]

Scève develops in both his love poetry and his philosophical poetry the central theme of man's dignity, his *vertu* as Scève puts it. The definition that Scève gives to this "virtue" is precisely that creative curiosity and drive without which artistic achievement and success would be impossible. What most characterizes the human condition for Scève is the power of the human mind and its struggle to understand and to create, even when confronted by seemingly hopeless odds. The virtue of artistic struggle is even praised by Scève as an ideal in itself, regardless of outcome. He announces this theme at the very beginning of the *Microcosme*, in the second stanza of the "Au lecteur":

> Ce *tems perdu* peut aux plus esbahis
> Gaigner encor son merite, et acquerre
> Son loyer deu, que mieux peuvent conquerre
> *Veille, et labeur* d'oisiveté haïs.[22]

Virtue is used specifically in other parts of the *Microcosme* to emphasize the struggle involved in attaining higher meaning. Scève is clearly describing here and revealing to the reader the great importance of the aesthetic of *difficulté vaincue*, of continually going beyond what he again calls "vexation" and "adversité" to reach a higher and more significant "entendement," as we first saw this idea in D94 at the beginning of this chapter:

> Lors l'homme humilié en sa peine, et sa faute
> Se r'assure eslevant sa pensée plus haute
> Par la *vexation*, qui luy eveille un soin
> De pourvoir diligent à son futur besoin.
> Son Genie meilleur pour sa garde ordonné
> Le voyant hors de soy tristement estonné
> En le heurtant luy dit: Où est celle *vertu*,
> Que forcer tu devrois de l'urgence abbatu?
> Si quelque chose encor te reste du pouvoir,
> Que divin je t'ay veu, et que tu peux avoir,

Icy employer faut tout ton virile effort:
Contre *l'adversité* se prouve l'homme fort.   (I, 441–52)

Even when the results of coming to terms with and capturing poetic *vertu* may not immediately seem rewarding,

Ceste experimentant quelquefois se deçoit
De curieux desir toujours insatiable,
Et en invention subtile esmerveillable.   (II, 88–90)

Scève always upholds its intrinsically therapeutic and aesthetic value and higher purpose:

L'Homme se renforçant en son genre renforce
Son audace, et son cœur en sa virile force.   (II, 107–08)

In these examples from the *Microcosme*, Scève is stating his firm belief in the therapeutic value of artistic struggle and creativity. As evidenced also in the *Délie* by its continual and conscious juxtaposition with such expressions as "Par l'estonné de l'esbayssement" (D369), "Ie me deçoy trop vouluntairement" (D38), and "Qui mon certain à ainsi debatu" (D167), the poetic commitment to *difficulté vaincue* required by the *vertu*-concept represents his only means of coping with the elusive and thwarting aspects of a higher love which the poet has not been able to understand and control. Scève's struggle is a poet's continual struggle for understanding and insight, for poetic *vertu*:

> *Viuacité en sa ieunesse absconce,*
> *Docile esprit, obiect de la Vertu,*
> L'oracle fut sans doubteuse response,
> Qui mon certain à ainsi debatu,
> Qu'apres auoir constamment combatu,
> Ce mien trauail iamais ne cessera.
> Donc aultre Troye en moy commencera
> Sans recouurer ma despouille rauie,
> Comme elle seule à esté, & sera
> Mort de ma mort, & vie de ma vie.   (D167)

As I first suggested in my essay on "The Notion and Meaning of Art in the *Délie*" quoted above, and am now convinced of, the ideas presented in this poem which are crucial for understanding Scève refer to the poet and more specifically to his sustained poetic activity and itinerary, and not to Délie as they have usually been interpreted as doing. In his quest of the ineffable, the poet must develop and acquire an undaunted vigor ("viuacité") or perseverance, both mental and physical, and a malleability of mind-spirit in contemplation and art ("docile esprit") if he is to succeed in capturing this ineffable and elusive object of poetic virtue. These qualities are absolutely essential to him for poetic restructuring and renewal, as the oracle had informed the poet, for the enlargement of mind and travail of spirit required in coming to terms with the ineffable. The poet is here giving the reader (and himself) a self-reflexive assessment of the situation he faces, in art as well as in love. The poet recognizes in this important poem that coming to terms with Délie/*Délie* as "obiect de plus haulte vertu" means coming to terms with himself as "obiect de la Vertu," with the development and restructuring of the self to become a vehicle for *poetic virtue*. This poem is really about poetic self-identity and self-realization, and how to accomplish them. The poet is probing deep within himself to discover the means with which to define his own transcendent power and potential, to insure his own transcendent worth. This potential can be had only by the poet affirming the artistic implication of *viuacité* and *docile esprit*, as we shall see him do in this study in so many poems. Moreover, Scève is acknowledging in this D167 the paradoxical principle underlying his particular literary experience: uncertainty, bewilderment, obscurity – once again, the presence of conceptual resistances – are always necessary conditions for his continued poetic creativity ("Qu'apres auoir constamment combatu, / Ce mien trauail iamais ne cessera"). In Scève's case, the psychological and thematic uncertainty involved in coming to terms with Délie/*Délie* as both love object and love text leads, through artistic *vertu*, to renewal of expression and new poetic life: "Comme elle seule à esté, & sera / Mort de ma mort, & *vie de ma vie*." This creative response to a confusing reality is in fact the poet's attempt at resolving the existential dilemma through the reality of art by creating a more personal, more bearable, sublimer poetic reality to which he can better relate and thus best realize a total unity of self in mind and emotion. That is, the effects of Délie's/*Délie*'s *vertu* will produce an enhancement and even restructuring of both the poet's "sentement" and his "entendement." This creatively aesthetic potential of *vertu* and its reverberations within the poet's psyche are most fully described for us in D424, with emphasis again placed on the power of *vertu* to provide the poet a greatly sought unity of mind ("l'entendement") and emotion ("sentement"), a sense of contemplated wholeness viewed not only in the object of love (Délie "Parfaicte au *corps*, & en l'*ame* accomplie") but in the poet-subject doing the contemplation:

De corps tresbelle & d'ame bellissime,
Comme plaisir, & gloire a l'Vniuers,
Et en *vertu* rarement rarissime
Engendre en moy mille souciz diuers:
Mesmes son œil pudiquement peruers
Me penetrant le vif du sentement,
Me rauit tout en tel contentement,
Que du desir est ma ioye remplie,
La voyant l'œil, aussi l'entendement,
Parfaicte au *corps*, & en l'*ame* accomplie.

Through his rigorous preoccupation and struggle with capturing poetic *vertu*, both Délie's and his own, Scève will replace the unful-filled side of his real life with the elucidative and rewarding experi-ence of higher art. In Proustian accents, he will affirm the aesthetic notion that the literary experience is actually the more significant of the two.[23] Délie's ineffable beauty and spiritual attraction serve as the impetus or catalyst for the poet's own recognition of his artistic sensitivity and creative potential and drive. She furnishes the external means for the poet to realize an inner artistic poten-tial.[24] Her image increasingly becomes a projection of the poet's personality, a "medium" for expressing his own desires and feel-ings. In the end, the poet's *self*-awareness and *self*-realization are what will primarily benefit from the love experience. Scève tells us as much in D271:

Ie quiers en toy *ce, qu'en moy i'ay plus cher.*
Et bien qu'espoir de l'attente me frustre,
Point ne m'est grief en aultruy *me chercher.*

The struggle towards *vertu* is depicted again and again in the sense of love inciting the poet to greater understanding and artistic achievement. Scève's particular understanding and portrayal of this virtue always posit the problematics of language and poetic dis-course involved in the poet's struggle to capture and reveal the ineffable meaning of love. The kind of poetic virtue Scève is intent on pursuing can be acquired only in discovering and affirming the artistic, creative implication of desire, of capturing Délie as "obiect de plus haulte vertu." This goal is a continual source of renewal for the poet's vital and much-needed *désir de poésie*, for affirming his own identity of self through love and its expression in poetry:

Petit obiect esmeult grande puissance,
Et peu de flamme attrait l'œil de bien loing.
Que fera donc entiere congnoissance,

Dont on ne peult se passer au besoing?
Ainsi Honneur plus tost quicteroit soing,
Plus tost au Temps sa Clepsidre cherroit,
Plus tost le Nom sa trompette lairroit,
Qu'en moy mourust ce bien, donc i'ay enuie.
Car, me taisant de toy on me verroit
Oster l'esprit de ma vie a ma vie.   (D119)

In these very revealing last three lines, Scève is stating that the creative endurance and struggle of his life as a poet (cf. "Docile *esprit*, obiect de la Vertu" of D167) is for him the ultimate sustaining principle of life itself. For Scève, *vertu* is *difficulté vaincue*, and even more. As understood and practiced by Scève, poetic virtue does not merely overcome difficulty but consummates it. Arduous thought is Scève's poetic medium. At its best, a sense of relationship and purpose is what is revealed in it. *Vertu* is what is capable of producing the imagined object of feeling, whether that object be Délie or the poet's own self. This is what the poet means in D271 when he tells Délie that he also seeks in her himself ("Ie quiers en toy ce, qu'en moy i'ai plus cher"), and in D119 that in being silent about her he would be removing the vital, creative spirit from his own life ("Car, me taisant de toy on me verroit / Oster l'*esprit* de ma vie a ma vie"). As D119 so provocatively suggests also, the poet's sustained pursuit of higher artistic *vertu* has the potential of becoming the means for discovery and even enchantment. In artistic terms, it is this love poet's own *invitation au voyage*. Who knows where the poet's pursuit of *vertu* – of Délie and himself – will lead ("Que fera donc entiere congnoissance")? But, of course, the poet is determined to find out. Sooner would Honor, Time, and Fame cease performing their duties than will the poet let die in him his desire and struggle for knowledge of Délie and of himself.

As readers of the *Délie*, we should not continue to mistake the strenuous, even anguished presentation of a problem or situation by Scève for its solution or resolution. Textual obscurity and psychological anguish as obstacles to higher meaning are always temporary conclusions. For Scève as a determined love poet, the problematics of obscurity and anguish represented a means to an end. As we have seen, this is the same view that Boccaccio espoused and that Valéry, Flaubert, and Proust would subscribe to later on. In his pursuit of *vertu*, of higher meaning, ultimately of poetic paradise, Scève's initial, difficult, and perhaps even painful moments in fact prepare the way for the subsequent portrayal of the poetic and

26

psychological order or "diuine harmonie" of the love conscious-
ness, as it is the purpose of this study to show.[25]

Scève's obscure poetic art carries with it an aesthetic and thera-
peutic function in the *Délie*. The poet's final vision of beauty and
contentment, of the paradise that is the ineffable made effable, is
seldom arrived at, by the poet or the reader, through the easy access
of instant illumination, as another critical point of view on the *Délie*,
most recently argued by Paul Ardouin, would have us believe.[26]
Scève's love aesthetics, his sense of "Beaultée logée en amere doul-
ceur" (D9), reflect an achievement in and through difficult beauty
and art, not unlike the diaphoric portrayals of our modern symbolist
poets. Scève's love and art are built on difficulty, anguish, obscur-
ity, but the poet's higher restructuring of these resistances is what
makes his poetry and aesthetics the more meaningful and powerful.
To lose sight of this poetic process or devalue it in a rush to concen-
trate on its results is as critically inadequate as is the other tendency
of being blocked from the final celebration of aesthetic beauty
through excessive concentration on the poetry's anguish and
obscurity. Surely the aesthetic "truth" of Scève's poetry lies in
between these two prevailing critical understandings. Readers of
the *Délie* who rush straightway without pausse and reflection to praise
the work's overall sense of instant poetic beauty and pleasure over-
look, or at least underestimate, the aesthetic process itself of
struggle by which and through which the *Délie* achieves its triumph
in difficult poetic beauty and ecstasy. These kinds of readings do
not respond to the levels of challenge of the *via negativa* and the
underlying presence and meaning of darkness in Scève's thought
and his art. The marvel of Scève's poetry (like the process of lumi-
nous, soul-wringing refashioning of poetic perspective admired so
much by Flaubert and especially Valéry – a poetry/poet able and
determined to "se refaire selon ses clartés") is that this poetry
describes all the stages in its struggle from obscurity to clarity. It is
concerned as much with the process of refashioning and coming to
terms with obscurity as it is with the final product of clarity of
poetic perspective. A satisfactory critical reading must take this into
account. On the other hand, those readers of the *Délie* who overly
concentrate on its difficulty and anguish literally mistake the aes-
thetic process of conflict and struggle for the end result. Clearly,
for me, the higher meaning of the *Délie* – the poetic Beauty, Convic-
tion, and Contentment it can provide the reader – must be sought
somewhere in between these two extremes of interpretation. It is,
I wish to suggest in this book, finally to be found where Valéry

found the higher meaning and beauty of Mallarmé's obscure and difficult poetry to be, that is, in the primary task of art to lead both writer and reader from *vexation* to *entendement*, to help them both turn disorder into order and even perhaps into paradise. Valéry's statement on this purpose of art and life is worth quoting again:

Mais un homme qui se mesure à soi-même et *se refait selon ses clartés* me semble une œuvre supérieure qui me touche plus que toute autre. Le plus bel effort des humains est *de changer leur désordre en ordre* et la chance en pouvoir; c'est là la véritable *merveille*.   (I, 654)[27]

In this chapter, I have introduced the key issues this study will be concerned with: obscurity and anguish, struggle, the attainment diaphorically of a meaningful sense of poetic order and paradise. These ideas will be developed more fully in subsequent chapters. In order to attain that poetic virtue or "merveille" Valéry speaks of, Scève had a major obstacle to overcome. This problem and the poet's response to it are the subjects of the next chapter.

2

IN SEARCH OF LOVE'S EPISTEMOLOGY: AFFIRMING THE ROLE OF THE CREATIVE IMAGINATION

In his desire to give a higher meaning to the experience of love and to express the sublime effect it can have on his judgment and feelings, Scève was confronted by a fundamental artistic problem which he had to overcome. When he tried with the critical precision usually afforded by logic and reason to translate the wonderful infinity of love and its ability to transcend a whole world of human measurements, he did indeed end up frustrated and disappointed. There are many reasons for this impasse and they all seem to point in the same direction: Scève's higher poetic meaning, aesthetically centered on the beauty and infinite mystery of the sacred that is Délie, relies less on the brain than on the imagination for its ultimate portrayal and value. A central lesson that the poet is forced to learn is that Délie's "haulte value" (D275) – her "deité," her "diuine beaulté" her "beaulté esmerueillable Idée" – cannot adequately be measured by human logic:

> Tout iugement de celle infinité,
> Ou tout concept se trouue superflus,
> Et tout aigu de perspicuité
> Ne pourroyent ioindre au sommet de son plus.
> Car seulement l'apparent du surplus,
> Premiere neige en son blanc souueraine,
> Au pur des mains delicatement saine,
> Ahontiroyt le nud de Bersabée:
> Et le flagrant de sa suaue alaine
> Apouriroyt l'odorante Sabée.   (D166)

Délie's ineffable qualities – her sacred beauty, perfection, and infinity – go beyond the limits of the poet's intellectual comprehension. However penetrating his reasonings, however shrewd his judgments, they are *all* ("*tout* iugement," "*tout* concept," "*tout* aigu de perspicuité") inadequate and fail to reach the heights of her perfection (the "sommet de son plus") and to reveal the beauty of her divine being. What the poet is telling us here in D166 he tells us time and again in other poems. This desperate state of being blocked from a sacred revelation and understanding of the ineffable through rational means, which underscores the poet's limitations and thus inadequacy, constitutes his major dilemma and obstacle. As much as any impasse associated with unrequited love, this artistic impasse is a principal source of his anguish, frustration, and obscurity.

Scève exploits this epistemological dilemma of understanding and portraying the ineffable love object for one of *Délie*'s major themes. Solving this poetic and critical uncertainty is what projects Scève into the ranks of the great love poets. And trying to understand Scève's solution may be the most appealing task of his readers. In this chapter, I propose to work through the difficulty and uncertainties of several of Scève's better-known poems. My objective is to see if they do indeed succeed in finding a means of coming to terms with this dilemma caused by an adversarial relationship with Délie as ineffable object of poetic contemplation and writing. I shall be following here a word of advice given by Paul B. Armstrong: "The first premise of hermeneutics is that interpretation is basically circular. The classic formulation of the hermeneutic circle holds that we can only comprehend the details of a work by projecting a sense of the whole, just as, conversely, we can only achieve a view of the whole by working through its parts."[1] Both here and in chapters to follow, I shall be reading the *Délie* not only analytically but also synthetically and organically, and thus attempting to throw both a backward and a forward light on some of the difficult poems of the *Délie*. I shall undertake the explication of some of the obscurities and difficulties of individual poems with the hope of working towards a more overall appreciation of the great artistic theme of struggle and paradise, the difficult yet final attainment of an ineffable knowledge by the poet which ties them all together.

In a way, Scève's critics who continue to define the essence of his world view to be that of anguish and obscurity are partially correct, but for the wrong reasons. What has generally escaped notice in the *Délie*, in spite of the early effort by Staub in *Le Curieux Désir* to call our attention to it, is the shift of ground from existence to epistemology. The crucial point to keep in mind in reading Scève and in trying to understand Scève is that for him experience is synonymous with knowledge, and especially the struggle involved in acquiring a particular kind of knowledge. Scève's love lyrics dramatize much more than the simple experience and poetic of lamentation caused by unrequited love. They raise the greater epistemological issue of human knowledge and understanding, of the human *limitations* confronting the poet in trying to understand and communicate the sacred and ineffable side of his experience in love. (It is here, I believe, that Staub's otherwise perceptive and certainly suggestive thesis misses the mark. It is not a poetic of logic and reason, a "noetic" process of rational discernment ["l'élan noétique" as this critic defines it in his chapter on the *Délie*] that will enable Scève to come to terms with the ineffable. Rather, it is this love poet's higher, transcendent probing and affirming of the imagination, as we shall see in this chapter.) Scève even builds the cognitive antithesis between the sacred and the human, between Love-Délie as higher object of pursuit and Reason-the Poet as unfit subject of this pursuit, into the very structure of his poetic discourse. Scève's strain or tension in many poems does not stem as much from a dialectic of unrequited love as it does from a basic epistemological problem the literary origin and implications of which Augustine was one of the first to elaborate: "What can anyone say about you, O Lord, and yet woe to him who says nothing."[2] In his three famous "oui–non" poems – D181, D184, D362 – Scève presents this basic problem in this way: Can human reason, personified as "Non," adequately cope with and profitably pursue higher love, personified as "Oui"? For Scève, too, the problem seems to have been as difficult to articulate as it was to avoid. But there was for Scève, as for Augustine, a felt need and even obligation to express the sacred and ineffable, even if this appeared to be doomed to failure. His three "oui–non" poems thematically and structurally present this linguistic dilemma of ineffable writing. They also show, epistemologically, the extent to which human language and reason, in their striving for higher conceptualization, mirror their own limitations and ultimate failure. These poems do not achieve any stability, conviction, finality, or for that matter any thematic or structural purpose other than to point to their own tentativeness, doubt, irresolution – poetic frustration and obscurity. Here is what two of these poems have to say to the reader:

Ouy, & non aux Caestes contendantz
Par maintz assaultz alternatifz s'assaillent:

Tous deux a fin de leur gloyre tendantz
En mon *cerueau* efforcément trauaillent.
Et nonobstant, que bien peu, ou *rien vaillent*
Si longz effortz sans rien determiner,
Si sens ie en moy de peu a peu miner
Et la memoyre, & le sens tout confus:
D'ailleurs l'ardeur, comme eulx, ne peult finer:
Ainsi ie suis *plus mal*, qu'oncques ne fus.   (D181)

Ne du passé la recente memoyre,
Ne du present la congneue euidence,
Et du futur, aulcunesfoys notoyre,
Ne peult en moy la sage prouidence:
Car sur ma foy la paour fait residence,
Paour, qu'on ne peult pour vice improperer.
Car quand mon cœur pour vouloir prosperer
Sur *l'incertain d'ouy, ou non* se boute,
Tousiours espere: et le trop esperer
M'esmeult souuent *le vacciller du doubte*.   (D362)

    Like Délie, the ineffable and aesthetic object of inquiry and pursuit in them, D181 and D362 provide a Circean poetic encounter: a beguiling and frustrating enchantment full of ironies, paradoxes, reversals, twists, and turns (structural as well as thematic) which often elude the analytical mind of the reader-critic. These poems reflect the seemingly inaccessible character of Délie herself who, referred to as the elusive Hecate in D22, entices Scève the lover and then more often than not foils the intense scrutiny and reasoning of Scève the poet. They do, however, serve a definite purpose, and it is an intentionally negative one: to re-create an internalized and disoriented state of consciousness of a poet *rationally* trying to contemplate love. In D181, as in the other two poems, the personified Yes (Love) and No (Reason) hammer out their incompatibility and antagonism with lethal force ("aux Caestes contendantz" – with iron boxing gloves!) inside the mind of the poet-lover and within the confines of this epistemological dizain embodying the poet's dilemma ("en mon cerueau efforcément trauaillent"). D181 reflects the psychological and intellectual ups and downs of a mind totally overwhelmed by those elusive answers to questions and doubts raised by the meaning of the love experience, and so too do D184 and D362. They are excellent examples, in their own right exhibiting anti-closural closure, of the structural and generic strain under which Scève composed. They are also excellent examples of the epistemological strain under which Scève thought. The poet sees himself literally caught up, as he says in D184, "en tel suspend ou de non, ou d'ouy." That is, he pictures himself in a thoroughly distressing and thwarting situation.

In the structural and thematic indeterminateness of these poems can be found, though, a paradoxical poetic message: the poet is affirming the inadequacy of words, of language, of thought, of reason, of the noetic notion itself – cherished by the Renaissance – of teleology as a viable means of obtaining a higher level of meaning and certainty. Scève is telling us that some human phenomena (such as love and the capturing of it in a love poem) cannot always be adequately explained by *rational* artistic design. Consider again this observation made by the poet in D181:

> Et nonobstant, que bien peu, ou *rien vaillent*
> Si longz effortz sans *rien determiner*,
> Si sens ie en moy de peu a peu miner
> Et la memoyre, & le sens *tout confus*.

And this conclusion, even more revealing, on human limitation reached by the poet in D362:

> *Ne* du passé la recente memo‚re,
> *Ne* du present la congneue euidence,
> Et du futur, aulcunesfoys notoyre,
> *Ne* peult en moy la sage prouidence.

The poet's mind or intelligence is thoroughly confused and he has reached an impasse. Neither the recent memory of the past, nor the known evidence of the present, nor even the sometimes wise foresight of the future is able to serve the poet's purpose and extricate him from his uncertain dilemma. By emphasizing the futility of *all* of time itself in his pursuit of higher understanding and certainty, the poet (like the reader) is forced in these poems to draw the only appropriate conclusion: the anti-teleological, anti-closural conclusion which denies meaning. The only possible solution in these poems seems to be the affirmation of uncertainty, and thus D362's *last* words are: "le vacciller du *doubte*."[3]

Reminiscent of the epistemological vision which Nathalie Sarraute later popularized as "the age of suspicion" wherein rational conviction and certainty are viewed as self-deluding at best, other similar poems in the *Délie* draw an even sharper distinction between the limitations of the human mind in its attempts at understanding and the poet's none the less determined pursuit of higher meaning. A close look at Scève's use of the very concepts of "raison," "sens,"

33

and "pensée/penser" will reveal that they are being used to keep forever in the reader's mind the poet's epistemological struggle successfully to come to terms with the higher meaning of Délie as sacred and ineffable object, as "obiect de plus haulte vertu" whom the poet specifically calls the ineffable ("ô l'oultrepasse") in D230. The difficulty facing the poet is always the basic one of portrayal of this ineffable object. This central problem is what is being very clearly expressed again by the poet in D23. Since Délie's beauty and perfection are so close to those of the Gods, the poet avows his own artistic inadequacy and uselessness in trying to represent these qualities in his writing:

> Seule raison, de la Nature loy,
> T'à de chascun l'affection acquise.
> Car ta vertu de trop meilleur alloy,
> Qu'Or monnoyé, ny aultre chose exquise,
> Te veult du Ciel (ô tard) estre requise,
> Tant approchante est des Dieux ta coustume.
> *Doncques en vain trauailleroit ma plume*
> *Pour t'entailler a perpetuité.*

The poet is acknowledging the disappointing fact that Délie's virtue and manner, of finer substance than any precious human creation such as minted gold, can only be appreciated in the final analysis by the Gods in Heaven. Thus in vain would the poet's pen labor to capture Délie's sacred and ineffable qualities.

The overriding problem or constraint then for Scève became that of sacred meaning *versus* human understanding and portrayal. Scève's struggle to bring them together in the poetic act of language and image generates a strategy of poetic discourse that casts reading as a drama, interpretation as an ordeal that enacts and distinguishes the human predicament. When the poet turns to his "raison," "sens," or "pensée/penser" for help and enlightenment, he is more often than not thrown back on himself and extremely disappointed. They in fact work to block his desired progression towards higher understanding and portrayal and thus demonstrate the limits of human critical analysis in both its linguistic and its intellectual realms. Since the poet's rational faculties of perception always seem to fail him, it is little wonder he is often forced to conclude that he must give up his futile efforts to attain to the ineffable meaning of Délie. This is the conclusion the poet reaches again, and most poignantly, at the end of D97: "O vain desir, ô folie euidente / A qui de faict espere y paruenir" – that is, in his desire announced at the beginning of this poem "a contempler si merueilleux spectacle," his desire to understand and portray this "merueille a toute éternité" but in which he is forced to recognize yet again "que tout aigu d'œil vif n'y peult venir." This D97 is another example of a poetic text that can only hover around the ungraspable love object. There can be little doubt that Scève is here equating artistic impotence with conceptual impotence. The failure of poetic discourse (of *la plume*) is the failure of the process of rational discernment (of *la raison, le sens, la pensée*). Scève is even clearer on this point in D227. Indeed, Délie's ineffable character will certainly shine the better if the poet gives up trying to capture and communicate it:

> Pour m'efforcer a degluer les yeulx
> De ma *pensée* enracinez en elle,
> Ie m'en veulx taire, & lors i'y pense mieulx,
> Qui iuge en moy ma peine estre eternelle.
> Parquoy *ma plume au bas vol de son aele*
> *Se demettra de plus en raisonner,*
> Aussi pour *plus haultement resonner,*
> Vueille le Temps, vueille la Fame, ou non,
> Sa grace asses, *sans moy*, luy peult donner
> Corps a ses faictz, & Ame a son hault nom.

This D227, like so many other poems of the *Délie*, does embody a protracted contemplation of an epistemological void, an abyss between language as signifier and meaning, a gap that Scève found most conspicuous in his desired contemplation and portrayal of a higher love. This void, this abyss, this gap we are made to see very clearly in the extremely poignant recognition by the poet there of the inability of his pen ("la plume") to *raisonner* (to rationally contemplate) and thus its being unable to *résonner* (to communicate "haultement") in his love lyrics the ineffable qualities and meaning Délie incarnates. In all of the above poems, Scève is being introduced to the same, central lesson that other poets and theorists of the ineffable before him, such as Plotinus, had to learn on the difficulty involved in contemplating and communicating this ineffable: "The vision baffles telling."[4]

To be sure, the poet's conceptual faculties of "raison," "sens," and "pensée" are viewed more often than not as being destitute and utterly useless to him in his poetic experience in love. In the very beginning, in D1, we were warned about the shortcomings of rational conceptualization in the poet's attempts at interpretation of higher meaning: "Mon Basilisque auec sa poingnant' veue / Perçant

35

Corps, Cœur, & *Raison despourueue*, / Vint penetrer en l'Ame de mon Ame." The ineffable challenge posed by Délie even produces in the poet a state of mental and psychological warfare where he always finds his "sens" and "raison" so ineffective and powerless that they are removed from his very being:

> Toutes les foys, que sa lueur sur Terre
> Iecte sur moy vn, ou deux de ses raiz,
> En ma *pensée* esmeult l'obscure guerre
> Parqui me sont *sens*, & *raison* soubstraictz.   (D358)

This desperate theme of the failure of conceptual analysis in the interpretation and understanding of the ineffable Délie runs constantly throughout Scève's sequence. The poet's sense of disappointment and frustration in relying on conscious mind, that is, on the brain or reason for contemplation, is just as strong at the end as it is in the beginning:

> D'elle puis dire, & ce sans rien mentir,
> Qu'ell' à en soy, ie ne scay quoy de beau,
> Qui remplit l'œil, & qui se fait sentir
> Au fond du cœur par vn desir noueau,
> Troublant a tous le *sens*, & le *cerueau*,
> Voire & qui *l'ordre a la raison efface*.   (D410)

What the reader must keep in mind is that it is always the poet's *rational thought*, represented as "raison," "sens," or "pensée/penser" and their synonyms like "cerueau" above in D410, which seems to fail him. At any given moment in this love sequence when they are relied upon, their ineffectiveness to help the poet contemplate love is what always plunges the poet into darkness and obscurity:

> Ie sens mes yeulx se dissouldre en fontaine,
> Et ma *pensée* offusquer en tenebres.   (D200)

> Arcz de structure en beauté nompareille,
> A moy iadis immortel argument,
> Vous estes seul, & premier instrument,
> Qui liberté, & la *raison* offence.   (D270)

What are we to make of these negative views on poetic contemplation and writing? It seems to me that the dilemma Scève is presenting in these poems is that the brain that tries to understand an ineffable and sacred kind of love is, by itself, incapable of doing so.[5] In Scève's intense longing for understanding of this higher love, the human mind or intelligence really becomes this poet's primary adversary. His acute awareness of limitation and of being inextricably bound by uncertainty is rendered again very poetically in D393 as the tempest of thought which violently tosses the poet back and forth at sea. The description which the poet gives of himself, again of his "pensée," in D393 is a variation of what we saw happening to him in his "oui–non" poems:

> Ie voys, & viens aux ventz de la tempeste
> *De ma pensée incessamment troublée:*
> Ores a Poge, or' a l'Orse tempeste,
> Ouuertement, & aussi a l'emblée,
> L'vn apres l'aultre, en commune assemblée
> De doubte, espoir, desir, & ialousie,
> Me fouldroyantz telz flotz la Fantasie
> Abandonnée & d'aydes, & d'appuys.
> Parquoy durant si longue phrenesie,
> Ne pouuant plus, ie fais plus que ne puis.

This realization and depiction by the poet of limitation have staggering implications for a love poet like Scève and for the way his language must ultimately work in poetry. One of the results for the reader of the above epistemological poems is that they make him acutely aware, by having them demonstrated before his own eyes, of the inadequacy and invalidation of conceptual logic or rational thinking in poetry concerned with the ineffable, and yet of the poet's continued struggle to express the inexpressible. Scève's love lyrics are indeed grounded, at an initial stage anyway, in paradox and skepticism about the nature and communicability of higher love and its truth. His poems do embody a protracted contemplation of an epistemological void. These are poetic texts that depict consciousness at the limits of what mind and language can grasp. But this very negativity or questioning of reason and knowledge, and thus of meaning and writing, is what makes his continued writing possible and even necessary. And this brings us back to the saying of Augustine which, for Scève, I would change ever so slightly into: "*How* can I say anything about you, Délie, and yet woe to me if I say nothing." In the final analysis, Scève's "silent outcries" (D228), as with most successful poets of the ineffable, cannot and do not remain thwarted and silent.[6]

Through a mimesis of real-life conditions of inference, we as *rational* readers seeking measurable meaning in poems of the *Délie* are often surrounded by ambiguities, baffled and misled by appearances, reduced to piecing fragments together by trial and error, often left in the dark about essentials to the very end, literally the end of a poem. This makes at best for difficult unity. With both the poem and our interpretation of it becoming an obstacle course, the act of reading turns into a drama of understanding – conflicting observations, conceptual and logical impasse, reversal, discovery, and the like. For as we have seen, knowledge and understanding quite often become the knowledge of limitation and impossibility. Just at the point of achieving a higher insight into Délie's transcendent excellence, the reader, like the poet, is suddenly thrown back to an obscure position of doubt and uncertainty. The poet's presumption in coming to terms with (which always means in Scève the poet trying to contemplate – "estimer" – and to portray – "exprimer") Délie's ineffability ("Et sa vertu, & sa forme elegante," her "haultesse en magesté prestante") is compared to that of Dathan and Abiram in Numbers 16:1–35, who in their own audacity and subsequent defeat were swallowed up by the earth that opened beneath their feet:

> Mes pleurs clouantz au front ses tristes yeulx,
> A la memoire ouurent la veue instante,
> Pour admirer, & contempler trop mieulx
> Et sa vertu, & sa forme elegante.
> Mais sa haultesse en magesté prestante,
> Par moy, si bas, ne peult estre *estimée*.
> Et la cuydant au vray bien *exprimée*
> Pour tournoyer son moins, ou enuiron,
> Ie m'apperçoy la memoyre abismée
> Auec Dathan au centre d'Abiron.   (D165)

Or, as Scève describes the problem in another way imagistically in D397, the pursuit of a sacred revelation and higher meaning in love is like watching a cloud rise high into the heavens. The higher it progresses, the more it disintegrates and dissolves into nothing before the poet's own eyes, leaving him utterly abandoned and lost in his desired contemplation of it:

> Toute fumée en forme d'vne nue
> Depart du feu auec graue maintien:
> Mais tant plus hault s'esleue, & se denue,
> Et plus soubdain se resoult *toute en rien*.
> Or que seroit a penetrer au bien,
> Qui au parfaict d'elle iamais ne fault?
> Quand seulement [pensant] plus, qu'il ne fault,
> Et contemplant sa face a mon dommage,
> L'œil, & le *sens* peu a peu *me deffault*,

In search of love's epistemology

Et me pers tout en sa diuine image.

So it is for the poet. His rational faculties of sense and perception little by little seem always to fail him and even to mislead him in his desire for an ineffable meaning in love and its portrayal. Walking side by side with Reason (D180), the poet will always be led down the wrong path where true knowledge departs from purely rational assessment. The problem of interpretation and understanding is once again being acutely raised in the reader's mind. His commitment to the rationality of critical reading is being undermined at the same time as is the poet's commitment to the rationality of literary discourse:

> Quand pied a pied *la Raison ie costoye*,
> Et pas a pas i'obserue ses sentiers,
> Elle me tourne en vne mesme voye
> Vers ce, que plus ie fuiroys voulentiers.
> Mais ses effectz en leur oblique entiers
> Tendent tousiours a celle droicte sente,
> Qui plusieursfoys *du iugement s'absente*,
> *Faignant du miel estre le goust amer*:
> Puis me contrainct quelque mal, que ie sente,
> Et vueille, ou non, a mon contraire aymer.

What are we truly to make of the above portrayals? As his readers, we could stop here and proclaim Scève to be a great poet of failed, lamented love, which is after all the distinction and worthy contribution of many a good love poet. Louise Labé immediately comes to mind. But in spite of his passionate and all-too-human outcries, there is also in Scève the artist, an artist *par excellence* of the imagination. And it is this character and higher aspiration in Scève which his reader must come to understand and to appreciate. The result will more than repay the difficult effort required of the reader. I believe that it is this same notion of the artist in Mallarmé which Valéry admired so profoundly. Mallarmé's higher achievement was viewed by Valéry, as we saw in the last chapter, in his having undergone the sublimation or transformation that only art (and of course religion) can truly bring about: he succeeded in changing his "disorder" into "order," his "chance" into "law" in the miracle that is the new life of artistic creation. "C'est là la véritable merveille," Valéry concludes. Is it not possible that the very poetic depiction of limitation and lamentation which we have examined above in Scève was a necessary stage in the poet's evolution and quest of the ineffable to lead both him and us to greater

39

understanding and poetic certainty? I believe it was. The poet's picture of despair, anguish, and obscurity is symbolizing a flawed and failed artistic process as a prerequisite of a higher excellence, the working out of *Délie* as "obiect de plus haulte vertu." This great and perplexing body of love poetry that is the *Délie* turns upon itself to seek a resolution that is at once a denial and a sublimation of its initial portrayal of love defined by frustration and obscurity. This shift in poetic perspective corresponds to a transcendent strategy and objective: being aroused yet thwarted or unfulfilled by desire and its reliance on reason, the poet (and the reader) will be in a better position to be moved by the superior truths and insights of hard-won virtue (cf. my discussion of Boccaccio and others on this point in Chapter 1). The *Délie* as poetic text first baffles and excites and even seduces, then cleanses and resolves. The poet's initially negative and pathetic pursuit of the ineffable through reason becomes supplanted by a positive and constructive one. The poetic process or method of failed reason is reversed and an understanding and portrayal of higher values and truths as originally proposed made reachable, and only so by a newly acquired poetic of the imagination. Thus, even pain and conflict can have a positive meaning or purpose and are not their own ends. They are the difficult working out of an artistic ideal, necessary elements in the passage from disorder to order. In the end, it is only by a sustained effort to break free of the limiting process of purely rational discernment that the poet can progress beyond conflict and impasse to something of the ineffable vision. For both the poet and the reader, to find another means of making sense of the tortured and unyielding discourse, through the required interpretive effort of time, energy, and perseverance, is to gain a sense of being human, or at least this appears to be true for the poet. Scève's response to conceptual and artistic failure with its overwhelming effects of obscurity and anguish is always the glorious one of continued struggle. And this stuggle is the inner struggle of every artist with the forbidden desire of the ineffable, with overcoming one's "defects" so as to capture "la merueille d'vn si hault bien." By "defects," the poet means his rational faculty of judgment forever blocking him from attaining a higher level of understanding in love:

> Me desaymant par la seuerité
> De mon estrange, & propre *iugement*,
> Qui me fait veoir, & estre en verité
> Non meritant si doulx soulagement,

Comme celluy, dont pend l'abregement,
De mes trauaulx me bienheurantz ma peine,
Ie m'extermine, & en si [grande] hayne
De mes deffaultz i'aspire a la merueille
D'vn si hault bien, que d'vne mesme alaine
A mon labeur le iour, & la nuict veille.   (D384)

Having stressed the epistemological dilemma thwarting Scève's attempts at ineffable understanding and portrayal, I will only add that its manifestations are also associated, not only with "raison," "sens," and "pensée" and their variants such as "cerueau," "concept," and "iugement," but also with other, more obvious key words such as "voir," "contempler," "entendre," "comprendre," and so forth.[7] The reader's interpretive role is literally dramatized by an analogous process because of the same constraints on human reason, vision, and understanding. He too, like the poet, is constantly confronted by a standing challenge to interpretation and must overcome these difficulties if a higher meaning is ever to be accorded to the *Délie*. The limiting rational process of sight and understanding initially associated with the awakening of desire or poetic passion ("vertu") very quickly becomes in Scève the more sustained spiritual and artistic process of insight, and it is only in Scève's progression to the latter that his poetic success with metaphor and transcendence can be truly evaluated. Scève's real quest is always his desire for ineffable knowledge of Délie. This higher pursuit of insight results from the poet's felt need for more complete knowledge of the sacred love object and for more intense poetic contemplation and creation of it. For the poet does see significance in things above and beyond what he is truly able to see and assess through reason. It will take some means other than purely rational discernment to enable him to enjoy and reproduce the illumination and expressive virtue of this experience. Ordinary logic and reason alone will not take the poet where he wants to go. They will not lead him to either "vraye congnoissance" (D182) or to "entiere congnoissance" (D119). This is why the poet tells us in D227 that he must untrap or free up "the *eyes* of [his] *thought*" grounded in Délie ("Pour m'efforcer a degluer les yeulx / De ma *pensée* enracinez en elle"). For Délie has indeed entrapped and checked the poet's capacity for reason, for understanding, for vision. This accounts for the decision he makes in this poem to cease trying "to reason" the ineffable, trying to come to satisfying terms with it through his faculty of reason: "Parquoy ma plume au bas vol de son aele / Se demettra de plus en *raisonner*." The poet comes to see himself trapped not only by the ineffable Délie but by his very ability to know his own limitations.

Things will come together though for the poet precisely because he undergoes a profound change in perspective and method. His more successful meditations and reflections on Délie and higher love can no longer just be logical acts of thought but must embody, as Valéry would later define in the seminal essay on poetic art we have already referred to, that rare and miraculous combination of thought *and* feeling in the creative imagination so necessary for portraying a higher emotional-intellectual unity. Here is Valéry's definition of this epistemological-aesthetic triumph of phenomenological poetics as he sees it in Mallarmé's poetry:

Que voulons-nous, – si ce n'est de produire l'impression puissante, et pendant quelque temps continue, qu'il existe entre *la forme sensible d'un discours et sa valeur d'échange en idées,* je ne sais quelle union mystique, quelle harmonie, grâce auxquelles nous participons *d'un tout autre monde que le monde* où les paroles et les actes se répondent? (I, 647)

For Valéry, the truly remarkable poet (and by implication his successful reader-interpreter) is one who comes to associate the delights of poetry with the artistic struggle to affirm the creative imagination and its powers of combination. In a meaningful way, both poet and reader must learn "à associer le travail suivi de l'esprit et de ses forces combinatoires au délice poétique" (p. 646). And the accomplishment of this ineffable kind of diaphoric portrayal in poetry – of creating this harmonious, juxtaposed union of "the sensuous form of a poem and its exchange value in terms of ideas" through which both the poet and the reader may participate in "quite another world" – depends on the almost magical power of poetry simultaneously to transmit a fact or idea and to evoke an emotion. That is, the poet must combine in the same creative operation a seductive or emotive element ("la forme sensible") as well as a rational or conceptual element ("sa valeur d'échange en idées"). In other words, both the reason and the creative imagination must be brought into play in order to express the inexpressible, to portray the unportrayable, to capture the ineffable. And the important point is that this potentially higher expression of the ineffable will not always be logical, or at least cannot be only logical. For a poet of the ineffable like Scève or Valéry or Mallarmé, reason is never enough. Both mind and emotion, both "thought" and "soul" as Scève also puts it in D153, must be fully engaged if the poet, like the love cricket, is to perform profitably the labors and song of higher love, of "si saincte amytié":

> Morte esperance au giron de pitié,
> Mouroit le iour de ma fatalité,
> Si le lyen de *si saincte amytié*
> Ne m'eust restraint a immortalité:
> Non qu'en moy soit si haulte qualité,
> Que l'immortel d'elle se rassasie.
> Mais le *grillet*, ialouse *fantasie*,
> Qui sans cesser chante tout ce, qu'il cuyde,
> Et la *pensée*, & l'*Ame* ayant saisie,
> Me laisse vif a ma doulce homicide.   (D153)

In his recognition (and practice) of the importance of both the reason and the imagination to ineffable expression lie our love poet's recovery and his only hope of fully understanding and communicating the higher logic and seductive power of Délie as sacred and ineffable object. Here the poet's words may not always make logical sense, but they do make poetic, emotional sense:

> Haultain vouloir en si basse pensée,
> *Haulte pensée* en vn si bas vouloir
> Ma voulenté ont en ce dispensée,
> Qu'elle ne peult, & si se deubt douloir.
> Pource souuent mettant a nonchaloir
> Espoir, ennuy, attente, & fascherie,
> Veult que le Cœur, bien qu'il soit fasché, *rie*
> *Au goust du miel tous mes incitementz:*
> Et que le mal par la peine cherie
> Soit trouué *Succre* au fiel de mes tourmentz.   (D406)

In order to change his disorder into order, the poet must let his creative imagination perform the desired transformation. It (literally "haultain vouloir" and "haulte pensée" in the above poem) is what enables the poet to laugh ("au goust du miel," with honeyed laugh!) at all his passionate outcries and impasses and to process or swallow his failures and torments as if they were "Sugar." How far indeed the poet has come at this point! In the poems discussed earlier highlighting Scève's epistemological dilemma, all of Scève's contradictions, impasses, and paradoxes involved in applying conceptual logic alone (Reason) to his experience in love made honey taste bitter to the poet (cf. the discussion above of D180: "Faignant du miel estre le goust amer"). The poet's situation now contains a complete reversal: to him, anguish and obscurity have the sweet

43

taste of sugar. Scève's earlier poems on human limitation and lamentation were made cumulatively more obvious, painful, and bitter until in the ones just quoted the poet clearly makes a great shift in perspective, one that takes him and us out of the former, flawed, and closed system of conceptual rationalization into the latter aesthetic meta-system of the imagination, of palpable symbol and metaphor. The shift is a departure from the limiting way of discursive logic to the creatively expansive way of transcendent understanding and portrayal. *Délie*'s epistemological poems of impasse demonstrate well how problematic are logical attempts at expressing the ineffable and asserting poetic values. The proper corrective then for higher contemplation lies in an aesthetic perception more fundamental, more encompassing, more intimate than reason. The artistic import of this change in perspective is to signal a new and potentially more revealing and significant pattern of affective and sensitive poetic insight and being. The poet is still very much concerned with the verbally ineffable, but it is no longer the inexpressible and agonizing principle of vital experience. Its "content" will become what the poet perceives as beautiful, sweet, sensuous form; and this formal element is also to become the poet's "idea" which he is to convey in the *Délie*: Délie as sacred and ineffable "*obiect de plus haulte vertu*," Délie as "*beaulté esmerueillable Idée* (D275), in a word Délie as aesthetic object directing the poet towards the expressive virtue of higher art and insight. This unity of vision at the heart of phenomenological poetics is precisely what Valéry described to be the miracle and greatness of Mallarmé's poetic art. The powerful impression or aesthetic effect that exists when this poet combines "la forme sensible d'un discours et sa valeur d'échange en idées" is what enables Mallarmé as well as his reader truly to participate "d'un tout autre monde." Scève's most privileged moments in the *Délie* – his poetic paradises, as we shall see in the next chapter – are always the result of the same diaphoric operation of combining, of juxtaposing form with idea, body with soul, matter with mind in a singularly powerful and illuminating transcendent image. In those poems where this sweet sublimation of art takes place, there is also to be found a higher insight and contentment; in those poems which fail to create this harmonious blend, such as those we have seen in this chapter that rely only on conceptual reasoning, the result is always disappointment and despair, anguish and obscurity – bitterness. And a world of difference separates ordinary emotion from the kind of aesthetic emotion Valéry is talking about in Mallarmé, and that I am talking about in

Scève. The aesthetic kind of emotion is not so much the source, but the fulfillment of artistic labor, the personal emotive experience of revelation, the difficult process of insight and unity and recovery which Scève's ongoing struggle with ineffable understanding inspires. Being able to produce and enjoy this higher emotion of "ialouse fantasie" is what keeps our love poet *alive* ("vif") in his moments of "sweet dying" when his reason or thought (his "pensée") is replaced or at least being reinforced by his faculty of the imagination (his "Ame"), unitive moments when the poet's whole being is being brought into play and thus satisfied:

> Mais le grillet, ialouse fantasie,
> Qui sans cesser chante tout ce, qu'il cuyde,
> Et la *pensée*, & l'*Ame* ayant saisie,
> Me laisse *vif* a ma doulce homicide.   (D153)

It really is a matter of the higher sublimation of mind and art, the extremely difficult process which Scève presents diaphorically in D406 as the turning of "gall" into "Sugar." Scève will finally succeed in constructing a sweet unity of vision not only of Délie the ineffable object of contemplation but also of the contemplating poetic subject itself. The specific unitive forms of these two operations, of the poet's external vision of the contemplated love object and his inner vision of the contemplating subject of love, we will consider in the next two chapters, respectively. For now, our purpose is to see the poet discover and affirm the crucial role of the creative imagination without which neither of the two unitive operations of seeing and being just mentioned would ever have been possible. For Scève the love poet, disorder is always the dilemma of being able to perceive only sensuousness ("forme sensible"), on the one hand, or only spirituality ("idée"), on the other hand, in the love object. During these moments when the poet's "raison," "penser," and "sens" acting alone are of no use to him, feelings of obscurity and anguish color the love experience. When, however, the poet is able to combine in the same creative act, as he does in D434, both "la raison" and "la memoyre" in full contemplation of Délie's sensuous form ("sa grace") and her spiritual idea ("sa vertu"), the order and unity of love and life and art prevail. The poet is then truly able to enjoy a privileged moment in love, one full of sweet contemplation and vision:

> Ainsi absent la *memoyre* posée,
> Et plus tranquille, & apte a conceuoir,
> Par la *raison* estant interposée,

45

Comme clarté a l'obiect, qu'on veult veoir:
Rumine en soy, & sans se deceuoir
Gouste trop mieulx *sa vertu, & sa grace* . . .   (D434)

Scève's love is an imaginatively creative love and adoration of the sacred and ineffable object, often presented as comprehension of the unpresent object ("Ainsi absent"), an aesthetic creation by the poetic imagination which combines emotion and intelligence in order to achieve insight into a higher form of love. The poet's triumph always resides in the ability of his faculty of the imagination (often called "memoyre") and his faculty of the reason ("raison") to work together harmoniously in order to perceive both Délie's physical being (her "grace"), and her spiritual being (her "vertu"). This epistemological means of seeing and creating order and unity in the contemplated object of love is always an artistic triumph for the poet. When the poet is able to achieve these paradisal creations of the love vision, *his* whole being (*both* his "sens" and his "imaginative") has been fully realized and satisfied. At that sublime moment, a higher definition of love and the struggle of art to capture that definition come together in a glorious creation in which the poet-lover takes utmost delight:

Plus ie poursuis par le discours des yeulx
L'art, & la main de telle pourtraicture,
Et plus i'admire, & adore les Cieulx
Accomplissantz si belle Creature,
Dont le parfaict de sa lineature
M'esmeult *le sens, & l'imaginatiue.*   (D288)

The poet is telling us in this "portrait" poem what he had told us above in D434: the crucial point for a great love poet is to conceive of the ineffable's presence, even in its absence. And this is done above all through the creative imagination, which performs its difficult task not discursively through logic, but symbolically through image where even the experience itself becomes ineffable. For our love poet, only through the marriage, such as we have seen it in the above poems, of the intellect-reason (*le sens* or *la raison*) and the imagination-sensibility (*l'imaginatiue* or *la memoyre*) can a higher poetic logic ("haulte pensée," D406) be established, an emotive logic that is crucial if he is to succeed in capturing the full essence and meaning of an ineffable kind of love. It is the recurrent function of Scève's poetic art to discover its limitations of purely rational discernment and to impose this new perspective, with this aesthetic marriage being even more valid and meaningful because of the extreme care in the precedent psychological observations on limitation and the striving for unity of perception and expression. D288 and D434, and many others we will be considering in this book which go beyond an initial stage of epistemological obscurity and anguish, do not contain at all a fragmented vision, but a full vision of wholeness and unity as constructed in both the object and the subject of poetic contemplation. And this is possible because these poems rely not only on reason but also on the creative imagination for this higher vision and its portrayal. This new transcendent perspective of the creative imagination helping and crucial to establishing a sense-beyond-sense is the high ground of poetry viewed as religion. It is also what separates and distinguishes aesthetic emotion from ordinary emotion and what turns the poet into an artist:

> Mont costoyant le Fleuue, & la Cité,
> Perdant ma veue en longue prospectiue,
> Combien m'as tu, mais combien incité
> A viure en toy vie contemplatiue?
> Ou toutesfoys *mon cœur par œuure actiue*
> *Auec les yeulx leue au Ciel la pensée*
> *Hors de soucy d'ire, & dueil dispensée*
> Pour admirer la paix, qui me tesmoingne
> Celle *vertu* lassus recompensée,
> Qui du Vulgaire, aumoins ce peu, m'esloingne.   (D412)

The rewards to be found in a higher kind of poetic contemplation and writing are "peace" and "virtue": the peace of mind and even pleasure that ultimately come with the perception of sacred beauty, and the virtue of art, the *virtus imaginativa*, whose portrayal of love records and raises the whole contemplative experience above the common level to that of paradise. The poet is acknowledging in this poem the higher operation and importance of his imagination, as he will do so many times. This "vie contemplatiue," so much an integral part of the poet's being, can be sustained only through the continued working together of his faculties of the imagination and the reason, the uplifting feeling and creative activity ("par œuure actiue") of the poet's "cœur" and "yeulx" and "pensée" seeking together a higher awareness and definition of love. The serenity of great art is always a quality of its unified, transfigured energies in the creative imagination, as it is the purpose of D412 to convey.

The poet's newly acquired perspective comes from what we can variously call creative virtue, creative reason, or quite simply the creative imagination. The important point is that an aesthetic emotion, an intellectual and emotional unity, is what is always being generated – the higher perception and pleasure of, as Valéry called it, "un tout autre monde." The feeling of poetic paradise is being created and experienced in both body and mind, in both its physical and spiritual significances: these are always supreme unitive moments in the poet's "vie contemplatiue" during which, as he puts it above in D412, his creative imagination (this time his "cœur par œuure actiue") raises both his eyes and his thought – both the sense and the intellect – to a higher contemplation and contentment. Only then can the poet truly understand and perhaps even portray the ineffable nature and higher meaning of Délie, as in fact so many of his poems tell us and show us:

> Ce lyen d'or, raiz de toy mon Soleil,
> Qui par le bras t'asseruit Ame, & vie,
> Detient si fort auec la veue *l'œil*,
> Que *ma pensée il t'à toute rauie.*   (D12)

> Qui *la pensée*, & *l'œil* mettroit sus elle,
> Soit qu'il fut pris d'amoureuse liesse,
> Soit qu'il languist d'aueuglée tristesse,
> Bien la diroit *descendue des Cieulx*,
> Tant s'en faillant qu'il ne la dist Déesse,
> S'il la voyoit de l'vn de mes deux yeulx.   (D44)

> Si de sa main ma fatale ennemye,
> Et neantmoins *delices de mon Ame*,
> Me touche vn rien, ma pensée endormye
> Plus, que le mort soubz sa pesante lame,
> Tressaulte en moy, comme si d'ardent flamme
> Lon me touchoit dormant profondement.   (D159)

> Ces tiens, non yeulx, mais estoilles celestes,
> Ont influence & sur *l'Ame*, & *le Corps*.   (D243)

> Et par son *tainct Angeliquement fraiz*
> Rompt ceste noise a nulle aultre pareille.   (D358)

> Par diuers acte, & mainte inuention
> Ie la contemple *en pensée rassise.*   (D363)

> Pour esmouoir *le pur de la pensée,*
> Et l'humble aussi de chaste affection,
> Voye tes faictz, ô Dame dispensée
> A estre loing d'humaine infection:
> Et lors verra en sa parfection
> Ton hault cœur sainct lassus se transporter:
> Et puis cy bas Vertus luy apporter
> *Et l'Ambrosie, & le Nectar des Cieulx,*

In search of love's epistemology

Comme i'en puis tesmoingnage porter
Par iurement de ces miens propres yeulx.   (D380)

In these poems, there is no longer any failure or dissociation of poetic sensibility, any real break between love words and the higher meaning they seek to translate, between the intellect-reason and the creative imagination. The poet is actually working towards a *reconstruction* of sensibility, towards the supreme state of a harmony and marriage of mind and matter which the poet's portrayal of Délie and of himself will culminate in. The specific forms of this poetic marriage, embodying, and urging the reader to accept, the emotive and even at times seemingly irrational logic of a sense-beyond-sense, will be the subject of our discussion in the remaining chapters of this book.[8]

To see even better Scève's progression from an epistemology of love based solely on reason, resulting in frustration and skepticism, to one based also on the imagination, which alone has the potential of leading to paradise, there is one final and crucial effect with serious ramifications for the poet which Délie and love produce in him and which I would like to discuss now. I have already alluded to this effect in the above section. It has to do with the implications of Scève viewing poetry as a kind of religion, as an activity and process for renewal of his faith in love and his creative imagination. Here I am not talking about his success as an artist, which I believe can only be assessed in his actual portrayals of Délie and love, and which we will begin addressing in the next chapter. Rather, what I am talking about has to do with his revival and even survival as a love poet, without which his paradisal portrayals would never have been possible. In the *Délie*, this constant theme of poetic struggle and revival carries with it always the heavy metaphorical burden of death, repentance and renewal. These ideas, I believe, are precisely the important ones the poet is developing in D69, in spite of the fact this poem has been interpreted very differently by other readers. I consider this D69 to be a pivotal poem which helps greatly to take us from the poetic limitations and lamentations of an old epistemological order to the imaginative art of a newly created poetic order and consciousness very much alive and paradisal in form and content. In reading D69, my thesis again is that Scève was much less concerned with any notion of unrequited love than with the contemplation and expression of the sacred and the ineffable. The principal source of Scève's obscurity and anguish is not to be found in the all too familiar reality-depicting condition and theme of unrequited love, but in his intense desire for an ineffable understanding and portrayal of higher poetic love. All analyses of this great symbolic poem which I have read take for granted that its theme is precisely unrequited love, with Délie's husband being cast in the role of the "Tyrant" forever preventing the poet's access to her:

> Par le penser, qui forme les raisons,
> Comme la langue a la voix les motz dicte:
> I'ay consommé maintes belles saisons
> En ceste vie heureusement maudicte,
> Pour recouurer celle a moy interdicte
> Par ce Tyrant, qui fait sa residence
> Là, ou ne peult ne sens, ne prouidence,
> Tant est par tout cauteleusement fin.
> Ce neantmoins, maulgré la repentence,
> I'espere, apres long trauail, vne fin.

Even McFarlane, in his extremely helpful commentaries on Scève's poems in his critical edition, which have rescued this reader from many a pitfall in pursuing Scève, takes the situation being described in D69 to be that of unrequited love. For example, he advises us to understand the verb *consommé* in line 3 in the sense of "waste"; *Tyrant* in line 6 as "Délie's husband, who thus conforms to a long literary tradition"; *sens* in line 7 as possibly meaning "scheming" (as indeed subsequent translators of this poem have used); and finally, *repentence* in line 9 is attributed to Délie.[9]

Other critics have gone even farther in viewing this poem as a realist narrative of unrequited love full of obscurity and anguish. Here is what Dorothy Coleman has to say on it, in effect expanding McFarlane's position:

Again there is deep reflection on the value of his life, which is wasted and paradoxically *heureusement maudicte*. The analysis he gives of a three-way relationship is embedded in the literary tradition of Augustan poets. Thus in Propertius, II.23 the poet specifically mentions the husband who may at any time come home and find his wife engaged in adulterous activities. . . . And so it is here in the dizain that *ce Tyrant* resides in *Délie* and takes love-rights over her body which is legally his. And yet the poet is hoping that after lengthy devotion and worshipful service to Délie he will in the end be rewarded. Délie will become an unfaithful wife in the strictly legal sense but in spite of her remorse after giving in to her lover they will be united by much stronger ties than purely human ones. . . . But when we put the companion dizain alongside the theme of the tyrant/husband and when we realise that love and death are really overlapping worlds we begin to see that this woodcut with death as the prime motif does open our minds to the whole problem of death as seen by a poet who was not like the Pléiade (poetry vanquished death) but was simply affirming that love for Délie conquers death.[10]

Perhaps D69 does justify some of the above interpretations. But I believe it also calls for more. There is indeed a "three-way relationship" being described in this poem, but I fail to see how it really involves Délie's husband as any kind of tyrant, or that it involves only that. What it involves as well is once again the central epistemological dilemma of the poet, his reason-language, and portrayal of the ineffable, with these three categories very cleverly being made to correspond to the rhyme scheme of *dicte/maudicte/interdicte*: the poet's rational faculty of *penser* (and of *sens* later in the poem) in dictating words (*dicte*) – because its meaning is *maudicte* and thus its desired result *interdicte* – is what is blocking the poet once again from the ineffable. Formulaically stated, for the poet's *penser* alone to conceive and say words (*dicte*) is to speak words that are damnable (*maudicte*) and thus words that prevent the poet from truly "telling" (*interdicte*). It is not the lover's life that has been "wasted," but the poet's contemplation and writing through *le penser* and its defective operation and language. This poem implicates the poet in the damage caused by him in having committed some kind of sin or fault, some kind of error. The real tyrant in this poem is the unfit working of the poet's *penser*, of mortal thought and words trying to overcome the barrier of the forbidden ineffable. For this love poet, *le penser* can never truly form ideas but can only dictate the failure of "tongued" words in its endless repetition of "raisons." It alone is not sufficient to enable the poet to "recover" the sacred and ineffable since this "Tyrant" that is mortal thought and language "fait sa residence / Là, ou ne peult ne sens, ne prouidence." In other words, this Tyrant resides where neither intelligence ("sens") nor wisdom ("prouidence") can truly prevail, in spite of, or perhaps better yet, as a result of its attempts at being so "cauteleusement fin," that is, so "deceitfully clever."

Love, perceived and articulated through *le penser* and its *raisons*, is itself a kind of Fall and is incompatible with the attainment of the higher ideal and the fulfillment of transcendent art required by *Délie, obiect de plus haulte vertu*. But despite this predicament, and in spite of the unfit way and artistic error of his *penser* and *raisons* (of mortal thought and language) in need of repair, amendment, and redemption, the poet always vows, as we are told in D69, to continue in his struggle to succeed in coming to higher terms with Délie as ineffable object and with *Délie* as sacred writing: "Ce neantmoins, maulgré la repentence / l'espere, apres long trauail, vne fin." The poet tells us as much again in another poem, in D34, which helps to shed light on the notion of the poet's "repentence" so crucial to an understanding of D69. I do not believe that this D34 is just another example of a poem concerned with unrequited love, that it was written to convey a simple anecdote and to depict the poet's frustration in love, as it too has been interpreted as doing:

> Ie ne l'ay veue encor, ne toy congneue
> *L'erreur, qui tant de coulpe m'imposa:*
> Sinon que foy en sa purité nue
> Causast le mal, a quoy se disposa
> Ton leger croire, & tant y reposa,
> Que ton cœur froid s'y mit totallement:
> Dont i'ay en moy conclu finablement
> *De composer a toute repentence,*
> Puis que ma vie on veult cruellement
> Pour autruy faulte offrir a penitence.

Since the poet does not even know what *erreur* he is guilty of committing in what he considers to be his unblemished and uncorrupted faith in love, his "foy en sa purité nue," he decides "de composer a *toute repentence.*" He will repent in his writings for *all* his errors and faults. And to repent as far as writing and poetic art are concerned means to rewrite and especially to keep writing. This is his burden, his fate, the penance and devotional sacrifice he must perform to show sorrow and to amend it. And for Scève the artist, this amendment of life, of perspective, of unfit former ways must mean the death of *la raison*, of *le penser*, of *le sens* if he is to keep on writing and striving for an ineffable understanding in love. Ultimately, this must also mean the death of the perceived tyranny that Délie's beauty has been exercising over his rational consciousness. *Tyrant* has a double meaning for Scève, and both of these meanings take us back to the central problem of the epistemology of the ineffable. It stands for both his defective *penser* and its ineffable object: Délie's divine beauty and the poet's desperate but failed attempts through *le penser* to understand and communicate it. This Tyrant is indeed that "Beaulté logée en amere doulceur" (D9) – this alien, unhuman, and murderously disturbing beauty that surpasses human understanding and literally "unwinds" (in the sense of the title of Emblem VIII – "La Femme qui desuuyde") or kills the poet's rational faculty of understanding, as the poet assures us again below in D306. Beauty in art, like love in life, is always cruel and bitter (i.e., tyrannical) when it remains unattainable, when it blocks a poet's desire for knowledge and possession of it:

> Ta *beaulté* fut premier, & doulx *Tyrant*,
> Qui m'arresta tresuiolentement:
> Ta grace apres peu a peu m'attirant,
> M'endormit tout en son enchantement:
> Dont assoupy d'vn tel contentement,
> N'auois de toy, ny de moy *congnoissance.*[11]

Thus, the poet's reason (i.e., "le penser" in D69) in its failed attempts to "recover" the ineffable Délie will have to be replaced, or at least amended, if he is ever to attain to a higher poetic understanding and meaning, that is, "knowledge" not only of Délie but of himself. And this will require of the poet a special kind of death and rebirth. The diaphorically reconstructive and life-giving aesthetic of *la beauté qui tue* becomes central and necessary to Scève's poetic vision of love. I would even suggest that Scève goes farther than did Ronsard with this motif of beauty-that-kills which symbolizes in Scève the death of an old poetic order (grounded in reason) and the aesthetic rebirth of a newly created poetic order (reconstructed through the imagination).[12] Scève will give to this theme of beauty-that-kills a sustained intensity and ultimate resolution which I have only seldom been able to find in Ronsard. For in the *Délie*, the poet as well as the reader is dealing not only with *la beauté qui tue* but also with, as I shall call it, *la beauté qui fait revivre.* As in Ronsard, however, this beauty in Scève is also what ravishes and utterly kills:

> Au receuoir de tes esclairs
> Tu m'offuscas & *sens*, & *congnoissance.*   (D80)

> Tes beaulx yeulx clers fouldroyamment luisantz
> Furent obiect a mes *pensers* vinque,
> Des que leurs rayz si doulcement nuisantz
> Furent le mal tressainctement inique.
> Duquel le coup penetrant tousiours picque
> Croissant la playe oultre plus la moytié.   (D212)

> Arcz de structure en beaulté nompareille,
> A moy iadis immortel argument,
> Vous estes seul, & premier instrument,
> Qui liberté, & *la raison* offence.
> Car qui par vous conclut resolument
> Viure en aultruy, en soy mourir commence.   (D270)

53

Toutes les foys, que sa lueur sur Terre
Iecte sur moy vn, ou deux de ses raiz,
En ma *pensée* esmeult l'obscure guerre
Parqui me sont *sens*, & *raison* soubstraictz.   (D358)

And above all, what Délie's tyrannical beauty ravishes and kills in
Scève is the poet's "pensée," "sens," and "raison," as these poems
confirm once again. But especially in Scève, not only does this
beauty kill (and it is always the poet's ability to reach an understand-
ing of the ineffable Délie through rational conceptualization that is
killed), but it also revives and redeems, it leads to the emergence
of the poet's higher creative intelligence or imagination.[13] Scève's
concern with and portrayal of death and rebirth appear through-
out his sequence and are a strong indication of this poet's con-
scious struggle for renewal against anguish and obscurity, with
renewal being both psychological and artistic. Scève discovered
in death – and in particular in that very special form of it I have
been describing as Beauty-that-kills – a liberating energy for
higher contemplation and writing, for the higher life of the poetic
imagination. Here are just a few of the many metaphorical affir-
mations of this idea which await the reader throughout the *Délie*:

Non de Venus les ardentz estincelles,
Et moins les traictz, desquelz Cupido tire:
Mais bien *les mortz, qu'en moy tu renouelles*
Ie t'ay voulu en cest Oeuure descrire.   ("A sa Délie")
En sa beaulté gist ma mort, & *ma vie*.   (D6)

Quoy que du temps tout grand oultrage face,
Les seches fleurs en leur odeur viuront:
Prœuue pour ceulz, qui le bien poursuyuront
De non mourir, mais *de reuiure encore*.   (D11)

Si donc le Cœur au plaisir, qu'il reçoit,
Se vient luy mesme a martyre liurer:
Croire fauldra, que la Mort doulce soit,
Qui l'Ame peult d'angoisse deliurer.   (D114)

Comme elle seule à esté, & sera
Mort de ma mort, & *vie de ma vie*.   (D167)

Toutes les fois qu'en mon entendement
Ton nom diuin par la memoire passe,
L'esprit rauy d'vn si doulx sentement,
En aultre vie, & plus doulce trespasse.   (D168)

Car tu y vis & mes nuictz, & *mes jours*,
Voyre exemptez des moindres fascheries:

Et ie m'y meurs en telles resueries,
Que ie m'en sens haultement contenté.   (D216)

Tout en esprit rauy sur la beaulté
De nostre ciecle & honneur, & merueille,
Celant en soy la doulce cruaulté,
Qui en mon mal si plaisamment m'esueille,
Ie songe & voy: & voyant m'esmerueille
De ses doulx ryz, & elegantes mœurs.
Les admirant si doulcement ie meurs,
Que plus profond a y penser ie r'entre:
Et y pensant, mes silentes clameurs
Se font ouyr & des Cieulx, & du Centre.   (D228)

En qui Nature à mis pour sa plaisance
Tout le parfaict de son diuin ouurage,
Et tellement, certes, qu'a sa naissance
Renouella le Phoenix de nostre aage.   (D278)

Qui par ses yeulx me rend mort, & *viuant.*   (D352)

O si tu es de mon viure amoureuse,
De si doulx arcz ne crains la fureur telle.
Car eulx cuidantz donner mort douloureuse,
Me donnent *vie heureuse, & immortelle.*   (D390)

These poems containing a death-to-life itinerary are beautiful examples of Scève's diaphoric art of transcendence based on the *via negativa*. They posit an ultimately higher life-affirming goal to be attained through the death of anguish and obscurity, through the loss of purely rational understanding and its portrayal. Scève's poetry not only affirms the conquering of death, like the Pléiade's, but does lead to new and more essential life. It is never a poetry of the reason, one intent on fulfilling the dictates and design of *raison*, *pensée*, or *sens*, that would permit a love poet like Scève to progress from the potentially negative view of beauty-that-kills to the redeeming and constructive view of beauty-that-revives. This progress can only be had in opting for another kind of poetry: a paradisal poetry of the imagination. For me, there is even an unmistakable trace in the above poems of reversal and renewal highlighting not only "la Beauté qui tue" but also "la Beauté qui fait revivre" of the New Testament teaching that he who would save his life must first lose it; that only in reaching one's end does one discover a new beginning, does one reach his desired destination of paradise. Only in this new life of the imagination that comes from death can the poet, "haultement contenté," truly experience this "aultre vie, &

plus doulce," this "vie heureuse, & immortelle." It seems to me that in this group of poems, in Scève's death-to-life portrayals, the reader is driven to find a second and more profound level of understanding of the poet's meaning, the higher reality the poet refers to in D402 as "plus seconde chose." And this higher reality so deeply sought by the poet is psychological, epistemological, and especially artistic, by definition. The above poems are not at all highlighting a love discourse of silence and death, but propose a confrontation by author, text, and reader of the limits of awareness. At these limits, both the ineffable and the ineffable experience the poet is undergoing become not negation and defeat but creation and triumph. I must quote a very special poem in the *Délie*, one that we all have encountered before and which is very much about poetic death and recovery and which once again provides us another beautiful portrayal of the deathly state of "penser" being redeemed and replaced by the higher life of the poet's creative imagination, which he this time calls his "ame rauie." This D79 contains one of Scève's best expressions of the transcendent metaphor of beauty-that-kills with its redeeming, imaginative corollary of beauty-that-revives. The death-like state of the poet's "penser" in its futilely reasoning grief is shown to give way to the illuminating life of the poet's "ame rauie," to the soul of the poet's creative imagination:

> L'Aulbe estaingnoit Estoilles a foison,
> Tirant le iour des regions infimes,
> Quand Apollo montant sur l'Orison
> Des montz cornuz doroit les haultes cymes.
> Lors du profond des tenebreux Abysmes,
> Ou mon penser par ses fascheux ennuyz
> Me fait souuent percer les longues nuictz,
> *Ie reuoquay a moy l'ame rauie*:
> Qui, dessechant mes larmoyantz conduictz,
> Me feit cler veoir le Soleil de ma vie.

Far from providing the reader a poetic description of limitation and lamentation and impasse, this poem dramatically presents the artistic struggle to recover new life. The poet's nightlong struggle with his faculty of reason – which takes him to the very depths of the "tenebreux Abysmes" where it, his *thought*, his *"penser,"* makes him undergo many a long, obscure night – is being relieved by the break of day, by the recovery of his "ame rauie," of his imaginative faculty which gives him vision of the ineffable. The tension in Scève's verse, that tension which is the life of his poetry, resides in his struggle for something which the poet feels his intellect alone cannot accept and grasp. So he transfers the pursuit of the idea of transcendence, of the sacred and ineffable Délie, to the realm of art, to the purview of the creative imagination. The all-too-familiar struggle and conflict depicted again in this poem (the poet's *thought* lost in dark abysses, wasted in wearied grief, in tears, in long nights) exist because, in Scève's view, it is the poet's supreme duty to discern and illuminate order even amid chaos, an order which for a poet like Scève is the highest kind of all – an aesthetic order which enables him, finally, to see clearly and to communicate clearly his vision: "Me feit cler veoir le Soleil de ma vie." In the triumph of the supreme line "Ie reuoquay a moy l'ame rauie," Scève is showing himself, in his molding of the recalcitrant and dark materials of love into a higher order and creation and meaning, to be a greater poet of the imagination than he is a poet thwarted by reason. This poem reveals what I consider to be the central tenet underlying Scève's particular vision of love: adversity and struggle do indeed serve to introduce a poet to the ineffable love object of his contemplation and writing, but to do this, they must also serve to introduce a poet to himself, to make him aware of the potential and power of the creative imagination which he may contain within himself.

It is only through the revival and higher operation of the creative imagination (what the poet variously calls his "memoyre" or his "ame rauie" or his "cœur par œuure active" or his "imaginatiue"), or at least of the poet's "raison," "pensée," and "sens" qualified and amended as such, as we have seen it presented in this chapter ("Raison *par vraye congnoissance*" [D182], "pensée *rassise*" [D363], "le *pur* de la pensée" [D380], "*haulte* pensée" [D406], "*plus haut* sens" [D432], and so forth) that Scève is able to create and communicate what Valéry called the "powerful sense" of a poem: "the sensuous form of a poem [Délie's "forme elegante"] and its exchange value in terms of ideas [Délie's "vertu"]." Higher thought and higher reason and soul, heart, imagination are often interchangeable terms in the *Délie*. Scève is often at a loss to describe and name this power, which I believe may be best called simply the creative imagination. Since it is the faculty by which the poet and the reader commune with the sacred and the ineffable, it transcends all human efforts to designate it as it transcends being confined to the logical limits of language.

Surely the predominantly artistic relevance of Scève's struggle is becoming apparent. *Raison, penser, sens* – imperfect forms of sight operating through rational discernment – comprise the faculty by which the poet perceives the world and its objects, such as Délie's "beaulté" or "forme elegante," as Material. Utilitarian, sensuous, and divisive, this lower form of sight for higher understanding is indispensable but incomplete. Through it alone, the poet's world is essentially literal, static, uncreative, and meaningless. The higher insight provided by the imagination is what enables the poet *also* to perceive the higher ideal (Délie as "vertu" or "Idée") which is the innate reality and spiritual beauty of the love object. As we have seen, the crucial and constructive role played by this imagination always endows Scève's poetic world with newly discovered unity and life, and thus with higher meaning. Without it, Scève would never have been able to portray Délie and *Délie* as "*obiect* de plus haulte *vertu*," both her and its "*beaulté* esmerueillable *Idée*" (D275).

The problem we have been considering in this chapter of Scève's impasse in contemplation of the ineffable love object containing both the bodily ("forme elegante" or "beaulté") and the spiritual ("vertu" or "Idée"), both extrinsic and intrinsic beauty, did frustrate many a Renaissance love poet and love artist in their attempts at portraying this object fully and successfully. This problem of knowledge and portrayal also led to much theoretical speculation on the ability of the mediums of poetry and painting to respond to the challenge. Our modern critical concern with the notion of specularity, be it the self-questioning and self-reflexive nature of the art of writing or that of the art of painting, is rooted in a sort of epistemological crisis perceived by the Renaissance poets and painters themselves, which they struggled to overcome, some successfully, some unsuccessfully. This was in essence the same dilemma Ronsard faced: the problem of how to transform his initial contemplation of his love object in its overwhelming sensuous physicality into contemplation of higher "Idea" as achieved by the creative imagination. For it is always the imagination, not reason, which enables a poet to connect a spiritual meaning to a portrayal of physical form. Ray Ortali has studied very nicely this aesthetic progression in Ronsard's love poetry and shows how it reflects the ideal of art advocated by Marsilio Ficino:

Lorsqu'aux beautés du corps s'ajoutent, comme chez la bien-aimée de Ronsard, "les valeurs" de l'âme, on est bien proche de l'état décrit par Ficin, dans lequel les amants "ne voient plus l'aimé dans sa simple apparence perçue, ils le contemplent dans l'image modifiée par leur *âme* à la ressemblance de son idée [i.e., the same operation performed by the creative imagination – the "ame rauie" and the "imaginatiue" – of Scève's poet-lover], plus belle que le corps."[14]

The artists of the Renaissance period were also struggling with the same problem of how to render a more perfect portrayal of the full and complete essence of love and woman. Some of them, relying on the same inexpressibility topos which we have seen to inform much of Scève's early epistemological thinking on the subject, concluded finally that, in the medium of art and portraiture, it was impossible. Other artists and most notably Leonardo Da Vinci demonstrated that it could be done, that the full representation of extrinsic beauty (body) and intrinsic beauty (soul) could be accomplished. Elizabeth Cropper has convincingly shown this higher portrayal by Leonardo to have been the true challenge and triumph of this great love artist: "Leonardo accepted the challenge of the *paragone* more aggressively than his contemporaries, determining to express the beauty of the *soul* through the representation of the graceful movements of the *body*. . . . Responding to the poet's challenge, he represented the *form* and character of an individual woman as the effigy of the perfect *idea* in the lover's heart."[15]

In Scève, as we have already seen, the perfect idea and image of Délie as aesthetic object are also to be found in the lover's "heart" ("mon cœur par œuure active" – D412) which, along with his "soul," is the site of the creative imagination. Scève goes much beyond the mere theoretical speculation involved in identifying and affirming the value and role of the imagination in ineffable writing. Important as are his statements and beliefs on this faculty and its contribution to poetic production, the embodiments of the ineffable he provides the reader, showing the imagination (heart and soul) at work, are much more meaningful and significant. These ineffable creations testify to his successful struggle of surmounting the epistemological problem of representation. Scève will succeed at acquiring a "knowledge" of the ineffable Délie, at merging spiritual Idea with sensuous Form (which we shall consider in detail in the next chapter), and this paradisal blend will always mirror the difficult yet complete representation of Délie as ineffable love object:

> Quand ie te vy orner ton chef doré,
> *Au cler miroir mirant plus [clere] face,*
> Il fut de toy si fort enamouré,
> Qu'en se plaingnant il te dit a voix basse:

Destourne ailleurs tes yeux, ô l'*oultrepasse*.
Pourquoy? dis tu, tremblant d'vn ardent zele.
Pource, respond, que ton œil, Damoiselle,
Et ce *diuin, & immortel visage*
Non seulement les hommes brule, & gele:
Mais moy aussi, ou est ta propre image.   (D230)

This image of Délie being reflected in a clear mirror from which, in turn, radiates an even brighter face ("l'oultrepasse" – the *ineffable* Délie) shows the profound specular nature and power of Scève's transcendent poetic vision. It is this "*beyond*" that haunts Scève, this beauty of Délie which the poet feels beyond his reach and vision, but which he also feels he must somehow grasp and communicate. This reflected representation of Délie's "diuin, & immortel visage" is the poet's intense desire to be utterly absorbed by it and to possess it completely. In this way, the lyric portrayal of beauty and the ineffable does often become its own object. The specular paradox of a poetry of the imagination transmitting the discernment of something more beautiful, of a sense-beyond-sense or of a beauty-beyond-beauty, what Valéry calls "un tout autre monde" beyond the ordinary world, does seem at times to displace the very object of contemplation itself by the poetic act or image. This becomes the ultimate test of Scève's poetic imagination and art: he is often forced to close his eyes to his object, so to speak, as he tells us in D165, in order better to contemplate and portray it. Once again, for the reality-depicting condition of "tearful" anguish and obscurity is being substituted a higher vision of the imagination and its workings, one which succeeds in capturing Délie's full essence of physical form and spiritual idea:

Mes pleurs clouantz au front ses tristes yeulx,
A la *memoire* ouurent la *veue instante*,
Pour *admirer*, & *contempler trop mieulx*
Et sa *vertu*, & sa *forme elegante*.

Thus, even absence, or better yet presence-in-absence, in the *Délie* can serve a positive purpose. The absence of the love object is what quite often triggers the more significant working presence and potential of the poet's imagination. In Délie's absence, it is the poet's faculty of the imagination (presented below again as "memoyre") which, working now in unison with the poet's faculty of reason, enables him better to contemplate and communicate, indeed to "enjoy," both Délie's extrinsic and intrinsic beauty, that is, her full essence which is always one of *vertu* and *forme elegante* (or else *grace* as the latter quality is called in this poem):

> *Ainsi absent* la *memoyre* posée,
> *Et plus tranquille, & apte a conceuoir,*
> Par la raison estant interposée,
> Comme *clarté a l'obiect*, qu'on veult veoir:
> Rumine en soy, & sans se deceuoir
> Gouste trop mieulx *sa vertu, & sa grace*,
> Que ne faisoient presentez a sa face
> Les sentementz de leur ioye enyurez,
> Qui maintenant par plus grand'efficace
> Sentent leur bien de leur mal deliurez.   (D434)

These three poems just quoted – D230, D165, and D434 – in depicting and affirming an ineffable presence or reality above and beyond the problematics of obscurity, anguish, and absence, point to a higher, more intensely imagined love-form and art-form. They are good examples of what Julia Kristeva has called in love poetry its intense specular desire to communicate a "message d'elle-même, signe de l'intensité amoureuse," of love poetry consumed with transmitting much more than the bare and ordinary sentiments, the reality-depicting anxiety and frustrations of an unrequited love. As we have already begun to see in the *Délie*, in this kind of intense poetry, the beloved object quite often becomes "simplement un destinataire imaginaire, prétexte de l'incantation." The ultimate value which Scève seeks to capture is not so much love as it is the ineffable art of poetry itself. This is what I mean when I say that Scève viewed poetry as religion. Of course, there is absolutely nothing incompatible with this notion of art as religion and the kind of higher love Scève envisioned. Indeed, the two go hand in hand. The "message" reflected in these poems is the poet's struggle to merge with and to possess Beauty and Perfection. For Scève, the poetic art of the ineffable is always more than a rational and logical process: it both takes possession and itself demands to be possessed. This aesthetic longing and its creation of "forms of attention," as another critic has called them, are what are truly being mirrored for the reader in the presence-beyond-absence and sense-beyond-sense message of D230, D165, and D434. These poems *are* the poet's *via negativa* highlighting his sense and portrayal of a *mise en abyme*, of the poet not just finding presence in absence but being able to see there a more complete and satisfying essence defined always as sensuous Form and spiritual Idea. This highly emotive and seductive portrayal, grounded in a metaphysics of literary specular meaning, is also what compels from the reader a meta-physics of literary response.[16]

Délie is often depicted as being absent in other ways, but her strong presence in the poet's creative imagination is none the less perceived and communicated, and even better so (as the poet sees it) because of her absence. These specular portrayals again reflect the greater aesthetic experience the poet is undergoing more than any amorous experience. Scève's images of Délie's imagined presence through her absence are metaphors of poetic and sacred writing. Whether it is her "diuin, & immortel visage" being reflected in the mirror image above of D230, or her "secrette, & digne chose" which is being disclosed in another mirror image in D257, or the "sainct miroir de voz sacrées vndes" of the water and fountain in D235 which reflect Délie's "holy" presence after she has bathed in them, Scève uses the pretext and condition of absence in order better to portray presence and essence. These mirror images serve primarily to provoke a mental reconstruction, not so much of Délie as the object of poetry, but of poetry itself as object in which they serve as figures in the reflecting pool of imagined consciousness. This way, and with Délie necessarily absent, the poet is truly able to endow emotive form with higher idea, to bring together the sensuous and even sensual and the spiritual in the singularly complete and imagined Délian image of Beauty-Idea. The poet pledges himself to this higher, transcendent portrayal and vows to employ whatever artistic means necessary to achieve it. In D275, the poet specifically acknowledges and sets for himself this intense artistic goal of creating and combining "the sensuous form of a poem [Délie's 'beaulté'] and its exchange value in terms of ideas [Délie's 'beaulté' becoming also 'esmerueillable Idée']." In this proclaimed commitment to ineffable reflection and writing of a high religious intensity combining the intellect and the imagination, Scève is embracing the art of poetry at least equally as much as he is Délie:

> Pour m'incliner souuent a celle image
> De ta *beaulté esmerueillable Idée*,
> Ie te presente autant de foys l'hommage,
>
> .   .   .
>
> Reueramment, te voyant, te salue,
> Comme qui offre, auec son demeurant
> Ma vie aux piedz de ta *haulte value*.

In the end, the real "value" that the *Délie* attempts to assert is that a non-present, a non-rational, an almost non-portrayable understanding and revelation of the sacred and ineffable love object are not only worthwhile but possible.

The remaining chapters of this study will continue to view the obscurity and anguish of Scève's love lyrics as potentially positive qualities and will focus on specific techniques of the poetic imagination used in the *Délie* to capture higher contemplation and creation. It is not logical or rational comprehension (sight through reason) that will lead a poet to a full and satisfying knowledge of the ineffable, but the freeing up and affirming of a higher power and potential (insight provided by the creative imagination). Though not developing this idea in reference to Scève's love lyrics, Claude-Gilbert Dubois has shown this aesthetic principle of the imagination to be crucial to an understanding and appreciation of the other Renaissance poets and writers he considers in his seminal book *L'Imaginaire de la Renaissance*.[17]

Since a resistant and adversative impulse pervades Scève's poems, one that always seeks to check the poet's attempts at capturing the poetic ineffable, we will never be far removed from the drama of poetic struggle and the poet's recognition of the constant need for perseverance. In Scève, obscurity and anguish are a constant quality of vision. They serve to generate this vision. They do not, in the final analysis, mirror any dissociation of sensibility, but are a most revealing reflection of the way in which he conceived of the art of poetry and its difficult pursuit of aesthetic beauty. Scève's purpose and desire are always strong and persistent; it is what they drive him towards that sometimes makes his poems appear obscure and anguished. He is constantly trying to come to terms with the ineffable, and it always seems to be eluding him. His poems enact this struggle. The poet-lover invites his reader to embark on a quest parallel to his own: an imaginative reassessment and metaphoric re-creation of love in concrete, transcendent terms. Only in being able to portray Délie in both body-form and spirit-idea can the poet truly succeed in conveying her sacred, transcendent meaning, her "beauté esmerueillable Idée." This challenge is nothing less than an attempt to achieve the diaphorically transcendent principle of art admired so profoundly by Valéry. Our poet's success in embodying this unitive principle of love and of art will enable him and the *Délie* to progress to the "marvel" of poetry as defined by Valéry, that is, the turning of disorder into order in the poetic image combining sensuous form and spiritual idea.

For Scève, there can be no literary ontology, no literary creation, no literary being or existence without knowledge of the ineffable Délie, a knowledge which must be discovered through the struggle of literary creation. This constitutes, in my view, the great artistic love theme of the *Délie*.[18] In his love lyrics, Scève does acquire and communicate knowledge, a poetic knowledge of the ineffable Délie as contemplated object (our subject in the next chapter) and of the ineffable contemplating self (our subject in Chapter 4). Both of these ineffable portrayals and poetic triumphs he accomplishes through Valéry's definition of the supreme unitive-luminous principle of poetic contemplation. This malleable, transfigured principle of mind and art highlighting a transcendence of the creative act is what will enable our poet to capture Délie's/*Délie*'s *vertu* and *forme élégante*, and thus to demonstrate his own *vertu*, to realize the potential of the poetic self as "obiect de la Vertu" (D167).

3

EMBODYING THE SACRED AND INEFFABLE: POETIC FORMS OF TRANSCENDENCE AND PARADISE

This chapter will explore how Scève creates the aesthetics of transcendence and paradise. It will be concerned with how the poet acquires knowledge of Délie, with the external forms and portrayals of the love object in which Scève captures both the body and the soul, the matter and the spirit, of poetic contemplation, both Délie's "forme elegante" and her "vertu" (D165). There awaits the reader in the *Délie* not only striking epiphoric portrayals of Délie achieved through lexical embellishment and imagistic intensification, but even more powerful diaphoric portrayals of her through the highly developed aesthetic techniques of transfiguration and transillumination. It is especially in these intense creations where the reader can best see the poet's imagination combining the ideal of love with the concrete image to reveal the true and full essence of Délie's "haulte value" (D275), her transcendent worth. All of Scève's poetic ways of seeing and portraying Délie are for the purpose of glorifying her, of aggrandizing and ennobling her, truly for the purpose of deifying or sacralizing Délie as the sensuous object and form of a higher love. These portrayals are the poet's way of participating in "un tout autre monde," of constructing *Délie*'s "Parolle saincte en toute esiouissance" (D278) which offers the reader marvelous poetic creations combining sensuous form and spiritual idea. These extremely seductive portrayals will support Valéry's notions on poetic art which we have been applying to Scève throughout this book. They will highlight the imaginatively creative and form-giving function of emotion regarded not as a feeling merely, but as a process of investigation and revelation, an adventure by our poet in the diaphoric malleability of transcendent art.

In his own experience with these portrayals of the sacred and ineffable love object, the reader will find an even greater and more intense and almost always paradoxical emphasis being placed by Scève on the blending of the physical and the spiritual. This should now come as little surprise. Scève's diaphorically ineffable portrayals connecting the spiritual and the physical represent his highest and most difficult achievement in composing aesthetic metaphor. And the success of this portrayal, each time Scève achieves it, is what continually paves the way for and sustains the new, ever-emerging poetic perspective of the imagination. This diaphoric portrayal of the sacred, of Délie's and *Délie*'s "Parolle saincte," begins with this poetic and metaphysical principle found in John 1:14: "The Word was made flesh and dwelt among us." So too does the great difficulty involved in expressing this principle: to demonstrate that the sacred, in its spiritual and physical wholeness, can be revealed in human speech; to show that mortal words, grounded in perceived physicality, and the sacred, containing an ineffable spirituality, can be brought together in the linguistic and poetic act of transcendence.

To be sure, all successful portrayals of the Word are paradoxical and problematic and disturbing whether in Christ, in Scève, or in Mallarmé. Mircea Eliade was one of the first to call our attention to this problem which he termed the "dialectique du sacré." The problem is deceptively simple: how to face and portray a spiritual truth in its physical beauty and body. There can really be only one solution. It proposes that sacred portrayal and writing can be fully realized only by a creative act of the imagination embodying both spiritual insight and sensuous perception. The success of this sacred mode of writing Eliade calls the creation of "hierophanies," when a human thing or object ceases to be merely profane and acquires a new "dimension" of sacredness.[1] This sacred dimension of a higher contemplation and writing can be reached only through transcendent, metaphorical portrayal of the love object. In the *Délie*, we are presented this sacred dimension which the poet creates through his diaphoric images and portrayals of a highly transfigured and transilluminated art-form. Scève develops and perfects the aesthetic technique of transfiguration (the poet will change the appearance of form, he will spiritualize physical form or matter in diaphoric images of spirit-in-matter) and the aesthetic technique of transillumination (the poet will endow matter with light, he will let light pass through matter or physical form in diaphoric images of light-in-dark). In the end, these two techniques will serve the poet's purpose, announced in the sequence's sub-title, of portraying Délie as "*obiect* de plus haulte *vertu*."

There is no finer poet in whom to study and appreciate this sacred dimension of a higher art-form than Scève. Through an artistically analogous act patterned on the biblical Incarnation, Scève celebrates a love which is more than human, a "divine" love which truly comes from the "Deity." This love cannot be communicated to us through the intellect or rational sense alone, but requires the "volenté sainctement obstinée" (D421) of the poet's creative intelligence or imagination. The purpose of this kind of imagining is always to reveal the sacred love object's most intimate workings in the poet's heart or soul. Délie's sacred influence on the poet's soul and heart, providing them insight, recovery, and renewal, is a constant theme in the *Délie*. Scève connects the activity of the heart and soul to the creative imagination (the coupling of "cœur–memoire," "ame–fantasie," "cœur–œuvre active–longue prospective–vie contemplatiue," "ame–vertu," and so forth in the examples below) and its role of feeling deeply and of relating these feelings:

> Mon Basilisque auec sa poingnant' veue
> Perçant Corps, Cœur, & Raison despourueue,
> Vint penetrer en l'Ame de mon Ame.   (D1)

> Si le desir, image de la chose,
> Que plus on ayme, est du cœur le miroir,
> Qui touiours fait par memoire apparoir
> Celle . . .   (D46)

> Tant ie l'aymay, qu'en elle encor ie vis:
> Et tant la vy, que, maulgré moy, ie l'ayme.
> Le sens, & l'ame y furent tant rauis,
> Que par l'Oeil fault, que le cœur la desayme.   (D49)

> Celle, de qui la rencontre m'estonne,
> De qui la voix si fort en l'ame tonne.   (D92)

> Renaist soubdain en moy celle aultre Lune
> Luisante au centre, ou l'Ame à son seiour.   (D106)

> Meites la flambe en mon ame allumée.   (D121)

> Lors ie sentis distiler en mon ame
> Le bien du bien, qui tout aultre surmounte.   (D133)

> Mais le grillet, ialouse fantasie,
> Qui sans cesser chante tout ce, qu'il cuyde,
> Et la pensée, & l'Ame ayant saisie,
> Me laisse vif a ma doulce homicide.   (D153)

Et le parfaict de ta beaulté croissant
Dedans mon cœur tousiours se renouelle. (D176)

Et par ce nom encor ie t'en adiure,
Qui en mon cœur escript te perpetue. (D325)

Mont costoyant le Fleuue, & la Cité,
Perdant ma veue en longue prospective,
Combien m'as tu, mais combien incité
A viure en toy vie contemplatiue?
Ou toutesfoys mon cœur par œuure actiue
Avec les yeulx leue au Ciel la pensée . . . (D412)

This list could be extended with many more examples. As I have said earlier, it is typical of Scève's perception and portrayal of the sacred love object that he does not always clearly distinguish the faculty performing these operations – the heart, the soul, higher reason, and so on. The explanation is that he considered all of them in their highest significations to be manifestations of the divine and immortal part of the sacred object and of the subject contemplating this object. I do not believe that Scève was overly concerned with naming this higher faculty, and neither should we be. The crucial point is that in finding a home for the sacred object in the soul, it is possible for the poet to discover and enjoy a supreme state beyond reason which he always identifies with divine love and which, paradoxically, in its ontological flashes of insight, is made possible only by the "death" of ordinary reason and life. Here is how the poet presents this picture in D443, turning to myth for personal and poetic clarification:

Combien qu'a nous soit cause le Soleil
Que toute chose est tresclerement veue:
Ce neantmoins pour trop arrester l'œil
En sa splendeur lon pert soubdain la veue.
Mon ame ainsi de son obiect pourueue
De tous mes sens me rend abandonné,
Comme si lors en moy tout estonné
Semeles fust en presence rauie
De son Amant de fouldre enuironné,
Qui luy ostast par ses esclairs la vie.

This higher and glorious "death" is what produces in the poet the loss of all his senses, just as Semele, in the ravishing presence of her own Beloved (Jupiter), was struck down by death. In both cases, the "death" of the poet and that of Semele, its importance is above all symbolic. This death does not mean that the sacred cannot be felt and that experience portrayed, but that they must be done so differently. The workings of the poet's higher imagination do spring from his perceived limitation (usually viewed as death) of sight and reasoning which cannot direct him to the knowledge and portrayal of the sacred. But one kind of death can become an opening, as we saw in the last chapter, to a different kind of life, to another world viewed and created symbolically in the imagination through the aesthetic perception and embodiment of the sacred.[2] Délie as "death," as "la beauté qui tue," is also our poet's only hope for unlocking the door, his only hope for bridging the gap between heaven and earth.

Scève's symbolic and creative imagination constructs higher meaning through a metaphoric network of hierarchical analogy and linkage, of the human to the divine, of the low to the high, of love's sensuous and even sensual desire ("la couleur de paille") to love's spiritual principle ("ce cler," "ce neigeant"), with the appropriate understanding of symbol and sign being crucial to this poetic portrayal and process:

> Ce cler luisant sur la couleur de paille
> T'appelle au but follement pretendu:
> Et de moy, Dame, asseurance te baille,
> Si chasque signe est par toy entendu.
>
> . . .
>
> Et ce neigeant flocquant parmy ces fentes
> Est pure foy, qui iouyssance honnore.   (D377)

In the poet's vision of a sacredly *requited* love ("qui iouyssance honnore"), in this blending in the color symbolism of D377 of light and white with yellow, the key figure sustaining this vision and making it work poetically and hang together structurally is Délie portrayed as transcendent object. Her influence in coloring the love experience ties the poet's human love to the anticipated longing and enjoyment of a sacred love. And it is the perceived possibility of this ideal and not its actual attainment which is enough to keep the poet searching and writing. What the poet does acquire in the end is a creative and honorable discipline of the will of an artist. Paradise – higher love and art – is a difficult and elusive aspect of reality which must always seem to remain just beyond the poet's final reach. This is why the reader of the *Délie* often has the impression that the ideal has been captured even as it escapes the poet's grasp. Although perhaps never fully realized by the poet, it has somehow been validated, and the poetic imagination that can conceive of it has thereby fulfilled itself even in defeat. But the important point for Scève is to conceive of the sacred and ineffable, and he does that here and now. Through representation in human terms of transcendent image and symbol, the sole means after all of communicating the ideal in poetry and of making it effable, Scève establishes contact with the sacred world. Much more is involved here than simply making poems out of abstract ideas. Scève's kind of poetry is always an exercise in conceiving clearly and feeling deeply, of informing and connecting mortal words and image ("la couleur de paille," "ces fentes") with the likeness of what is perhaps paradisal ("ce cler," "ce neigeant"). This kind of diaphoric juxtaposition accounts for the great emotional intensity of the *Délie* which many of its readers experience. It is precisely this new poetic life, full of the hidden intensity and arresting force of the sacred, which the poet must feel and portray if he is to find truth, poetic truth, and express it. It is only through metaphoric concentration, which paradoxically leads to expansion, of a sacred essence in physical form that the poet can ultimately provide the imagination and the intellect with higher beauty and truth. As a trope, a subjective component of poetic truth, Délie's "diuin visage," her "beaulx yeulx clers," in a word her "forme humaine," are felt and interpreted by the poet as so sacred that he is able to experience paradise right here on earth. But this revelation and understanding are not as easy for him as they might appear. It takes the commitment and courage of a great love poet to see and come to rest in the worldly meaning of Love's Transcendence, to perceive this "Ange en forme humaine" and to understand and accept this "gracieux domaine / Du Paradis terrestre en son visage" as the real object of poetic activity and struggle:

> Apperceuant cest Ange en forme humaine,
> Qui aux plus fortz rauit le dur courage
> Pour le porter au gracieux domaine
> Du Paradis terrestre en son visage,
> Ses beaulx yeulx clers par leur priué vsage
> Me dorent tout de leurs rayz espanduz.   (D409)

Scève's struggle in "apperceuant cest Ange en forme humaine, / Qui aux plus fortz *rauit le dur courage*" is that of all love poets in coming to acceptable terms with and in giving substantive reality to a sacred and ineffable ideal. Here is how Diotima in Plato's *Symposium* describes this transcendent progression and end of the love vision and its portrayal:

When a man has been thus far tutored in the lore of love, passing from view to view of beautiful things, in the right and regular ascent, suddenly he will have revealed to him, as he draws to the close of his dealings in love, *a wondrous vision*, beautiful in its nature; and this, Socrates, is the final object of all those *previous toils*.[3]

This "wondrous vision" arising out of Scève's own poetic "toils" is "ce cler" and "ce neigeant" in D377 and "cest Ange en forme humaine" in D409. For the poet, Délie's light answers in earthly form the light that is surely to be found in the sacred and ineffable world. In Scève's epistemological pursuit of the ineffable, the poet in his struggle for cognition and understanding of this object relies ultimately on the human acts of imagination that allow him to make experience meaningful. He examines this side of mental activity and creativity, which I call his transcendent paradisal mode, and makes important advances in the effort to unravel its nature. As we shall see in this chapter, the poet's transcendent vision will give many other marvelous and substantive forms and shapes to Délie and to love throughout the poems of the *Délie*.

The sacred drama of Scève's poetry, artistically and paradoxically his transcendent portrayal being achieved through the creation and illumination provided by the diaphoric act, really begins with the "coming" of Délie into this world. Here is the poet's description of Délie's introduction into the world in D7:

> Celle beaulté, qui embellit le Monde
> Quand nasquit celle en qui mourant ie vis,
> A imprimé en ma lumiere ronde
> Non seulement ses lineamentz vifz:
> Mais tellement tient mes espritz rauiz,
> En admirant sa mirable merveille,
> Que presque mort, sa Deité m'esueille
> En la clarté de mes desirs funebres,
> Ou plus m'allume, & plus, dont m'esmerueille,
> Elle m'abysme en profondes tenebres.

Délie's descent in the form of human flesh ("ses lineamentz vifz") is perceived through the poet's struggling ascent to the divine vision. The emergence of his "clarté" is the result of contemplating Délie's living features. This poetically upward gaze responding to the sacred downward act pivots on the paradoxical brilliance and beauty of the mystery of the Incarnation: Délie as sacred object who has become flesh and in whom we can see, as the poet does, "sa chair precieusement viue" (D349). The diaphoric paradox of

D7 mirrors that dialectical reality central to all sacred creation and meaning: the mysterious and disturbing illumination that arises from perceiving and portraying the profound depth of sacred matter (Délie's "Deité" – "celle beaulté" and "ses lineamentz vifz" – which leads to "Ou plus m'allume, & plus, dont m'esmerueille, / Elle m'abysme en profondes tenebres"). The paradox of the emergence of spiritual insight and illumination being associated with a downward movement of perception and consciousness is always the result of the sacred manifesting itself in or being intimately connected to something concrete and physical. The poet reports what is there to see and suggests, in moments of heightened and often disturbed awareness, the profound depth of feeling aroused:

> L'esprit, qui fait tous tes membres mouoir
> Au doulx concent de tes qualitez sainctes,
> A eu du Ciel ce tant heureux pouoir
> D'enrichir l'Ame, ou Graces tiennent ceinctes
> Mille Vertus de mille aultres enceinctes,
> Comme tes faictz font au monde apparoistre.
> Si transparent m'estoit son chaste cloistre
> Pour reuerer si grand' diuinité,
> Ie verrois l'Ame, ensemble & le Corps croistre,
> Auant leur temps, en leur eternité.   (D127)

Scève's transcendent vision is indeed earthly: the poet does begin to see the sacred unity and harmony of Délie's spirit ("esprit") and her physical features ("tes membres"). Scève even reveals to us in this poem, I believe, the diaphoric foundation and purpose of his particular poetic vision and art. If the poet were only able to see through Délie's external appearance or physical form, her "chaste cloistre" as he puts it, into her spiritual being, then he would be sure of communing with the sacred here and now. He would then be able to see in this world the divine unity of Délie, both her "soul" and her "body" growing together – "*auant leur temps*" – in eternal perfection. But can this transcendent goal really be accomplished? Our love poet is determined to find out.

Just as Christ was seen to embody the Holy Spirit in this world, so the poet increasingly sees Délie as embodying in her human features a divine essence and illumination whose purpose it is to change and uplift the condition of the poet and the world. After all, Délie was "produced," as the poet tells us, that is created, in Heaven and sent by Heaven to this "dark" and "erring" Earth for the latter's illumination and recovery and renewal:

Produicte fust au plus cler ascendant
De toute estoille a nous mortelz heureuse:
Et plus de grace a son aspect rendant,
Grace aux Amantz toutesfois rigoureuse.
Le Ciel voyant la Terre tenebreuse,
Et toute a vice alors se auilissant,
La nous transmit, du bien s'esiouissant,
Qui en faueur d'elle nous deifie.
Parquoy depuis ce Monde fleurissant
Plus que le Ciel, de toy se glorifie.   (D319)

The purpose of these verses, and of many others charged with an intense exhilaration and excitement, is to communicate a joyous rediscovery and reaffirmation of life seen through its amelioration and renewal in Délie. That "bien" sent by the Heavens "en faueur d'elle" ("in the form of" Délie) to this dark and erring World was for the purpose of changing it for the better, even of perfecting and "deifying" it: "Qui en faueur d'elle *nous deifie*." This recognition by the poet is a crucial one. This central theme of life's betterment and renewal through Délie's perceived presence and influence is represented time and again in the *Délie* and gives this body of love poetry such a high level of religious intensity and aesthetic emotion as is not to be found, in my estimation, in any other collection of French Renaissance poetry. This experience of renewal and its portrayal which even encompass nature and the external world always produce an aesthetic insight in which matter is seen as constantly being imbued with *spirit* and thus acquiring new life, as we saw above in D377 ("Ce *cler* luisant sur la couleur de paille / . . . / Et ce *neigeant* flocquant parmy ces fentes") and can see again in D11:

Quoy que du temps tout grand oultrage face,
Les seches fleurs en leur *odeur* viuront:
Prœuue pour ceulz, qui le bien poursuyuront
De non mourir, mais de reuiure encore.

This is another poem which dramatically expresses a transfiguring pressure of opposites bringing life out of decay and death by merging matter ("Les seches fleurs") with dynamic spirit ("en leur odeur viuront"). This extremely insightful little image appearing early in Scève's sequence in D11 is paradigmatic of Scève's poetry as a whole: the poetic mind, intimately aware of the imperfection and ultimate destruction of the things of this temporal world, strains for signs of order and unity and permanence within and without. Such a theme is aptly articulated by a verse whose basic stresses are between disintegration and renewal, freedom and control. The sense of control and renewal that Scève seeks to affirm and confirm in his love lyrics is the recovery of a higher kind of life itself, as the conclusion the poet draws from the floral image-analogy testifies to: "Prœuue pour ceulz, qui le *bien* poursuyuront / De non mourir, mais de reuiure encore." The "highest good" ("bien") referred to here in D11 and the very same "bien" depicted above in D319 are both designations of the correcting and perfecting influence which Délie provides the poet and the whole world (cf. also above D7: "Celle beaulté, qui *embellit le Monde* / Quand nasquit celle . . ."). This influence is what enables the poet and the world to "*flourish*" (D319), that is, be seen in and enjoy a new light: light (white) decorating the yellow of straw, snow-color being perceived in dark crannies, perfume emanating from dried flowers – fine examples of Scève's transcendent, transfiguring vision at work. The extraction of higher sense from the inner world of the poet as well as the world around him is always Scève's objective. And this higher sense is always Délie who informs, illuminates, and renews this "dark" and "erring" world (D319) with the "*cler* de sa *presence*" (D368). In the eyes of the poet, Délie is, or at least is connected to, *all* the paradisal images above we have been considering thus far.

In consistently portraying Délie and his love for Délie transfiguratively, the poet's divine perception of her is what intermittently threads and thus holds his poems together sequentially; this is what gives ultimate direction and meaning to this love sequence: "Et le parfaict de ta beaulté croissant / Dedans mon *cœur* tousiours se renouelle" (D176). Scève the lover and poet was often in paradise – an earthly paradise, a "Paradis terrestre" as he says in D409, which is to be found in Délie, and especially in the poet's success at "apperceuant cest *Ange en forme humaine.*" This ever-increasing principle of beauty which is always being renewed within the poet's "heart" (i.e., in the creative imagination) shows itself again and again in Scève's poetry as either paradise brought to earth and given human form, or as earth raised to paradise and imbued with spiritual idea. Both portrayals exist to highlight the reality that higher life is possible only when the imagination and its object are in love-unison. Such a paradise – which is always the result of Délie viewed as transfigured or transilluminated object – exists whenever the poet, contemplating a present actuality, finds his soul and spirit and heart wholly blest in this communion, without further desire or unrest. Just as God appeared to Moses as a burning bush (Exodus

3:2), the transcendent vision often sees a spirit-flame blazing in the actual, and it is felt to be alight with spiritual and prophetic significance:

> Seule raison, de la Nature loy,
> T'à de chascun l'affection acquise.
> Car ta vertu de trop meilleur alloy,
> Qu'Or monnoyé, ny aultre chose exquise,
> Te veult du Ciel (Ô tard) estre requise,
> Tant approchante est des Dieux ta coustume.
> Doncques en vain trauailleroit ma plume
> Pour t'entailler a perpetuité:
> Mais ton *sainct feu*, qui a tout bien m'allume,
> Resplendira a la posterité.   (D23)

All is presented and seen in these transilluminated portrayals through highly illuminated imagery:

> Quand l'œil aux champs est d'esclairs esblouy,
> Luy semble nuict quelque part, qu'il regarde:
> Puis peu a peu de clarté resiouy,
> Des soubdains feuz du Ciel se contregarde.
> Mais moy conduict dessoubs la sauuegarde
> De ceste tienne, & *vnique lumiere*,
> Qui m'offusca ma lyesse premiere
> Par tes doulx rayz aiguement suyuiz,
> Ne me pers plus en veue coustumiere.
> Car seulement pour t'adorer ie vis.   (D24)

In thus being portrayed luminously transfigured as the poet's "sainct feu" and "vnique lumiere," Délie is being shown to be the poet's only means to find true love and happiness. This portrayal also points intratextually to the poet's sustained efforts to define and display the real nature of the object of his "humanly sacred" desire:

> Ie vy aux *raiz* des yeulx de ma Deesse
> Vne *clarté* esblouissamment plaine
> Des esperitz d'Amour, & de liesse,
> Qui me rendit ma fiance certaine
> De la trouuer *humainement haultaine*.   (D105)

As I have been trying to show, Scève's poetic handling of transcendence relies on natural, vividly physical imagery. This is a very important feature of *Délie*'s transcendent art which distinguishes it from other overly idealized Neoplatonic love sequences. Otherwise, Scève's sacred portrayal would lose its human paradigm, which is the very foundation of this poet's love vision and love art.

In the *Délie*, ideal love and emotive intensity are conveyed by very tangible human features – such as Délie's fingers and voice in D196 – asking to be touched, felt, heard:

> Tes *doigtz* tirant non le doulx son des cordes,
> Mais des haultz cieulx l'Angelique harmonie,
> Tiennent encor en telle symphonie,
> Et tellement les oreilles concordes,
> Que paix, & guerre ensemble tu accordes
> En ce concent, que lors ie conceuoys:
> Car du plaisir, qu'auecques toy i'auoys,
> Comme le vent se ioue auec la flamme,
> L'esprit diuin de ta celeste *voix*
> Soubdain m'estainct, & plus soubdain m'enflamme.

As this poem reveals, Scève's sacred portrayal accomplishes its end through the physicality of this world – the body of a beautiful woman – in which is found or associated a coherent network of analogies. The poet creatively combines in Délie emotive form with higher idea, which is another way of saying he informs an intuitively creative act with symbolic meaning: the image and, for him, the reality of human *fingers* not plucking the sweet sound from the lyre, but creating the angelic harmony of the high heavens; his intense pleasure at hearing the sacred sound of Délie's celestial *voice*. In this seductively perceived interpenetration of Délie's body and spirit, in the hearing of Délie's "celestial voice," the poet is making a metaphysical, a sacred, and an artistic statement. Délie's higher perfection or essence, her "Angelique harmonie" and her "esprit diuin," are being revealed through her lesser human features, such as her fingers and voice, and both of these dimensions, the heavenly and the human, are being revealed through the poem in its combining of emotive form with higher idea. In these poems, the image of Délie as aesthetic object is also being identified with the spirit of glorious contentment with life itself. The process of her image fading and then being revived within the poet's consciousness is what brings him ever closer to paradise. For me, this is the meaning of the last two lines of D196 above ("L'esprit diuin de ta celeste voix / Soubdain m'estainct, & plus soubdain m'enflamme").

In many other poems, other physical features of Délie will be portrayed in intimate association with a higher spiritual quality and meaning. In presenting the picture this way, the poet is consciously endowing emotive form with higher idea, the poetic process we saw earlier praised so highly by Valéry. D2 is where the poet actually begins his transcendent and transfigured presentation of Délie, his diaphoric portrayal of her *"beaulté* esmerueillable *Idée"* (D275). Nature has brought the poet a "marvelous work" in the form of a "perfect body" which will provide him analogies to higher syntheses:

> Le Naturant par ses haultes Idées
> Rendit de soy la Nature admirable.
> Par les vertus de sa vertu guidées
> S'esuertua en *œuure esmerueillable.*
> Car de tout bien, voyre es Dieux desirable,
> Parfait vn *corps en sa parfection,*
> Mouuant aux Cieulx telle admiration,
> Qu'au premier œil mon ame l'adora . . .

In D80, it is Délie's powerful eyes which show the poet the way to the higher ideal:

> Au receuoir l'aigu de tes *esclairs*
> Tu m'offuscas & sens, & congnoissance.
> Car par leurs *rays* si soubdains, & si clairs,
> I'eu premier peur, & puis resiouissance:
> Peur de tumber soubz griefue obeissance:
> Ioye de veoir *si hault bien allumer.*

In D96, it is Délie's laughter, smile, and face which renew the poet's desire for sacred meaning and communion:

> Te voyant rire auecques si grand grace,
> Ce doulx *soubris* me donne espoir de vie,
> Et la doulceur de ceste tienne *face*
> Me promect mieulx de ce, dont i'ay enuie.

In D159, it is the "touch" of Délie's hand, a symbol as the poet puts it for the "delices de [son] Ame," which brings him forth from a state of death to intense consciousness:

> Si de sa *main* ma fatale ennemye,
> Et neantmoins delices de mon Ame,
> *Me touche* vn rien, ma pensée endormye
> Plus, que le mort soubz sa pesante lame,
> Tressaulte en moy, comme si d'ardent flamme
> Lon me touchoit dormant profondement.

In D207, it is again Délie's eyes and her face which perform the sublimated miracle of the merging of mind and love with matter:

Mais les *deux feuz* de ta celeste *face*,
Soit pour mon mal, ou certes pour mon heur,
De peu a peu me fondirent ma glace,
La distillant en *amoureuse humeur*.

In D208, the poet addresses and encourages his beloved and already renowned Rhône River to become even more "illustrious" by "swelling" in the "perfection" of Délie's life-giving splendor:

Tu cours superbe, ô Rhosne, flourissant
En sablon d'or, & argentines eaux.
Maint fleuue gros te rend plus rauissant,
Ceinct de Citez, & bordé de Chasteaulx,
Te practiquant par seurs, & grandz batteaulx
Pour seul te rendre en nostre Europe illustre.
Mais la vertu de ma Dame te *illustre*.
Plus, qu'aultre bien, qui te face estimer.
Enfle toy donc au parfaict de son lustre . . .

In D313, it is again Délie's physical "Grace," and her spiritual "Virtue," which together have completely inflamed and captured the poet's heart:

Grace, & *Vertu* en mon cœur enflammerent
Si haultz desirs, & si pudiquement,
Qu'en vn sainct feu ensemble ilz s'allumerent,
Pour estre veu de tous publiquement . . .

In D322, it is Délie's "rare qualities," and in particular her "celestial hands," which are enough to cause the poet to persist in his sacred quest:

Merueille n'est, Deesse de ma vie,
Si en *voyant tes singularitez*
Me croist tousiours, de plus en plus, *l'enuie*
A poursuyuir si grandes raritez.
Ie sçay asses, que nos disparitez
(Non sans raison) feront esbahyr maints.
Mais congnoissant soubz tes *celestes mains*
Estre mon ame heureusement traictée,
I'ay beaucoup plus de tes actes humains,
Que liberté de tous tant souhaictée.

In D358, several of Délie's sacredly physical, human features are being described, thanks to which the poet may enjoy seeing her, hearing her, touching her: the "earthly radiance" of her eyes ("Toutes les foys, que sa *lueur* sur Terre / Iecte sur moy vn, ou

78

deux de ses *raiz*"), her Angel-fresh complexion ("Et par son *tainct* Angeliquement fraiz"), her voice ("Et quand sa *voix* penetre en mon oreille"), and her hand ("Là ou sa *main* par plus grande merueille"). In D372, the poet describes Love opening Délie's mouth and pulling from it "celle [doulceur] *celestement humaine,*" this mouth from which is breathed "(ô Dieux) trop plus suaue *alaine,* / Que n'est Zephire en l'Arabie heureuse." Finally in D424, it is Délie's combined perfection of body and soul which once again activates the poet's own faculties of sight and insight and thus fills him with complete joy. This poem presents the acquisition, after much difficulty, of the symmetry and unity of both the object of love and its contemplating subject. Délie's combined perfection of body and soul is being viewed by, and providing great pleasure to, the poet's own body and soul:

> De *corps* tresbelle & *d'ame* bellissime,
> Comme plaisir, & gloire a l'Vniuers,
> Et en vertu rarement rarissime
> Engendre en moy mille souciz diuers:
> Mesmes son œil pudiquement peruers
> Me penetrant le vif du sentement,
> Me rauit tout en tel contentement,
> Que du desir est ma ioye remplie,
> La voyant l'*œil*, aussi l'*entendement*,
> Parfaicte au *corps*, & en l'*ame* accomplie.

The poetic truth that Scève is always confirming is two-fold: adversity and struggle do indeed serve to introduce a love poet to the sacred object of his desire. But to do this, they must also introduce a poet to himself. If the sacred and ineffable object is to be fully grasped, poetic struggle must make him see and understand the difficult nature of unity to be found in both the subject ("La voyant l'*œil*, aussi l'*entendement*") and the object ("Parfaicte au *corps*, & en l'*ame* accomplie") of higher contemplation.

The above poems are just some of the many illustrations in the *Délie* of the diaphorically aesthetic techniques of transfiguration (Scève's spirit-in-matter portrayals) and transillumination (his light-in-matter and light-in-dark portrayals) through which the poet achieves a transcendent paradisal state. All of these creations exist to satisfy the poet's desire for fulfillment in portraying Délie as sacred object containing emotive form and higher idea. They provide the possibility of "un tout autre monde" of the poet's imagining: Délie viewed as embodying a "sainct feu" (D23), as being the poet's "vnique lumiere" (D24) whose eyes emit such a "clarté esblouissamment plaine" that the poet can remain confident of finding her "humainement haultaine" (D105), or, as the poet also says in D372, "celestement humaine." An even more powerful diaphoric image of transillumination appears in D59 where the poet tells us that concealed in his choice of the name for his beloved is the symbol of Délie as the night-light:

> Car ie te cele en ce surnom louable,
> Pource qu'en moy tu luys la nuict obscure.

Here again, human words and higher, illuminating image are working together to reveal the ideal which Délie incarnates in both her form and her very name, just as the literary analogue *Délie, obiect de plus haulte vertu* does. As in so many of Scève's poems, this all-important renewal image and illuminating principle of Délie as the light in the dark – repeated elsewhere as light shining forth from night, as the physical body containing but not eclipsing the luminous soul, as Délie's body enclosing yet radiating the divine – must be appreciated for the way in which they illuminate the sacred tenet on which Scève's poetry and his faith in love depend. It is always "celle *vertu*, qui tant la faict *reluire*," as the poet describes his "eternelle amytié" in D66, which sustains him. For Scève, the sensuous and the physical are often very special *forms* of revelation. The light-in-dark and spirit-in-matter paradox is a mysterious and powerful symbol of Délie as embodiment of immanent and transcendent idea and meaning: she is to be found in the deepest and darkest recesses of physical creation or matter in the form of the perfected (and reflected) light of its soul or essence. This can all be seen in the highly diaphoric mirroring image in D229, which is another good example of Scève translating spiritual idea *through* a particular concrete image:

> Dens son poly ce tien Cristal opaque,
> Luisant, & cler, par opposition
> Te reçoit toute, & puis son lustre vacque
> A te monstrer en sa reflexion.
> Tu y peulx veoir (sans leur parfection)
> Tes mouuementz, ta couleur, & ta forme.

This paradoxical image of Délie's form being clearly mirrored in and shining through a distorting object such as opaque cristal, whose normal function is the opposite blurring or distortion of true meaning and proportion, reflects the mystery and the triumph that

Scève obviously intended his diaphoric art of transcendence and transillumination to portray. The poet is not only endowing matter with light, but, in letting this opaque object reflect the visible side of Délie (her movements, her color, her form, in a word her "Graces"), the poet is overturning a rational mode of perception and portrayal for a highly imaginative one. And the real reason for doing this is given in the last part of this poem. The poet's diaphoric portrayal of Délie is intended to emphasize this greater diaphoric principle of poetic activity and insight:

> Mais ta vertu aux Graces non diforme
> Te rend en moy si representatiue,
> Et en mon cœur si bien a toy conforme
> Que plus, que moy, tu t'y trouuerois viue.

This principle which we have already seen so many times before is, once again, the following: it is the creative feeling of the imagination ("Te rend *en moy si representatiue,* / *Et en mon cœur* si bien a toy conforme") which must perform the difficult yet marvelous transcendent task of capturing the sacred and ineffable (Délie's "vertu") and bringing it to life (making it "viue"). Scève as poet-lover *is* the "Cristal opaque" in this poem, that is, in his newly acquired and different and captivating way of seeing and reflecting the full essence of the love object in its diaphoric unity. Like the "Cristal opaque," the poet's heart perceives Délie *totally* ("Te reçoit toute . . ."), and the heart's own illumination then is diligent in showing her in its reflection (". . . & puis son lustre vacque / A te monstrer en sa reflexion"). The hypothetical goal that the poet set for himself above in D127 is no longer hypothetical. In D229, as in so many other poems of the *Délie*, the poet has made the "cloister" of Délie "transparent." He has captured and validated Délie's "grand' diuinité" in its contemplated, combined unity of "Body" and "Soul":

> Si transparent m'estoit son chaste cloistre
> Pour reuerer si grand' diuinité,
> Ie verroit l'Ame, *ensemble* & le Corps croitre,
> Auant leur temps, en leur eternité.

Clarity or unity of vision through diaphoric insight, not obscurity or fragmentation, is the end of Scève's transcendent contemplation, reflection, and poetic art. D229 makes this point very clearly: "Dens son poly ce tien Cristal opaque, / Luisant, & cler, par opposition . . .".

81

Although Scève's poetic experience of the sacred and ineffable love object is addressed and engaged by both epiphoric and diaphoric portrayals, the latter are what insures the success of his transcendent art. It is, therefore, by far Scève's favorite and most striking mode of portrayal in the *Délie*. We have, however, already seen many good examples of Scève's reliance on epiphor. D166 immediately comes to mind:

> Car seulement l'apparent du surplus,
> Premiere neige en son blanc souueraine,
> Au pur des mains delicatement saine,
> Ahontiroyt le nud de Bersabée:
> Et le flagrant de sa suaue alaine
> Apouriroyt l'odorante Sabée.

Scève's epiphoric handling of image or metaphor constructs a comparative sense of "is/is more" or, as in the case of D166, of "is/is much more." These kinds of images disclose something of greater value in comparison to something else we already know. The literal is metaphorically transcended, not abolished or denied; we are still in a world of the familiar and the understood. The reader's focus is shifted, letting him see beyond the literal and ordinary into the realm of the supraliteral and extraordinary. D166 above is indeed a good example of how Scève's epiphoric portrayal works. The poet sees Délie's physical beauty as like a first snow, *sovereign* in its whiteness; he sees it as like, but much more than, the renowned beauty of Bathsheba; he sees the fragrance of Délie's sweet breath as like, but much greater than, that of Arabia, the land of perfumes.

To give another example, epiphoric portrayal is used by the poet in D141 to compare and to connect the perceived value of his love to a much greater value. The sustenance and replenishment the poet receives from Délie's eyes ("Ie me recrée aux rayons de ses yeulx") are like those given to flowers which feed upon the vital and generous rays of the Sun in Springtime ("Comme des raiz du Soleil gracieux / Se paissent fleurs durant la Primeuere"). Again, the literal (the effects on the poet of Délie's eyes) is being metaphorically felt and transcended (these eyes which are also *like* the Sun's warm rays in Springtime). The standard semantic transference of epiphoric comparison has again been accomplished. The poet has established a similarity between something well known to him (Délie's eyes or light – the semantic tenor) and something which, though of greater worth or importance, is more abstractly or obscurely known (the resplendent light of the Sun in Springtime

– the semantic vehicle connecting to a spiritual realm or dimension). Each time it is used by the poet, epiphoric comparison permits the love feeling and its vision to see, with the help of something else, beyond the ordinary and to capture the subject of the poem – the ever-present and renewal-effecting power of Délie's eyes or light – a metaphoric operation the poet himself acknowledges in D141:

> Si que le Cœur, qui en moy la reuere,
> La me [fait] *veoir en celle mesme essence*,
> Que feroit l'Œil par sa belle presence,
> Que tant ie honnore, et que tant ie poursuys.

This metaphoric development of epiphor produces poetic wonder and delight, but not the intense mystery and vital tensions so often at the heart of Scève's poetic *ravissement*. This kind of feeling can be achieved only through diaphoric images of transfiguration or transillumination, as in D9, already discussed, whose "mirable merueille" results from the poet acquiring "clarté" and "espritz rauis" in contemplation of Délie's spirit-in-matter (of her "Deité" residing in her "lineamentz vifs") and in D229, whose opaque crystal reflects the spiritual luster of Délie in both it and the poet's own, most intimate domain of matter – his heart.

Scève's diaphoric portrayal always serves to incorporate and help create the vital tensions and awarenesses fundamental to the spiritual dimension of human existence. This portrayal does not point to but *embodies* the ideal. In contrast to the epiphoric image, the diaphoric image is what confronts us as paradoxical, making our rational methods of comparison and analysis almost useless as well as our conventional modes of understanding. Yet it is this diaphoric portrayal which profoundly opens us to new possibilities, to new ways of seeing, to a sense-beyond-sense. Diaphoric insight reflects the triumphant, redemptive mystery within reality itself, and Scève's best transcendent poems where he truly manages to capture the ineffable Délie are, in their very creation, diaphoric: the reality of the spiritual being revealed *through* (*dia*), and not just in a comparative relationship with, the physical. Whereas Scève's epiphoric portrayals succeed in conveying similarities, his diaphoric portrayals create new meanings through the sheer juxtaposition of at first seemingly irreconcilable or at least dissimilar elements. The diaphoric image always creates an arresting effect. Through diaphor, the unity of a poem is not a unity of logic and reason but a unity of aesthetic effect, the ultimate poetic vision and creation of a truly affective stylistics. Scève's use of diaphoric portrayal, which works

through the juxtaposition of opposing images, is what especially
ensures the tensive character and purpose of his metaphoric mean-
ing. This higher meaning (i.e., spirit, light, clarity, a poem's "idea")
is more often than not being generated and processed *through*
something material or concrete (i.e., matter, darkness, obscurity,
a poem's "sensuous form"). A partially concealed essence and pres-
ence of spirit or light are made more mysterious, obvious, and
meaningful by them being juxtaposed with, that is, filtered and seen
through, matter and darkness. Indeed, what better way of giving
body to spiritual light than by setting this light off against physical
darkness? All this emphasis by our love poet on *seeing* Délie's
sacred essence "in human form" (D409), on "*Touchant* sa chair
precieusement viue" (D349), on "*Sentant* ses mains, mains *celeste-
ment* blanches" (D367), all this physicality revealing the spirituality
of the "Deité en [son] esprit empraincte" (D149), in a word, this
soul/heart-consuming and art-consuming preoccupation with the
spirit-in-matter paradox (like that also perceived by the poet in
D407 where Délie's "vertu . . . *viuant* soubz verdoyante escorce, /
S'esgallera aux Siecles infiniz") – all these diaphoric connections
and illuminations are what make paradise possible for Scève as love
poet. In the above poems, the abstract or ideal and the concrete
are perfectly related. However abstract the ideal, its expression is
always concrete; indeed, the poet's vision is not complete until it is
embodied in sensuous language. The main purpose of this highly
diaphoric vision and art, it is worth repeating, is the poet's intense
desire to possess as intimately and poetically as possible, and almost
to become, the object of his contemplation and writing. As the poet
says in the close of D229, his heart contains and reflects an even
truer *living* picture of Délie than it does of himself ("Que plus,
que moy, tu t'y trouuerois viue")! These diaphoric creations of the
poet's transcendent imagining work through images of transfigur-
ation and transillumination to reveal a poet's way of seeing, hear-
ing, smelling, touching, and feeling the love object. They satisfy his
desire for a total (spiritual-sensuous) relationship in love; artisti-
cally and aesthetically, they also enable him to express what Valéry
later will prize most in poetic creation, that is, the combination of
la forme sensible and *sa valeur d'échange en idée*. In his own combin-
ing of these poetic parts, Scève manages to convey what is not and
cannot be expressed by either of the parts alone. Neither sensuous
form nor spiritual idea, seen and taken by itself, is enough to serve
this love poet's purpose. Transcendent poetic value and the power
so necessary to achieve a poetic of the ineffable can only be had by

their combination, their juxtaposition, by their being brought into contact producing a fresh and new meaning. This, I believe, was Scève's intention when he chose for the *Délie* the sub-title "*obiect de plus haulte vertu*": the continual presentation and re-presentation (as opposed to "representation") of diverse and even contradictory particulars in a newly designed arrangement always forming a new whole. This kind of ongoing poetic activity must strive, over and over again, to merge and reconcile opposite or discordant qualities, hence the great importance of poetic struggle. In all the various and different poetic "forms" of transfiguration and transillumination we have been looking at in this chapter, Scève has been showing us how new combinations and new wholes and new meanings (poetic order) can emerge, can come into being, out of previously ungrouped words and images. Such diaphoric synthesis of sensuous form and spiritual idea is the essence of Scève's love vision and love art. It is indispensable to the construction and unity of *Délie* as a poetic sequence whose primary purpose is to arrange, to present and re-present, to portray and re-portray the ineffable Délie as sensuous form and spiritual idea, as "obiect de plus haulte vertu." This diaphoric aesthetic wherein all dualisms are resolved, wherein there is no longer any tension or conflict between the ideal and the actual – Scève's portrayals of the immanent Délie as sacred object living "in human form" as well as informing and perfecting all created matter and of the transcendent Délie as human object or receptacle for "plus haulte vertu" – is forever working variations on itself. The poet's satisfaction with a completed act of transcendence, of the actual becoming the ideal and of the ideal being embodied in human form, never lasts for long. He is driven to create more, to discover more, to take delight in the prospect that the form is the higher reality sought, Délie as both sensuous woman and ineffable deity.

If, in the above discussion of poems containing Scève's paradisal vision and portrayal of Délie as transfigured object, there remains any doubt that Scève as a great love poet was seriously and intensely concerned with experiencing and conveying primarily an artistic emotion through the creation of the diaphorically aesthetic image, I have saved D418 for final discussion. In this supreme poem, the ideal and the concrete, the spiritual and the physical, emotion and idea, are once again so perfectly and so beautifully re-presented in art-form as almost to defy interpretation, in the sense, of course, of rendering it unnecessary. There are, after all, some ineffable experiences of the sacred which do not need to be discussed and analyzed. They beg to be heard, seen, touched, or, in the case of D418, simply to be read and enjoyed:

> Soubz le carré d'vn noir tailloir couurant
> Son Chapiteau par les mains de Nature,
> Et non de l'art grossierement ouurant,
> Parfaicte fut si haulte Architecture,
> Ou entaillant toute lineature,
> Y fueilla d'or a corroyes Heliques,
> Auec doulx traictz viuement Angeliques,
> Plombez sur Base assise, & bien suyuie
> Dessus son Plinte a creux, & rondz obliques
> Pour l'eriger Colomne de ma vie.

Just as the Corinthian column was deemed sacred and was a constant source of revelation to Diana, so it is to the poet. In its exquisite artful form (in spite of the customary disclaimer by the poet in line 3 to the contrary), in its sacred combination of emotive form and higher idea, its being the most ornate yet lightest embodiment of any architectural design, this "Column" symbolizes in concrete form, and stands as a physical sign of, the link between human love and sacred love, the low and the high, the physical and the spiritual, earth and heaven. Indeed, these two realms are actually being brought together in this image. This Column in its intricate blend of the profane and the sacred ("Y fueilla d'or a corroyes Heliques, / Auec doulx traictz viuement Angeliques") supports all the stress and strain of the poet's transcendent imagination. This poem in its one-sentence condensation whose transcendent thrust thrives on physicality ("Ou entaillant toute lineature") narrows the distance between human love words and higher ineffable meaning. In *his* cumulatively artful concentration and amplification of trope after trope, the poet is making it perfectly clear that he knows he has only ten lines in this dizain form to bear the burden of human invention to express what lies beyond it. It is with a sheer sense of the triumph of *difficulté vaincue* when the poet (as well as the reader) reaches the tenth line with its marvelous transcendent turn and image – "Pour l'eriger *Colomne* de ma vie" – which points beyond itself, beyond that point on which it must bring the creatively restless efforts of poetic language and image-making of the preceding nine lines to rest. This poem is an exemplary model of Scève's transcendent, sacred art. It, as well as Scève's other diaphoric poems of transfiguration and transillumination, strives towards that higher meaning which great love poetry must somehow miraculously and triumphantly embody and reveal within the limitations of form. Above all for Scève, this transcendent vision of "si haulte Architecture" must be communicable, and forcefully so. The poet's struggle and frustration come from his desire to attain a higher understanding of the sacred and ineffable, and to attain it and communicate it entirely through the medium of poetry. Scève must have believed that a kind of unity or clarity would be found in the poems he wrote, for one can hardly mistake in them the determined sense of creative newness, of struggle and triumph, which the poet developed there.

So Scève creates his own paradise on earth. Whenever the creative mind finds itself in union with its contemplated world, or some part of that world, we have what Diotoma in Plato called the "wondrous vision" (cf. p. 71), the contented and even ecstatic vision of lover-poet who blends, in the aesthetically diaphoric image, the divine and the human into a glorious creation. The essence of Scève's poetry is its adoration and celebration of this higher perfected emotion of poetic paradise:

> Mais si Raison par vraye congnoissance
> Admire en toy *Graces du Ciel infuses*:
> Et Graces sont *de la Vertu puissance*,
> Nous transformant plus, que mille Meduses:
> Et la Vertu par reigles non confuses
> Ne tend sinon a ce iuste debuoir,
> Qui nous constraint, non seulement de veoir,
> Mais d'adorer *toute parfection*:
> Il fauldra donc, que soubz le tien pouoir
> Ce Monde voyse en admiration.   (D182)

For Scève, the diaphoric process whereby emotive form ("Graces") may be combined and given an exchange value with idea ("Vertu") – whose dual apprehension by the creative imagination constitutes the "vraye congnoissance" of Reason – is what makes the poetic ineffable attainable. This is so because love's physical Graces have the potential of becoming, in his eyes, the powerful instruments of love's spiritual Virtue. Scève's preoccupation with the aesthetics of sacred living form, with a poetry of paradise and its diaphoric principle of immanence-transcendence, gives to emotive energy and mortal form a higher idea, purpose, and meaning, and this emotive form breathes new life into his paradisal poetry. The truth that Scève always erects in his transcendent poems, as again above in D182, is an emotive truth central to the Imagination and to Art. Because of their ability to transcend the limiting testimony of rational mind and its language, Scève's diaphoric constructs of the poetic imagination form a world of ineffable beauty and meaning all their own, an aesthetic world which provides the poet great pleasure. They also give this body of love poetry its very special transcendent power and authority. Art's Diaphoria is the body and soul of the Renaissance achievement in literary aesthetics, an achievement Scève worked towards perfecting: "La raison renaissante n'est plus ce chapelet de raisons qu'on égrène, c'est une danse de l'esprit discursif qui se met *en divine extase, unissant aux figures terrestres les modèles de l'idéal.*"[4] Essential and perceivable reality or, better yet, *being*, is what is being revealed by the creative imagination in D182: a poet's sense of "toute parfection." Poetic language is being used in the only way it can function to capture the ineffable: the poet is not analyzing or explaining this ineffable but, in being face to face with it, he is using language to construct higher, growing vision, to indicate the intense personal joy of "seeing" more and more, of "admiring" and "adoring" more and more. It is this strong sense of a harmony of feeling and vision – of poetic insight emanating from the *being* and the *presence* of the ineffable – and not obscurity of vision that permits the poet to proclaim: "Il fauldra donc, que soubz le tien pouoir / Ce Monde voyse en *admiration.*" Scève too believed in and strove to capture "l'écriture comme *présence*" as opposed to "l'écriture comme absence," as Gérard Defaux recently has so sensibly and so beautifully argued to be the case with other Renaissance writers.[5] D182 presents a vision of the ineffable and of the unity of being which is always the definition of this ineffable ("toute parfection" – Délie embodying physical "Graces" in which is also found spiritual "Vertu") that *is* the writing of the ineffable. This vision and this writing can only come at the expense of ordinary mind and language: at that limit where contradictions cease to conflict and differences merge, where language is diminished in that it ceases to highlight its inherent divisions, in a word, where "saying" or "telling" yields to *seeing* and *showing* and *adoring*. For Scève, the ineffable can be "expressed" only through the showing of its being, not through the explaining of it or even the understanding of it when this understanding depends on explaining. D182's successful portrayal of the ineffable can tell us a lot about the "other" language Scève uses and which we have been seeing at work in the poems discussed in this chapter. Without wishing to digress too far into the complex areas of the nature and philosophy of language and consciousness as implied by the epistemological orientations of deconstructive poetics (Derrida) and phenomenological poetics (Husserl), it is clear and largely accepted that conventional language (an analytic/epiphoric kind, anyway) can only operate through categories of division and difference and thus those likely to produce fragmentation. This language in seeking to describe and explain quite often falls back on itself ("erases" itself) in defeat because of *its* inherent categories of division, its endless recognition and repetition of polarity and resulting fragmentation. From this viewpoint of the functioning of language, language *is* division, negation, absence – non-being. It is incapable of grasping the ineffable and showing *its* inherently powerful condition of unity. As we saw in Chapter 2 of this study, Scève begins his poetic quest of the ineffable with this language but fails, necessarily. He does, however, find and succeed with another language: an aesthetic (diaphoric) language of the imagination that shows (constructs) ineffable unity and being and presence through concrete, material objects, an aesthetic language through which the poet sees and does understand "showingly" the paradisal/mortal meaning (being) of Délie as "*obiect* de plus haulte vertu.*" This ineffable meaning shown and celebrated is always the showing and celebration of the content of the poet's insight or creative imagination (i.e., heart). Scève's aesthetic portrayal of Délie as Unity/Being/Presence is always the poet's way of capturing through showing the transcendent being of the ineffable. This is why form is so crucial to Scève's ineffable vision. D182 highlights one of the major reasons why this book on Scève's love aesthetics was written: to demonstrate how Délie's ineffability – her unity of being or "toute parfection" – baffles the poet in his telling, in his reasoning and explaining, but not the poet in his seeing and adoring, in his showing.

Délie's "imaginary" form is full of this kind of transcendent, diaphoric language, of the poet's sense of the ineffable which is revealed because he creates, textually, a material place for it which will be known as Presence, and even Paradise. This constructive principle of love and art is presented again, this time with axiomatic assurance as self-evident truth, in D219. Since Délie's ineffability is indeed self-evident, a language of referentiality is useless, or at least the kind that attempts, but fails, to explain and describe the ineffable, to fix it and limit it. The only appropriate language is a more simple, personal one, an aesthetically transfiguring language that says nothing or very little but sees and shows a lot. Such a language presents and asserts but can never explain. In a most meaningful way, this language informs Scève's ineffable portrayals and statements and thus is always silently but showingly present at the center of personal/textual being. This can all be seen in D219. Délie's "dignified presence," that is, her "physical features," the poet assures us, enables him to *see* her and to *show* her as the living embodiment of *all* divine creation. This poem expresses a simple though profound vision of constructive malleability which embraces all creation:

> Authorité de sa graue presence
> En membres apte a tout diuin ouurage . . .

Délie is here once again seen and presented as both immanent and transcendent: her ineffability is being intimately associated with a worldly contextual/poetically textual presence. Scève's aesthetic of the ineffable is the diaphoric affirmation of images: his love vision is not nourished by and directed towards some lofty being far removed from human experience, but illuminates and gives life to the abstract and ineffable by seeing them and presenting them in concrete, human terms, in the form of Délie's "membres." Scève was able to see, in the form of earthly or human objects such as Délie and her physical features (and also in dried flowers and straw as we discussed at the beginning of the chapter), what William Blake two centuries later was to see in a grain of sand or a wild flower, and also in "Human Form" itself. It is a vision in which concrete image and spiritual meaning perfectly fuse. The concrete image or physical form is, in fact, the basis of the ineffable vision. At the heart of this experience is the incarnation or embodied presence of the ineffable object of love, and its reincarnation in poem after poem: Délie always being viewed "en *membres* apte a *tout diuin ouurage*." Just as Blake was able to give his contemplated object an intense feeling of continuous creative energy, so Scève was able to see in Délie the eternal act of creation. In both poets, seeing succeeds where understanding (reasoning) fails; showing replaces telling and explaining. As Blake put it: "To see a World in a Grain of Sand / And a *Heaven* in a Wild Flower, / . . . / God appears . . . / [and] does a *Human Form Display* / To those who Dwell in Realms of Day."[6] And in this chapter we too have been seeing the various ways and forms through which Scève also saw and depicted this same ineffable unity and presence in Délie: "Apperceuant cest *Ange* en *forme humaine*, / . . . / Du *Paradis terrestre* en son *visage*" (D409). The art of the *Délie* is the shaping of life-forms within the creative imagination to house the sacred and ineffable love object and, thus, the shaping of poetic renewal of self in order and beauty. This humanly sacred process of the poet affirming Délie the beloved object's (and thus *Délie* the love text's) *vertu* in human form – of establishing in the art of poetry an "exchange value" between sensuous form and spiritual idea – is the ultimate *résistance vaincue*, as Valéry will later praise and call this same accomplishment in Mallarmé.

This understanding and practice of a humanly sacred poetic is what consumes Scève in his desire to realize an earthly paradise. St. Paul reveals how this human desire and reality of spirit-in-matter can be attained in Romans 8:2.[7] As we were told in D2, Délie too was not only made but was *created* (Old French *naturer*, "create, fashion" – McFarlane, p. 368) in the "diuine *image*" (compare "ta diuine image" in D3, "le sainct de ton image" in D194, "sa diuine image" in D397, and so forth), "image" being a word which sets a definite premium on her visible and perceivable physicality. Similarly, Christ was given perceptible form, was made flesh, was created with the same physical suggestion in the "image of God" (2 Corinthians 4:4) and even revealed "the stamp of God's very being" (Hebrews 1:3). Délie too bears the divine imprint, as we saw the Graces bearing witness to in D149: "La Deité en ton esprit empraincte." What I am leading up to is that there is no doubt, in my mind, that Scève had the Bible in mind when composing his diaphorically transcendent poetry and that this accounts greatly for his formulation and creation of the aesthetics of sacred living form. (The intertextuality of the *Délie* and the Bible seems to me to be an obvious and important subject that begs to be pursued further by Scève's readers.) For as it is said of Christ (2 Corinthians 4:6), so it can be of Délie, with a pointed emphasis on the body, that the glory of God truly *shines* in her "face":

> Pour contrelustre à ta diuine face   (D124)
>
> Couure, & nourrit si grand' flamme en ta face   (D201)
>
> Mais les deux feuz de ta celeste face   (D207)
>
> Qu'elle estoit seule au lustre de sa face   (D387)
>
> Ainsi qu'Amour en la face au plus beau,
> Propice obiect a noz yeulx agreable,
> Hault colloqua le reluysant flambeau
> Qui nous esclaire a tout bien desirable,
> Affin qu'a tous son feu soit admirable.   (D445)

Furthermore, in the light of Paul's description of Christ as "the image of the invisible God" (Colossians 1:15) and of the "image" of Délie reflecting in the mirror of D230 an even greater and more luminous image than can be seen with human eyes ("Au cler miroir mirant plus [clere] face"), Délie, as a Christ-figure, is aesthetically the physical representation of the unseeable, but not unportrayable, ineffable – "l'oultrepasse" whose "diuin, & immortel visage" the poet never the less in the art of his love lyrics manages to capture and to convey. This divine perception and image-making by the poet of sacred writing and meaning are what turn the *Délie, obiect de plus haulte vertu* into a *living* monument of the creative imagination. That "living virtue" which the poet speaks of in the last poem of the *Délie*, and which so many critics have interpreted purely along the traditional Neoplatonic thematic lines of immortality, that "*vertu, qui viue* nous suyura / Oultre le Ciel amplement long, & large" (D449), is also very much the sum total of the acts of diaphoric re-creation and re-living of Délie and of love which the poet had so artfully and faithfully portrayed in so many ways and forms in the preceding 448 poems of his love sequence. And even here in the poet's last love poem, his desire to be able to experience and portray a sense-beyond-sense, a beauty-beyond-beauty, and a meaning-beyond-meaning is possible only to the extent that this meaning has been *formally* embodied and intensely seen and felt already here and now, as the triumphant, transilluminated image at the beginning of D449 so confidently shows us:

> *Flamme si saincte en son cler durera,*
> *Tousiours luysante en publique apparence,*
> Tant que ce Monde en soy demeurera,
> Et qu'on aura Amour en reuerence.

Scève's poetic idealization, or better yet his artistic embodiments of the ideal, is grounded in the creative and living forms of reality and experience of this world. This diaphoric achievement more than anything else explains why Scève can have such a hold on the reader, such a literary relevance for the secular sensibility of many modern readers. He provides us a poetic context and reality for our own fears and desires, and not only the reality of human anguish and obscurity, but more importantly the possibility of human paradise. Scève's poems we have been analyzing in this chapter are a paradisal celebration of having successfully achieved a higher *human* synthesis in love. The miracle of the *Délie* is the miracle of the poetic principle of immanence-transcendence: the sacred and ineffable Délie made woman and beloved object. Scève's poems are realizations in human terms of the celestial potential in Délie, in the poet, and in man. In the sacred dialectic these poems had to come to terms with, the less than perfect and even imperfect features of the human condition are not only transcended but incorporated in the poet's ideal. A transfigured and transilluminated marriage of body to spirit, matter to light, form to idea takes place. All of Scève's great poems seek to perfect the notion and portrayal of a spiritual body as free as possible of human limitations and as full as possible of paradisal features and yet immediately applicable to and satisfying the requirements of human identification and worth – the seeing of something "celestement humaine". This may be in the outside world as seen in "Les seches fleurs en leur odeur viuront" (D11), or in the portrayed object of love itself as seen in "celle [doulceur] celestement humaine" (D372) of the breath of "cest Ange en forme humaine" (D409), or in the inner world of self as seen in the poet's personal recognition:

> Car sa vertu par voye perilleuse
> Me penetrant l'Ame iusqu'au mylieu,
> Me fait sentir celle herbe merueilleuse,
> Qui de Glaucusià me transforme en Dieu.   (D436)

In the final analysis, this process really is the difficult discovery and revealing of Art's spiritual body – its "vertu" in "forme elegante" – of endowing the Word with earthly and material form and thus bringing it to life. Throughout time, certain creators of literary masterpieces, and especially love poets, have recognized and attempted to fulfill this humanly transcendent end of the love vision and its expression in art, from the Bible to Scève, Blake, Valéry, and Mallarmé, among others. In these works, the human element and the physical element are always admitted in higher love and in sacred poetry. This kind of poetic love must be perceived and portrayed through a dual entity, body and soul, and must be felt, to one degree or another, by both of these faculties simultaneously. In his perception of paradise, Scève's poet must include the body in it, which will become a thing of joy, without losing its physicality but in gaining a spiritual component. Here, the poet's vision is transformed not by negating the physical element in the celebration of a purely idealized spiritual love, but by the fine, *mutual* development of total being – by employing the physical in the service of the spiritual and the latter in the service of the physical. This is truly the "effect mutuel" advocated by Love in D372, with its emphasis on an experience "celestement humaine." This ongoing diaphoric achievement of unity in opposites to give a higher meaning to love prevents the reader, as well as the poet, at any given moment from reaching a definitive conclusion on such a love. Both the readerly and the writerly process is non-ending. It must be revalidated by the poet and the reader continually; this kind of poetic love must forever pass the difficult test of unified experience and its portrayal.[8]

For some readers, this diaphoric portrayal by Scève, containing both the heavenly and the human, may appear a precarious victory, but it is from another perspective the more successful because of the opposition it has met and absorbed. One only has to look at the other poems in the *Délie* which present the problem of higher meaning and sacred portrayal in its unresolved state to see how far Scève has come in his transcendent poems, artistically and psychologically. As we saw in the former poems in Chapter Two, Scève repeatedly equates love with an imperfect and even fallen state devoid of any higher meaning. The poet in relying on reason for analysis and understanding feels a failure of descriptive language to convey his experience. We saw in these unresolved poems the standard themes and images of frustration, emotional disturbance, and intellectual derangement – the poet presenting the picture of love as the loss of paradise. To resolve this into order and fulfillment was to be the work of Scève's transcendent poems, which synthesize higher love and the human state into a unified and glorious compound. These poems come into being, at least in the poet's heart and soul (that is, in his creative imagination), to celebrate the rewarding experience of a higher poetic love. The poet's perception and expression of this higher love can only be attained through mind *and* emotion working harmoniously together (a *self*-referential as well as object-defining operation for poetic identity which we will explore in the next chapter) to produce love's and art's "effect mutuel" (D372). To create and take delight in this mutual effect of higher love requires, as we have seen in this chapter, the bringing together of "la forme sensible" and "sa valeur d'échange en idée," of "une substance précieuse de pensée" and "[une] séduction immédiate" (Valéry), or else of "vertu" and "forme elegante" as Scève calls these same, mutually dependent qualities of the love vision and its portrayal. Scève's transcendent poems which manage to capture this marvelous blend of Délie as "si doulce pensée" (D232), which achieve this artistic synthesis of sweet, sensuous *forme* and spiritual *fond* (*idée*) in their portrayals of Délie, hold out a confident promise of human fulfillment – not only in love, but also in the contemplative and creative life of art itself, a wonderful potential that is both "celestement humaine" (D372) and "humainement haultaine" (D105).

4

BECOMING WHAT ONE SEES: THE UNITY AND IDENTITY OF POETIC SELF

This chapter is also about knowledge, the self-knowledge the poet acquires of the contemplating subject of love. Seeing and discovering, that is, creating a unity of sensuous form and spiritual idea in one's object of contemplation, not only permit a poet to merge the emotive meaning of love with its intellectual worth in intimate imaginings of harmony and beauty, but they also open up the even greater possibility for the poet-viewer to see and enjoy this same unity of mind and matter at work within the contemplating subject or self. An acquired unity and sense of order of exterior vision is what enables our love poet to acquire a sense of unity of interior vision. Scève, like Baudelaire and Valéry and other symbolist writers later on, felt that he could work upon the visions he experienced and communicate them in his poems, and even perhaps understand them in spite of the fact they might point to something contrary to, or above and beyond, logic. As Baudelaire would later put it, this paradisal perspective – be ii outward vision of love object or inner vision of poetic self – is fundamentally a "call to order," just as Valéry too would later view the process to be a "turning of disorder into order." And the "order" being highlighted by both of these poets is one of aesthetics, not of logic. In his famous *Poëme du haschish*, Baudelaire talks about these writers (and readers) who have enjoyed "de belles saisons, d'heureuses journées, de délicieuses minutes" in vast, paradisally luminous perspectives "pleines de clartés nouvelles." He goes on specifically to describe this higher poetic state as truly "paradisal," and paradisal and luminous only because, however briefly, it reflects a unity and harmony of mind and sensuous matter working together in contemplation to provide much-needed relief to the "heavy obscurity" of one's everyday existence:

96

cet état exceptionnel de l'*esprit* et des *sens*, que je puis sans exagération appeler *paradisiaque*, si je le compare aux lourdes ténèbres de l'existence commune et journalière. . . . Je préfère considérer cette condition anormale de l'esprit comme une véritable grâce, comme un *miroir magique* où l'homme est invité à *se voir en beau*, c'est-à-dire tel qu'il devrait et pourrait être, une espèce d'excitation angélique, un *rappel à l'ordre* sous une forme complimenteuse.

Above all, this paradisal vision which is a product of the creative imagination – what Scève depicts very often as the combination mind and heart-soul in full contemplation – is aesthetic and psychologically therapeutic in its nature and purpose. It works primarily to free a poet from uncertainty and suffering: "cet état charmant et singulier où l'*imagination*, quoique merveilleusement puissante, n'entraîne pas le sens moral dans de périlleuses aventures; où une sensibilité exquise n'est plus torturée . . .".[1]

This higher life-creating and life-affirming principle of contemplation and being and art is precisely what Valéry too is emphasizing when he says: "*Je suis ce que je suis, je suis ce que je vois*" (II, 514; Valéry's italics). Like Scève, Valéry was to become preoccupied in the struggle with the poetic ineffable, coming to terms and even identifying with the objects of his contemplation. This harmonizing principle of a unity of mind and matter connecting the contemplating subject to its contemplated object is the very creative substance of one of Faust's monologues, itself another of Valéry's definitions of the art of poetry, in his *Mon Faust*. As we just saw in Baudelaire, Valéry too is stressing a poet's ability not only to see the ineffable but to commune with and to communicate it, to "live" the ineffable, which for both Valéry and Baudelaire means creating it in one's art:

Serais-je au comble de mon art? je vis. Et je ne fais que vivre. Voilà une œuvre . . . Enfin ce que je fus a fini par construire ce que je suis. . . . Il n'y a plus de profondeur. L'infini est défini. . . . C'est un état suprême, où tout se résume en vivre, et qui refuse d'un sourire qui me vient, toutes les questions et toutes les réponses . . . VIVRE . . . Je ressens, je *respire mon chef-d'œuvre*. . . . VOIR, c'est donc aussi bien voir autre chose; c'est voir ce qui est possible, que de voir ce qui est . . . De quel prix de fatigue dois-je payer à présent, sous mes paupières, la durée, la netteté et *l'éclat des objets que j'essaie de me former*? Et quelle foi intense, quelles macérations obstinées, quelle oraison excessive pourrait se créer un *soleil* comme celui-ci qui *luit* et verse si généreusement son sang de pourpre, pour tout le monde? (II, 321–23)

To be or to become what one *sees*, to be truly *living*, to be *feeling* and *breathing* one's *masterpiece* – in a word, to be able to produce and enjoy the "éclat" (luster and life) of one's object of contemplation – these insights by Valéry into a heightened state of unified poetic "living," like those of Baudelaire I have turned to thus far in this chapter on the meaning of paradisally self-luminous moments in Scève's poetry, underscore a crucial and fundamental principle that I am leading up to in Scève. This principle is the ultimate love principle of mind and matter united, of both psyche and soma (Baudelaire's "esprit" and "sens") working together harmoniously to ensure what by the end of this chapter we shall see Scève too calling love's "illustrious *order*." This supreme self-referential and self-defining state of contemplation represents also for Scève "un rappel à l'ordre sous une forme complimenteuse," a throwing of "une lumière magique et surnaturelle sur l'obscurité naturelle des choses," his attempt to "respirer [son] chef-d'œuvre," in a word, Scève's own intense desire to be "éclairé du dedans" in order to "se voir en beau."

Through this exhilarating principle of love and of art, Scève is still very much portraying Délie as sacred and aesthetic object, but he is portraying much more: himself and his own unique, most intimate relationship with this beloved object. Certainly one of the major thrusts of Scève's love poetry is the poet's attempts to achieve and relate this poetic and psychological principle of mind and matter united, from the point of view both of the poet contemplating Délie and the poet contemplating himself in the contemplation of Délie. In developing and espousing this principle of unity and harmony of vision, Scève is also following a distinguished Renaissance tradition: that of Speron Speroni, Leone Ebreo, and other more "Aristotelian" love theorists of the time who were advocating a more realist view of love than had been formulated by such "Neoplatonists" as Ficino and Pico. This view stressed the importance of the intellectual-spiritual *and* the physical in contemplated forms of poetic love. The emergence, and considerable influence, during Scève's time of an Aristotelian naturalism as a poetic reaction and counterpoint to the prevailing Neoplatonic idealism have been very convincingly argued and well documented in an extremely important and useful book by A. J. Smith, *The Metaphysics of Love: Studies in Renaissance Love Poetry from Dante to Milton*.[2] Ironically, as Smith also gives ample testimony for, this more realist treatment of love was viewed by the poets themselves as providing a body of love poetry a greater degree of transcendent meaning than did the overly rarefied and idealized kind of love poetry being cultivated by the Neoplatonists. For Renaissance love poets sharing to whatever degree the Aristotelian view of love, it was axiomatic that love is of brain, soul, and body, and that the operations of brain and soul depend on the body. For these poets, love must engage and sustain the mind, the spirit, and the senses. Smith also quotes this important and most revealing passage from Speroni, who of course had a great influence on Scève, a passage which clearly shows the unitive-luminous principle of mind *and* body being advocated by the Aristotelians in the contemplation of love:

Whoever is such a fool in love that he has no care of his appetite, but as simple disembodied intelligence seeks solely to satisfy his mind, can be compared to him who, gulping his food without touching it or masticating it, more harms than nourishes himself.   (p. 204)

Whether Scève as a Renaissance love poet was a Neoplatonist or an Aristotelian (or somewhere in between, which is where I would place him) is not that important for this study of his love aesthetics (though there is little doubt, I believe, that the Aristotelian side of his love thought and love art has been generally neglected). The important point is to be aware of the two Renaissance views on love and to see what Scève borrowed eclectically from both camps in formulating his own particular vision of love and its portrayal. It is clear that for Speroni, Ebreo, and other influential love theorists of the time, mind and body were inextricably mixed in love and both were considered necessary for its successful contemplation. Scève does not so much theorize on this notion, he demonstrates it time and again in the love portrayal of his lyrics, as we saw so many times in the last chapter in Scève's portrayals of unity of the love object and as we shall see now in regard to the portrayal the poet gives of the contemplating subject coming to terms with his own unity and sense of identity.[3]

In the *Délie*, the usually clear, sharp division and antagonism between body and soul (or else body and mind or body and spirit) normally associated with a Neoplatonic perspective give way to the view of the indivisibility of body and soul, earth and heaven, not only in the portrayed object of love but also in the portraying subject of love. An emotive union of lover and beloved, of poetic subject with poetic object, and an artistic unity of mind and matter within the poet himself are being worked towards. (The latter is, I believe, what specifically connects Scève to later symbolist writers, as I attempted to suggest at the beginning of this chapter; moreover, this connection seems to me to be another subject well worth pursuing at some length in a separate study.) The spirit–flesh dichotomy developed by so many Neoplatonic poets does appear in various poems of the *Délie*, but it is not Scève's final statement and picture of love. For him, it is a central problem to be worked out, to be resolved, and not the ultimate portrayal he desired to give to love. D367 is an excellent poem on this Aristotelian meaning of union and unity in the *Délie*, in spite of the fact the poet seemingly (prudently?) places this poem in a Platonic context:

> Asses plus long, qu'vn Siecle Platonique,
> Me fut le moys, que sans toy suis esté:
> Mais quand ton front ie reuy pacifique,
> Seiour treshault de toute honnesteté,
> Ou l'empire est du conseil arresté
> Mes songes lors ie creus estre deuins.
> *Car en mon corps: mon Ame, tu reuins,*
> Sentant ses mains, mains celestement blanches,
> Auec leurs bras mortellement diuins
> L'vn coronner mon col, l'aultre mes hanches.

In the beginning of this poem, Scève does introduce the theme of the spirit–flesh, body–soul dichotomy, but here it is being used to emphasize the painful separation of the two lovers. The separating factor in a poem with this theme may be time, as it is in D367 ("Asses plus long, qu'vn Siecle Platonique, / Me fut le moys, que sans toy suis esté"), or space, or a combination of the two. But the main problem is always the notion of separation viewed as apartness or division. Being separated from his beloved, the poet cannot function as a whole; under such a condition, the poet feels and sees a division of the self. Only upon reunion with the beloved can the whole self again be reconstituted ("Mais quand ton front ie reuy pacifique, / . . . / Mes songes lors ie creus estre deuins. / Car en mon *corps*: mon *Ame*, tu reuins.") The loss of paradise is always the picture of loved ones as separated from one another, and that of the poet as being divided in himself. The regaining of paradise is always envisioned as the sacred and joyous reunion of the poet with the beloved, which brings about a similar and harmonious reuniting within the poet of his own body and soul, mind and matter, which being brought together again in union and unity are then capable of conveying the divine contentment that the poet experiences in love's embrace, in his being totally enveloped and satisfied by these hands "celestement blanches" and these arms "mortellement diuins." (This poem in particular must have pleased

Scève's contemporaries inclined towards the Aristotelian love view. Few truly Neoplatonic poets of the period, if any, were envisioning love's contentment as coming from having one's "hindquarters" embraced.) The very cultivation, simultaneously, by Scève of a richly sensuous and at times sensual love poetry, on the one hand, and a searching paradisal poetry, on the other hand, reveals something vitally significant about the intensity and the complexity of the *Délie*. This body of poetry succeeds in portraying the transcendent love vision of a greater, a more complete and meaningful unity which in poetically inferior hands and imagination often either remains dialectically and antithetically strained, or else overly idealized and thus too removed from reality and unsatisfying. In D367, however, as in so many of Scève's poems, the sense of union and unity created by and enjoyed in the poetic imagination provides our love poet a full and meaningful sense of sacred contemplation: "Mes songes lors ie creus estre *diuins*."

The paradisal perspective of love's union and unity cannot be made of mind, or body, alone. For Scève's vision of higher love, as for Baudelaire's definition of higher vision above ("cet état exceptionnel de l'*esprit* et des *sens*, que je puis sans exagération appeler *paradisiaque*"), both brain and body, mind and matter are truly required to experience perfect love. Scève's vision and construction of Délie/*Délie* as "obiect de plus haulte vertu" always work towards the *full* realization and thus satisfaction of the contemplating subject of love (the poet's "sens, & l'imaginatiue" – D288; his "œil, aussi l'entendement" – D424) as well as the full portrayal of the object of love (Délie's "vertu, & sa forme elegante" – D165). Only then is the poet able, in love and through love, to "se voir en beau" (Baudelaire), to be living his masterpiece (Valéry). For Scève, love is above all an imaginative relationship. At its best, the poet's imagination sees its object of contemplation as well as itself as a whole self, mind and body together. As such, the poet gains insight not only into the object of love but also into the subject of love. Scève's ongoing struggle and determination to experience higher meaning will throw light on the inner world of the poet as well as his outer world; his love imagination will probe deep within itself so as to provide the poet's reason material which reason alone cannot perceive. For a love poet of the ineffable such as Scève, like the theorists of this ineffable throughout time, the soul or inner self suffers especially "when we withdraw from vision and take to knowing by proof, by the processes of reason. It is not our reason that has seen; it is reason's Prior [i.e., "the soul"], as far above

101

reason as the very object of that vision must be. Our self-seeing There is a communion with the self restored to its purity . . . a simple unity. . . . Only in separation is there duality."[4]

As we have seen, the poet's intense desire and struggle for attainment of this higher vision of union and unity always involve the difficult process of merging the spiritual with the physical, the supreme and overriding goal Scève indicates again, in axiomatic terms, to the reader in D392. This process is difficult because the poet always views it as the removal of contradiction:

> Les elementz entre eulx sont ennemys,
> Mouantz tousiours continuelz discors:
> Et toutesfois se font ensemble *amys*
> Pour composer l'*vnion* de ce corps.

Scève's kind of unity of vision, which always posits the removal of contradiction, must first be acquired by the poet in his contemplation of the beloved object, and this insight in turn triggers and makes the poet aware of the same unity in the subject of contemplation, the poetic self. The poet's contemplation of Délie's full essence, the sacred blend and harmonious interaction of *her* body and soul, her "vertu" and her "forme elegante," is what his mind and art are forever striving to see and to depict. The successful operation of the poet's imagination in full contemplation of Délie's beauty and perfection of body and soul is always the result of the combined participation of the poet's own emotive "sentement" and his intellectual "entendement." Only in thought and emotion harmoniously working together in the poet's consciousness is the poet truly able to experience and have knowledge of Délie's "vertu rarement rarissime," as well as of his own artistic worth, his own poetic *vertu*:

> De *corps* tresbelle & d'*ame* bellissime,
> Comme plaisir, & gloire a l'Vniuers,
> Et en vertu rarement rarissime
> Engendre en moy mille souciz diuers:
> Mesmes son œil pudiquement peruers
> Me penetrant le vif du *sentement*,
> Me rauit tout en tel contentement,
> Que du desir est ma ioye remplie,
> La voyant l'œil, aussi l'*entendement*,
> Parfaicte au *corps*, & en l'*ame* accomplie.   (D424)

Scève is here demonstrating his ability to "composer l'vnion de ce corps," a crucial contemplative principle and operation for the poet, announced in D392 and which he is always concerned with. In the composition of this "corps" (with the notion of "corps" in D424 clearly having meaning for both contemplated object and contemplating self), the poet is again showing his desire and determination to give unity and identity to *each* "body" involved in his love discourse. He is reconciling and merging Délie's *corps–âme* and his own *sentement–entendement*, and he accomplishes both of these identity-giving operations this time in the same poem. The phenomenological objective of Scève's poetry, as D424 so well demonstrates, is always to overcome, through union, the division between subject and object and the division between the mental (mind) and the material (matter) within the poet himself by examining consciousness and the object of consciousness simultaneously. The ultimate significance of this objective, when the poet is able to accomplish it, as he does in D424, is the construction of unity, clarity, and contentment in vision, in both its external form and internal form – the creative process of "befriending" (D392) of love subject with love object and of love subject with poetic self. In D424, paradisal relationships in love and in art are once again being made and highlighted. The poet's desire for union and unity presented in D392 is being fulfilled: love's discordant elements "toutesfois se font *ensemble amys.*"

It is D271 which provides the reader the very best portrayal of the great self-reflexive artistic theme of union and unity in the *Délie.* The poet is clearly and poignantly showing us in this poem that in pursuing and seeking to discover and reveal the full essence of Délie, he is also seeking to affirm the same sense of unity to be found within himself. One does truly become what one *sees* (Valéry) by creatively perceiving and perfecting the full potential of other which one already possesses in self. In throwing light on Délie's full essence, the poet is better able to reveal and to enjoy the same essence and light within himself:

> I'espere, & crains, que l'esperance excede
> L'intention, qui m'incite si fort.
> Car ià mon cœur tant sien elle possede,
> Que contre paour il ne fait plus d'effort.
> Mais seurement, & sans aulcun renfort
> Ores ta face, ores le tout [il lustre]:
> Et luy suyuant de ton corps l'ordre illustre,
> Ie quiers en toy ce, qu'en moy i'ay plus cher.
> Et bien qu'espoir de l'attente me frustre,
> Point ne m'est grief en aultruy me chercher.

In his primary desire ("intention") for union with the beloved, which more than anything else keeps him going, the poet's "heart" is already hers ("Car ià mon cœur tant sien elle possede"). Thanks to his even partial union with the beloved – and this is a most important and meaningful connection poetically since, as we have seen, the poet's heart is often viewed to be his imaginative faculty of creative feeling – the poet is able to feel and experience the illumination which even her physical being provides him. It is the poet's heart which creatively feels the *luster* of her face and whole being. And the point is, for the poet this experience is not just passive but active: to contemplate and enjoy the luminosity of Délie's face and whole being, the poet (his "heart") must actually create it ("Ores ta face, ores le tout [il lustre]"). Scève does indeed share and practice the same unitive-illuminating principle of art advocated by Valéry and Baudelaire and other symbolist poets, a view which I consider so important for understanding Scève that I spent some time discussing it at the beginning of this chapter. Scève will carry his luminous portrayal in D271 one specular step further. In being responsive to and in revealing the sacred "illustrious order" suggested by Délie's body, the poet is in fact seeking to discover the same order of matter and mind which he contains and considers most privileged within himself ("Ie quiers en toy ce, qu'en moy i'ay plus cher"). And although the hope of gaining insight into this higher order of mind and matter is often frustrating to the poet (the problematical idea used by the poet in the beginning of the poem: "I'espere, & crains, que l'esperance excede / L'intention . . ."), still it is not painful to seek one's own essence and perfection in another ("Point ne m'est grief en aultruy me chercher").

In D271, Scève is showing us once again his determination to express the beauty and idea of the spirit or mind through the portrayal and help of the body, and this time it is himself which he is highlighting and identifying. He is connecting and representing the extrinsic form and intrinsic worth of the beloved as the effigy of the perfect idea in the lover's *heart*. The "ordre illustre" which the poet creatively feels and sees in Délie *and* in himself (for it is his heart which illuminates this order – "[il lustre]") points to the emotively enlightened power of transcendent, diaphoric poetry to conceive and to embody the spiritual in words and matter. This aesthetic image of an "ordre illustre" is the perfecting creation of values already found in the poet. It is a reminder and demonstration of Valéry's notion: "Enfin ce que je fus a fini *par construire* ce que je

suis," a notion of being and becoming whose realization is the busi-
ness of great symbolic art. The poet's "ordre illustre" which he is
calling our attention to in D271 is also a reminder of Plotinus' view
that "the beholder" becomes "one with the beheld," and thus there
is "a unity apprehended": the beholder "*is become the Unity*" (VI,
ix, 11; Turnbull, p. 221). Scève's illustrious order in love, whether
of outer object or inner subject, is always both spiritual and physi-
cal. For Scève, higher love and art are really one and the same
thing and both require of the lover and the poet a price: that of
turning disorder into order, of creating right order and unity for
human accomplishment. It is the harmonizing art of an intense
poetry conveying the potential luminosity and order of higher mind
and feeling (again Baudelaire's "état exceptionnel de l'*esprit* et des
sens") which the poet truly desires to master and possess. Higher
love fulfills for the poet the spiritual and artistic need for self-realiz-
ation and self-completion. Its aesthetic experience for both poet
and reader is a compound of idea and form, imagination and per-
ception: the image in D271 of an "ordre illustre" is of an idea
of the mind, even an ideal, yet this image is being perceived and
illuminated by the senses – by the poet's heart. Once again, the
spiritual is being created in and revealed through the physical; the
poetic mind is operating through matter, and ridding it of its natural
obscurity. This is the pure diaphoric portrayal of an intense, pas-
sionate form of sacred love in which the poet *is*, or at least is *becom-
ing*, what he sees and feels. He is living in the realm of the imaginary
where he not only thinks about Délie but also becomes part of
Délie, and thus in uniting with Délie he is thinking about and unit-
ing with himself. The poet is rethinking and re-creating the self
through Délie, seeking his own unity and identity through her. This
is an expression of the popular Renaissance theme of Microcosm
and Macrocosm, which Scève will develop again in his other major
poetic work, the *Microcosme*: Man carries within himself the won-
ders he seeks to identify without. Scève's self-seeking and self-con-
scious poems are exemplary of a phenomenological kind of
reflexive writing working to reveal the author's *interior* mode of
consciousness: poetic texts whose purpose is the revelation and
awareness of the creative personality of their author; works mani-
festing themselves as the subjective correlate of the contents of
their focus, that is, of the love object and attendant imagery in
which the author's personal mode of awareness and feeling imagi-
natively projects itself. In the *Délie*, through imaginings of love's
union and unity, the poet is developing a self-referential meaning

in love of being and of art that increasingly becomes better known to him. The poet becomes absorbed in the act of feeling and seeing, the object seen, and the enlightening process of insight – the mind with the help of matter that sees and feels and creates: "Dont le parfaict de sa lineature / M'esmeult le sens, & l'imaginatiue" (D228); "La voyant l'œil, aussi l'entendement" (D424). By "understanding," as in the case of "heart," Scève means *imagination*. Above and beyond the defining of poetic object, Scève is revealing to us the process itself of the identifying of poetic self, the artistic implication of his desire, of "heart actively working" to unite mind and matter in his "contemplative life," as he presents the picture in D412: "mon cœur par œuvre actiue / Auec les yeulx leue au Ciel la pensée." Scève's *Délie* is a poetry of *becoming* and *being*; it comes into focus and acquires meaning when obscurity and anguish end and self-affirmation and self-identity begin. Seeing the unity of the beloved object and becoming this unity are the ultimate and glorious Life, the body ("Grace") and soul ("Vertu"), of the Poetic Imagination ("cœur") which alone can lead to Paradise:

> *Grace, & Vertu* en mon *cœur* enflammerent
> Si *haultz desirs*, & si pudiquement,
> Qu'en vn *sainct feu* ensemble ilz *s'allumerent*,
> Pour estre veu de tous publiquement.   (D313)

In pursuing the ineffable Délie and the ineffable self-meaning and self-identity she provides the poet in love, Scève can never remain just passive. The poet's "heart" ablaze with "si haultz desirs" and a "sainct feu" is always intensely and creatively *active* in the illumination and communication of the transcendent, as D412 and D313 above both tell and show us. His heart or faculty of the imagination, full of pride and purpose for all to see, is always striving to make the transcendent and ideal (Délie's "Grace, & Vertu" and the poet's own "haultz desirs") immanent through the medium of his poetry.

Délie's organic unity, a fine illustration of the poetic "miroir magique" and "lumière magique" Baudelaire speaks of, reflects a loving reconciliation and merger of thought and feeling in poetic matter (i.e., "Grace, & Vertu" above in D313 burning as a "sainct feu" in the poet's *heart*), a medium for the poetic mind in the act of higher creation, with the poet's imagination (his "cœur," "ame" "imaginatiue," "entendement") as the primary shaping, unifying, and reconciling power. For Scève, the poetic fire or light and life which are capable of transforming and triumphing over the natural obscurity of human things such as may be found in love are a clarity of mind and feeling and art acquired only in discovering and perfecting a dialectic, aesthetic unity and order in love. Scève's paradisal moments when mind and matter are united are always exhilarating, luminously triumphant moments for the poet's imagination when the struggle with duality ends and the unity of psyche and art begins. During these moments, as above in D271, the poet's love words seem to weld together fragments of disparate, contradictory experience (i.e., the inner world of the poet – his heart or imagination – creatively feeling and perceiving the outer world – the beloved's face and entire being), and the result for both poet and reader is an instantaneous flash of revelation – love's and art's "ordre illustre" being discovered and portrayed in a human object, in a "corps" (i.e., in both Délie and the poet's own self). D271 is a poetic text that confronts its own limits by trying to capture the uncapturable: Délie the ineffable object of contemplation and the ineffable self in the process of contemplating this "other" object. Scève came to know well and to perfect such moments of exhilarating certainty and unifying power when he depicted the imagination performing its work of synthesis: its diaphoric combination of mind and matter, of feeling and insight steadily progressing towards self-realization and self-possession ("Ie quiers en toy ce, qu'en moy i'ay plus cher / . . . en aultruy me chercher"). When a poet's imagination is working under this kind of intense pressure, the poetry may indeed seem to us obscure. This is so because the poet is making connections between apparently irreconcilable emotions and ideas; he is fusing seemingly different orders of experience, that is, different realms of knowledge. His very language and even his puns are being used to reveal, connect, and to construct a more meaningful relationship. The rhymed coupling in D271 of "illustre" and "[il lustre]" is not an inconsequential instance of poetic dalliance. Love's order can be "illustre" only because the poet's heart or imagination illuminates it ("[il lustre]") and makes it so. Scève's poems are indeed often obscure, but they are obscure because of their intensity of feeling and vision. It is not an intellectual obscurity as much as an emotional one, the use of the language and depth of feeling of secular love to describe the poetic experience of the sacred and the ineffable. This luminous, ineffable something "plus cher" often turns out to be, in addition to Délie, the poet's own inner creative faculty of the heart – the ineffable self – which the poet discovers to be both the tenor and the vehicle of poetic transcendence and paradise. In all of Scève's great self-reflexive poems, such as D271, the poet is discovering and developing and realizing a unity of self;

he is finding and creating his *own* identity as well as that of Délie. Put another way, the poet is both the one who is writing and the one who is written.

Scève as love poet was able to enjoy a highly desired unified meaning of being and of art in the love experience, a hard-won sense of "Paradis a tous espritz marriz" as he puts it in D324. For me, there is no finer achievement one can really ask of a love poet. Scève's "ordre illustre" is the highest accomplishment humanly possible of a poetic imagination and art-form clarifying a sacred and ineffable love world. The spiritual alone has no meaning, no value, no order until seen in its human context; and the same has to be said of the physical: it has to be given a higher meaning and order through its "exchange value" with higher idea (Valéry). This ultimate accomplishment in the poetic imagination – whether focused on the love object or on the love subject – of seeing and experiencing the spiritual "en forme humaine" (D409) brings about, each time the poet achieves it, a newly created rebirth of psyche and poetry – the poet's sense of paradise. Shakespeare too viewed the higher possibility of poetry in precisely these humanly self-transcendent terms. Of the many passages one could quote from him, here is one of his most famous, taken from *A Midsummer Night's Dream*, which is another good recognition of the unitive-luminous principle of poetic self-identity similar to Baudelaire's view ("cet état exceptionnel de l'*esprit* et des *sens*") and to Scève's ("le sens et l'imaginatiue"; "l'œil, aussi l'entendement"):

> The poet's *eye*, in a fine frenzy rolling,
> Doth glance from heaven to earth, from earth to heaven;
> And as *imagination bodies forth*
> *The forms of things unknown*, the poet's pen
> Turns them to shapes and gives to airy nothing
> A local habitation and a name.[5]

In the *Délie*, this poetic habitation or paradisal creation is also and always the spiritual ("plus haulte vertu") finding its home and identity in a concrete, human object – the "ordre illustre" seen and created by the poet in Délie/*Délie* and thus in himself. Scève's highest literary achievement is this symbolic marriage of mind to matter, the uniting of the sacred and ineffable ("things unknown," "airy nothing") to the material ("forms," "shapes," and so forth), in the poet's heart or imagination. The dizains we have been analyzing in this chapter belong to a long and distinguished self-reflexive, self-conscious poetic tradition. Scève's love vision is not only a prefiguring of Shakespeare, Baudelaire, and Valéry, but another echoing of Plotinus: "There are those that have not attained to see. The *heart* has not come to know the splendor There; it has not felt and clutched to itself that love-passion of vision known to the lover come to rest where he loves . . . made over into Unity" (VI, ix, 4; Turnbull, p. 216).[6]

Scève's love poet has attained to see – the unity both of Délie and of self. The epiphany he experienced in contemplation of Délie as love object was also a self-epiphany. His "heart" saw and felt the splendor of Délie's "*beaulté* esmerueillable *Idée.*" Délie is also "sensible au cœur" (Pascal) of this love poet, in whose own creative activity he too is able to see and understand and revere the ineffable object of his contemplation, as well as acquire knowledge of the poetic self performing the above luminous operations:

> Comme des raiz du Soleil gracieux
> Se paissent fleurs durant la Primeuere,
> Ie *me recrée* aux rayons de ses yeulx,
> Et loing, & près autour d'eulx perseuere.
> Si que le *Cœur*, qui en moy *la reuere*,
> *La me [fait] veoir* en celle mesme essence . . . (D141)

Just as important, Scève has shown that this deep love-passion of vision striving always to "se refaire selon ses clartés" (Valéry) as an activity and matter of heart, as that ineffable something "plus cher" which the poet contains within his heart, can also become *the* matter of art. In Valéryan terms, this diaphoric process of synthesis, whereby the spiritual or ineffable ("ordre illustre") is revealed through and illuminated by the physical and concrete ("[il lustre]" – the operation of the poet's heart), is the ultimate *résistance vaincue*, in art as in life. This unitive-luminous process of identifying and capturing and harmonizing poetic object and poetic self is how an illustrious poetic order, the *Délie* as "*beaulté esmerueillable Idée,*" came into being.[7]

5

STRUGGLE, LIGHT, AND LOVE'S "SAINCT LIEU"

In this chapter, I wish to come back to Scève's so-called "darkness" and to the critical assessment of it which I presented in my introductory chapter. More than any other aspect of the *Délie*, this darkness has quite literally haunted Scève's readers and critics over the centuries, and even blinded some of them to this work's higher meaning. Some of *Délie*'s most important and certainly most arresting poems have been and continue to be the object of rather severe criticism, and I wish to propose here a different reading of these poems. In the two preceding chapters, we considered Scève's concern with and success at developing the aesthetics of "showing," his diaphoric art of showing the being/unity of Délie as poetic object and the identity/unity of poetic self. There is, of course, another kind of showing of light in the *Délie*, a very powerful one always associated with Délie herself and intended especially for the spiritual-psychological benefit and renewal of the poet. Indeed, as we shall see, these poems and the light images they contain are absolutely vital to helping Scève construct and enjoy a love psychology of transcendence and paradise. In Scève's own terms, it is this light that will lead him to find and affirm love's "holy place" (D330).

Scève's transcendent goal or luminous pursuit, which I wish to continue exploring in this chapter, is implied in D218 when the poet recognizes that in spite of all his anguish and suffering he is indeed acquiring in the process the science of obtaining "more valuable things" in love ("Bien que i'acquiere en souffrant la science / De parvenir a choses plus prosperes . . ."). What Scève is referring to is a certain psychological understanding that can only be acquired by the poet through time and experience: the importance of a higher poetic perspective operating obstinately ("Ma volenté sainctement obstinée" as the poet says in D421) through earthly things and objects and which thrives in spite of, or perhaps as a result of, psychological pressure and obscurity; a psychological and artistic

110

ascent that often has been difficult and even painful but whose difficulty and pain merely add to the achievement. Throughout the *Délie*, we can observe this love psychology at work: death imagery, darkness, chaos, and disorder giving place to happier, more harmonious and radiant, aesthetically and psychologically more vital impressions and creations wherein the redeeming and ordering principle dominates. D158 is a good example of how this progression is achieved:

> L'air tout esmeu de ma tant longue peine
> Pleuroit bien fort ma dure destinée:
> La Bise aussi auec sa forte alaine
> Refroidissoit l'ardente cheminée,
> Qui, iour & nuict, sans fin determinée
> M'eschaulfe l'Ame, & le Cœur a tourment,
> Quand mon Phoenix pour son esbatement
> Dessus sa lyre a iouer commença:
> Lors tout soubdain en moins, que d'vn moment,
> L'air s'esclaircit, & Aquilon cessa.

For the poet, the road to recovery and renewal and peace and even to paradise can be very short. All it takes is that special kind of music and harmony, and especially light (as we shall see in this chapter), which only Délie can provide him. Then, in a split second, as D158 shows us, for the poet the air becomes cleared of all sadness, pain, and obscurity. The controlling image in D158 permitting this change for the better is a psychological and aesthetic turning point: Délie as the poet's Phoenix in whom the poet is able to find release and recovery from a morose, dark condition of obscurity and anguish. There are other significant light images of restoration which function in the same way as turning points to insure the poet's psychological progression away from a deathly state of obscurity and anguish. It is these powerful renewal images, more often than not presented in terms of chiaroscuro, that we will now focus on.

The inclination of our own age, which has accepted and incorporated to a large degree the often very helpful art of psychoanalysis into various paths of critical inquiry, has greatly contributed to the current emphasis which has been given to the *Délie* as the poetic mirror of a statically dark and forlorn mind. Many critics of Scève have found in his love poetry unresolved conflicts and tensions and thus have generally seen in him more darkness than light. I do not wish so much to refute these positions as to put the case differently, for there is indeed much darkness in Scève's world. But this darkness is important for reasons other than those some of his readers have expressed. It certainly has the structural and dramatic value of contrast and tension. The complexities and textual resistances found in poetic darkness are some of the sources of Scève's power and of his continued fascination for many readers. But there is also much more to be found in this darkness. Darkness is important for Scève, and even necessary, because of the light he was able to find in it. This situation really accounts for the intense, psychological drama of Scève's poetry and for the poet's continued desire to struggle. And within this poetic drama and struggle, light does emerge quite often triumphant, an aesthetic and psychological fact too often overlooked. If to some of his readers the progression in this love sequence towards the strenuously acquired order of art and mind is precarious, there seems no legitimate basis for misconceiving the real nature of Scève's undertaking or for seeing in it only an elaborate strategy to convey frustration and disorder. Otherwise, Scève as love poet would have to be considered a kind of failure – and that interpretation he certainly does not deserve. His own expressed goal or purpose is to come to terms, psychologically and metaphorically, with Délie the beloved and *Délie* the love text as "obiect de plus haulte vertu." We saw Scève achieve the metaphorical end of this purpose in the last two chapters. In order to fully accomplish this transcendent ideal, the poet must also turn "personal" anguish and obscurity into strenuous and acceptable clarity, as in fact Scève does in a most successful, conscious, and consistent way. If as his readers and critics we will allow this side of Scève to surface and will give it its intended place of textual prominence, many dizains in the *Délie* will become much less obscure while others will be seen in a more favorable light. Many of Scève's poems will lose their narrowly interpreted claim to "modernity" – that is, being viewed as representative of a crisis in art and in psychology – and will become again good and often superb Renaissance love poems. No longer will the reader-critic tend to overstate *Délie*'s "ambiguous language, tortuous and involuted syntax, and the poet-lover's *fragmented perception*," and so forth (Giordano, "Reading *Délie*: Dialectic and Sequence," p. 155). For example, the alleged textual and psychological obscurity of D446 will greatly recede if we approach the poem on its own terms and keep in mind what Scève is actually working towards, and accomplishes, in it. Modern critical notions such as "fragmentation," "verbal paralysis," and "painful dissonance," used by some critics to interpret Scève's poems such as this D446, really have little to tell us about this dizain:

> Rien, ou bien peu, faudroit pour me dissoudre
> D'auec son vif ce caducque mortel:
> A quoy l'Esprit se veult tresbien resouldre,
> Ià preuoyant son corps par la Mort tel,
> Qu'auecques luy se fera immortel,
> Et qu'il ne peult que pour vn temps perir.
> Donques, pour paix a ma guerre acquerir,
> Craindray renaistre a vie plus commode?
> Quand sur la nuict le iour vient a mourir,
> Le soir d'icy est Aulbe a l'Antipode.

This poem does indeed begin by presenting "the terms of co-existing contraries" Giordano, p. 155), but that is about as far as it goes along the modernist path, unless if what we really mean by "modern" is not that Scève was a poet thwarted by sensual conflict and psychological crisis, but that he was a great poet of transcendent symbolism intent on capturing a "vie plus commode," on creating poems that incarnate an ineffable or emotional experience that takes the poet and the reader ever deeper into illuminating subjectivism, and thus out of uncertainty and crisis. As symbolist, Scève does quite often detach a word or image from empirical reference or rational meaning, freeing it to express ineffable, spiritual, and emotional states, just as Mallarmé and other symbolists did later on. Even though Scève acknowledges the mystery or dark side of a thing or object, his poetry ultimately suggests, psychologically, an utter security and even delight in his union with it. In spite of the picture of his world which at times seems dark and meaningless, his poetry is always subjectivizing and clarifying a reality which finally can be known only through an understanding and portrayal of Délie as "obiect de plus haulte vertu" who informs and transforms the dark, concrete moment with the "cler de sa presence" (D368), the "authorité de sa graue presence" (D219). As such, Délie may be associated with the transcendent image of the *Aulbe* in D446 whose purpose it is to illuminate experience and to provide the poet light and renewal. In this way, Scève's use of poetic language and image is, I believe, very much like Mallarmé's and that of other symbolists. They both believed that the inherent obscurity of poetic creativity implies and can lead to a higher spiritual reality, just as Mallarmé's famous line "Une rose dans les ténèbres" suggests, as do so many of Scève's images which often substitute the metaphor of the *light* in the dark for Mallarmé's "rose."[1]

As rational readers, we are conditioned and trained to ask ourselves what "rose," what "light" are these poets talking about; do they really have any meaning? Perhaps the most appropriate answer to this question would be to suggest that insofar as the floral-illuminating memento is real, it would have to be a poem containing a definite vision. What kind of world-vision, then, is being endowed with meaning in the poetic language of the *Délie* and, for the moment, in the language and imagery of D446? The claim that the "itinerary of consciousness" being charted in D446 unfolds and fulfills the principle of a "haunting determinism" based on the final understanding and embracing of epistemological negativism (Giordano, p. 156) is hard for me to accept. The poet is actually affirming once again in this poem his desire and ability, with the help of the transcendent imagination, to go beyond an all-too-familiar, initial stage of uncertainty and negativity. In fact, as I see it, Scève's itinerary in this poem covers the same paradisal progression from the dark to the light of the love consciousness as we will see presented in so many of Scève's other poems. The dialectical and procedural dilemma presented in this one involves the conflict to be resolved between body and spirit, a commonplace in Renaissance writing. This central paradox of Petrarchan love is used to emphasize the lover's *temporary* emotional and mental confusion. It is also used to symbolize the central thematic conflict in Petrarchan psychology whose resolution or working out was deemed essential if a higher understanding in love was ever to be possible. In the poem's initial statement:

> Rien, ou bien peu, faudroit pour me dissoudre
> D'auec son vif ce caducque mortel:
> A quoy l'Esprit se veult tresbien resouldre . . .

the poet actually begins by *playing down* the importance of difficulty, of "co-existing contraries," in stating that it would take little or nothing to resolve this conflict between body ("ce caducque mortel") and spirit ("son vif" and "l'Esprit"), especially since it is his spirit or higher vital principle which encourages this resolution. The poet then states what the solution would entail, what the consequences of opting for a "vie plus commode" in love would be. He foresees the body initially made dead but then, with the spirit, finally made immortal, the change through spiritual conversion to life-in-death: "Ià preuoyant son corps par la Mort tel, / Qu'auecques luy

114

se fera immortel, / Et qu'il ne peult que pour vn temps perir." Since it would take very little to bring about this reconstitution of self through death, and since the poet's higher vital principle would benefit from this conversion,

> Doncques, pour paix a ma guerre acquerir,
> Craindray renaistre a vie plus commode?
> Quand sur la nuict le iour vient a mourir,
> Le soir d'icy est *Aulbe* a l'Antipode.

Through the light-in-dark composition of chiaroscuro, Scève's favorite aesthetic technique for relating his transcendent kind of love psychology, the poet does come to terms with his desire in this poem to understand, justify, and accept the central paradox in paradisal love of conversion, of the reconstitution of self, through life-in-death. This way, he will gain peace from his war: his conflict will be resolved. The poem's brilliant imagery has paved the way for only one solution, and it is that transcendent longing and leap of the spirit and the poet's very being that he will describe over and over again in his poems. Just as we saw in the last chapter, in the poet's desire for transcendence and paradise, and in his depiction of the struggle for unity (always a part of this desire), the body as well as the mind and spirit must be included. The body too must participate and be satisfied. In this context, it is not puzzling at all why the poet describes in this poem the body, and the spirit, being reborn *together*. To gain final peace and contentment, the poet will not be afraid to "renaistre a vie plus commode," to welcome this transforming experience, the unitive restructuring of body and spirit in a new life. After all, that "more favorable life," the poet assures us in the poem's supremely illuminated concluding line where even evening is eternally becoming dawn ("Le soir d'icy est *Aulbe* a l'Antipode"), is what will also provide him with the all-embracing prospect of light, illumination, clarity. Such is the course that will lead him ultimately to Délie, love, and life.

The experience of D446, as of others in his love sequence, represents, I believe, the successful attempt by a remarkable and persevering Renaissance poet to *diminish* as much as is humanly possible the obscure and anguished nature of his experience in love by placing it in a higher perspective. In this poem Scève is also expressing a central truth about lyric poetry, and one that needs to be constantly repeated, since so many of his readers today, as in the past, are unduly fascinated by the night-side of his love poetry. Great love poetry does indeed have the capacity, even the requirement to perform a mysterious act of enchantment, to produce a magical effect and meaning in its verses. However, the successful poet in the process can never be thwarted by that experience; rather he must have control over it. His goal is to attain that special kind of enlightened clarity and contentment through which he may best command his poetic talent and summon into the light the essence of the poem and of the love experience that lies hidden in the darkness. For Scève the symbolist, poetry is something akin to magic: it has the power of opening up the way to a metaphysical or transcendent life in the poet through the use of metaphoric, transcendent language – such as the renewal image of the *Aulbe* in D446 – which reveals in a flash and bestows a new meaning to an otherwise dark world. Transcendence through the metaphoric, creative act of illumination is truly Scève's itinerary in D446.

So too is it in D7, in spite of the fact that this particular poem has always been interpreted (literally) as the classic example of the dual, static nature of his love, as embodying the unresolved and forever strained psychological tension between carnal love and spiritual love. This view has led some readers to stress and be content with "the terms of co-existing contraries" (Giordano, discussed above), or the conflicting tensions of a "warring union" (Dorothy Gabe Coleman),[2] or the poet's dark and deep-seated "désespoir" resulting from his sensual anxiety and his inability to reconcile his ever-present awareness of "la coexistence essentielle de la vie et de la mort" (Henri Weber).[3] But must we stop here? Must this poem also be read in such a negative and unfinished light? Is Scève's aspiration "to an awareness of a higher good" in this poem truly "tinged with carnal appetite and doomed to failure" (Coleman, p. 128)? I do not take this to be the poem's message nor its final meaning:

> Celle beaulté, qui embellit le Monde
> Quand nasquit celle en qui mourant ie vis,
> A imprimé en ma lumiere ronde
> Non seulement ses lineamentz vifz:
> Mais tellement tient mes espritz rauiz,
> En admirant sa mirable merveille,
> Que presque mort, sa Deité m'esueille
> En la clarté de mes desirs funebres,
> Ou plus m'allume, & plus, dont m'esmerueille,
> Elle m'abysme en profondes tenebres.

Scève is performing in this exquisite poem the same creative, metaphoric act of illumination we saw him do above in D446. And once again, this act reflecting a love psychology of poetic triumph over difficulty is accomplished through transcendent metaphor and the diaphorically tensive, aesthetic technique of chiaroscuro. This poem has little to do with the agonizing, paralyzing dialectic of banal and sensual reality, but has a lot to do with poetic struggle and restructuring, as do most of Scève's great poems. The problem as I see it with arguments in favor of the former interpretation is that they assume that Scève in his poetic endeavor made futile efforts to write poems based on a transcendent, psychologically luminous love aesthetic. The experience that Scève is describing, or perhaps it would be better to say "showing," in D7 is an aesthetic one, one which seeks to go beyond the imperfections of human nature and love as the poet-lover knew them in order to capture his most precious and permanent beliefs – in this case, the divine beauty of Délie and its overwhelming and uplifting effect on his mind ("Mais tellement tient mes espritz *rauiz*"). As experienced by the poet, the infusion aesthetically of Délie's sacred beauty into this world is the means for a reconciliation of the poet's "desirs funebres." Délie's beauty and deity have the power not only to embellish and refine, to throw light on the outer world ("Celle beaulté, qui *embellit* le Monde / Quand nasquit celle . . ."), but also to do the same for the inner world of the poet ("A imprimé en ma lumiere ronde"). These renewal-effecting qualities and power of Délie's beauty and deity first produce ecstasy and then open ways for the poet beyond an initial feeling of intense excitement, of poetic *ravissement* ("Mais tellement tient mes espritz rauiz"), into a deeper peace and insight, that transcendent "clarté" subsisting at the heart of the seemingly endless agitation of the poet's "desirs funebres." Through symbolic art, the metaphoric direction implied in this poem is actually determined by the poet's retreat from the agony of objective reality, conveyed yet again through the renewal metaphor of life-in-death ("Celle beaulté, qui embellit le Monde / Quand nasquit celle *en qui mourant ie vis*"), to a deeper and deeper awareness and embrace of beauty, quietude, and illuminating subjectivity. The luminous and aesthetic center of this poem is the seemingly enigmatic line "En la clarté de mes desirs funebres." Therein lies the interpretive problem. For my part, this deep yet brilliant diaphoric metaphor exists to redefine the poet's situation as containing transcendent possibilities which are capable of freeing him from a world of sensual-psychological bondage. Délie's "Deité" awakens the poet-lover from a state of near death to one of great self-expansion that floods sensation, metaphysical uncertainty, and spiritual aspiration with radiance and thus illuminates his entire being, including his dark side. Put another way, Délie's beauty and deity are to the outer world what the poet's "clarté" is to his inner, dark desires: they exert a correcting influence in that they exist to illuminate and to perfect; they are the only means to guide the poet in his struggle towards a more positive and higher meaning to be found in the love experience.

Scève's diaphoric poetic experience in love thrives on a dialectic of the sacred, on the contradiction inherent in all transcendent art – the need to express the eternal (Délie's and the poet's own "clarté") by means of the material, and, as is the case in D7, by means of the poem's grounding in darkness and obscurity (the poet's "desirs funebres"). But this art does reach a higher meaning and the poet does move beyond his initial dark condition by realizing a synthesis between light and dark, by creating sequentially, as well as in the lines of a given poem, a set of analogies and relationships which call upon the creative activity of the reader to conceive the fullness and latent possibilities of these images, analogies, and relationships. A characteristic of the "vnique lumiere" of Délie's deity is that it always challenges the reader's (and the poet's) powers of rational explanation. The poet observes with both consternation and awe its ability to bring him to death only to effect his recovery. One additional quality of light that acquires symbolic importance in Scève, as we saw in our discussion of D24 (above p. 11), is its tendency to produce a blinding effect and thus to become even more associated with darkness. Scève quite often represents the mystery of encounter with the illuminating "deity" of Délie as a deep and dark and dazzling "abyss" ("Ou plus *m'allume*, & plus, dont m'esmerueille, / Elle *m'abysme* en profondes tenebres"). Scève's sacred myth of Délie is an autonomous act of creation by the mind working its way through darkness and matter: it is through this act of diaphoric searching, through this diaphoric enactment of a *mise en abyme*, that revelation and recovery are brought about. The creation or theme of descent, both Délie's to earth and the poet's to "profondes tenebres," is for the sake of the salvation of love and art, of the poet's higher creative life. Symbolic death and descent are for the purpose of finding new life, of undergoing spiritual recovery and self-renewal. A sacred value is thus being given to a material thing; the sacred is manifesting itself *in* a material thing: Délie's beauty and deity in the world, the poet's "clarté" in the darkness. As D7's crashing conclusion with its dynamic image of abysmal depth highlighting the diaphoric portrayal of the *via negativa* also suggests ("Ou plus m'allume, & plus, dont m'esmerueille, / Elle m'abysme en profondes tenebres"), the poet's descent, which plunges him into deeper darkness, may be associated with vitality and rebirth as well as with destruction. The darkening may be a brightening, a renewed springing forth, which of course is precisely the interpretation I have been arguing. D7 is exemplary of Scève's diaphoric art: as the poem progresses, new levels of significance are revealed and old meanings altered. The death-like obscurity to which the poet and the reader descend in this poem suggests that taking the way up may require taking the way down. This principle of the *via negativa* points to the necessity for death to come before life or a new beginning. The libido (the poet's "desirs funebres"), properly channeled and properly tapped, provides in the *Délie* a virtually endless source of creative energy and light. Stated aesthetically, the most intense and perfect revelation of the sacred or transcendent depends on and is almost always increased by darkness and obscurity in which, from which, and especially through which it acquires greater meaning and power. The way down is, for Scève, quite often the best way up, of finding and affirming the positive and even the paradisal in and through the negative. Metaphorically and axiologically, the implications of a symbol in the *Délie* are sometimes found to be rather different from what might logically be expected. For Scève, descent does give rise to ascent, light does come from dark, clarity or illumination can be found (created) in obscurity or matter. This newly generated meaning in D7 of "clarté" amid "desirs funebres" (like that seen above in D446: "Le soir d'icy est Aulbe a l'Antipode") provides a good indication of the success of Scève's diaphoric, transcendent art. The sacred theme found in D7 of excessive light producing darkness producing light is a very old one. This chiasm is rendered very poetically and diaphorically throughout the Bible. In Psalm 18:11, God in descending to earth is beheld in "thick darkness," for "he made darkness his covering around him." The reason for such darkness is explained in 1 Timothy 6:16: God "dwells in unapproachable light." The poetically metaphysical implication is obvious: light, for those incapable of beholding it, is darkness; darkness, for those capable and willing to behold it, is light. In his own love lyrics of the ineffable, Scève as chiaroscurist is both willing and determined to behold this light.

Scève's poetic efforts to understand and capture the deity and sacred beauty of Délie almost always involve or imply the transcendent, psychological state of life-in-death, with the aesthetic result of producing the uplifting ecstasy and radiant illumination we saw in D446, or the deep and profound inrush of quietude and enlightening serenity as they are presented in D7. This understanding of death within the death-and-rebirth pattern is envisioned not objectively as the end of life, but subjectively as the "quiescent *resolution* of affective excitement; the tendency to it is an effort of the organism to *restore* quiescent equilibrium."[4] This psychology is in Scève as well a felt need for greater psychic harmony and wholeness, for release and restructuring from sensual conflict and tension, and a transcendent impulse directed towards sublimation which actively and aesthetically realizes itself time and again in the poet's higher consciousness. Scève describes for us this very special meaning and purpose of death at the beginning of his sequence in his introductory poem:

> Non de Venus les ardentz estincelles,
> Et moins les traictz, desquelz Cupido tire:
> Mais bien les mortz, qu'en moy tu renouelles
> Ie t'ay voulu en cest Oeuure descrire.
> Ie sçay asses, que tu y pourras lire
> Mainte erreur, mesme en si durs Epygrammes:
> Amour (pourtant) les me voyant escrire
> En ta faueur, les passa par ses flammes.

It is not the simple exposition of his passion or sensuality, metaphorically the way of Venus and Cupid, which the poet ultimately wishes to convey and to highlight in his poetry, but rather the difficult pursuit and understanding of the "deaths," in the *plural*, renewed in him by Délie with the help of Amour, spiritual love. In other words, the natural obscurity of sensual reality is but a constant springboard from which better to portray this major theme of Scève's love sequence: the transcendent, paradisal state of life-in-death (light-in-dark) which requires that the poet go through obscurity and depth and beyond obscurity and depth in his struggle with anguish to recover new life. The sacred nature and influence of Délie's beauty, representing a totally different order of higher being, always produce an upheaval at the psychological level which initially proves fatal to the lover. And they do even more for the poet. These qualities make possible the passage from darkness to enlightenment, from disorder to order, from death to creatively renewed life. Such symbolism of the psychology of transcendence is paradoxical and almost impossible to appreciate at the literal and objective level, where images and statements can be interpreted as seemingly providing the poet (and the reader) a no-exit situation. Scève recognizes this problem of a literal interpretation of meaning when he says to Délie (and to the reader) in the above poem: "Ie sçay asses, que tu y pourras lire / *Mainte erreur*, mesme en si durs Epygrammes." But the poet-lover is forced to go where the dark and the light come together, where, in order to express and celebrate the higher awareness and significance of his kind of sacred or ineffable love, the necessity of transcending the pairs of opposites means abolishing the polarity that besets the human condition. The success of this poetic purpose and psychology depends also on the reader's ability to overcome what at first seem to be textual impasses and resistances. To this end, Scève's masterful handling of transcendent metaphor and its portrayal in chiaroscuro can be of immense help, as is the purpose of this chapter to show. The joyous turn of events described in the beginning of D7 with the coming of Délie prefigures the deliverance from and reversal of the poet's condition of anguish and obscurity. To the poet's great astonishment ("dont m'esmerueille"), Délie's beauty and deity perform the miracle of resurrection by *awakening* him and making him acutely aware of that higher part of himself and of the real purpose of his quest: that greater awareness and preservation of his own *clarté* ("sa Deité m'esueille / En la clarté de mes desirs funebres"). And the deliverance pointed to in D7 is to be found in the diaphoric, transcendent way of down and out, which in effect amounts to the same poetic method and direction we discovered in D446. In Scève, the aesthetic and psychological passage from darkness to enlightenment, from disorder to order, almost always involves the transcendent metaphor of life-in-death, of finding and highlighting *clarté* amid "desirs funebres," which leads in one of two directions – the up-and-beyond way of D446 or the down-and-out portrayal of D7. Regardless of direction, the purpose and result are always the same: the recovery of new and more essential life, of a higher state of "joyeux serain" (D365) which can only be reached by "clarté" or light "breaking through the thickness of agitated darkness," showing the poet the way through darkness to this higher life: "La Lune au plein par sa *clarté* puissante / Rompt l'espaisseur de l'obscurité trouble, / . . . / Me conduisant en son ioyeux serain."

The desire and struggle to escape from death, that is, to be transformed by it and to acquire in the process a new meaning, "choses plus prosperes" as the poet says in D218, or a "vie plus commode" as he insists on in D446, greatly concerned Scève. Through the love experience, Scève explores the positive and negative sides of death: the latter's prospect of unending life, and its transcendent corollary, life eternal. The poet makes a clear distinction between bondage to the world without hope of renewal (the error of his "desirs funebres") and the possibility of transcending death and of recovering new life (the promise of his "clarté"). These ideas already being developed in D7 will be tested time and again by Scève in his poems and thus become such permanent elements in his psychology and optimism in love that the poet will bring them together again at the end of his sequence in D442. How could it be, the poet asks himself in this poem, that the Gods caused him such anguish and suffering in love?

> Pourroit donc bien (non que ie le demande)
> Vn Dieu causer ce viure tant amer?
> Tant de trauaulx en vne erreur si grande,
> Ou nous viuons librement pour aymer?

But he immediately corrects this initial assessment of blaming the Gods in the remainder of this poem with the higher realization that his very special kind of love for Délie is both sacred and eternal, and thus cannot be tied down to the ordinary condition of destruction and darkness and death. His love is of a completely different nature. The poet's ongoing exploration and acceptance of his ideal bring with them a higher transformation of outlook and a greater degree of satisfaction, that is, once again the realization of the higher restructuring of the very meaning of the love experience:

> O ce seroit grandement blasphemer
> Contre les Dieux, pur intellect des Cieulx.
> Amour si sainct, & non poinct vicieux,
> Du temps nous poulse a eternité telle,
> Que de la Terre au Ciel delicieux
> Nous oste a Mort pour la vie immortelle.

The real escape from death is *through* death to the *clarté* of an eternal life in the "Ciel delicieux." This itinerary helps to clarify and balance the direction of Scève's thinking in many poems, as I have also suggested for the end of D7 and D446. With the glorious introduction of the transcendent word and metaphor "clarté" (or "Aulbe" in D446) and its potential power of making all clear and right, the poet opens the way for a change and reversal. The downward movement has the potential of swinging upward. Portraying this same psychological movement another way in D164, thanks to the higher nature of his love for Délie, the poet envisions hope emerging from the dark depths of his despair:

> Comme corps mort vagant en haulte Mer,
> Esbat des Ventz, & passetemps des Vndes,
> I'errois flottant parmy ce Gouffre amer,
> Ou mes soucys enflent vagues profondes.
> Lors toy, Espoir, qui en ce poinct te fondes
> Sur le confus de mes vaines merueilles,
> Soubdain au nom d'elle *tu me resueilles*
> *De cest abysme, auquel ie perissoys*.

Another good portrayal highlighting this process of recovery is to be found in D266, where we find again the illuminating image of the *Aulbe* functioning as a psychological and aesthetic turning point for the poet's renewal. Relying here once again on the triumphant portrayal of chiaroscuro, light is shown to come from darkness. The poet is showing us again that the obscurity of successful transcendent art always leads to clarity:

> *De mon cler iour ie sens l'Aulbe approcher,*
> *Fuyant la nuict de ma pensée obscure.*
> Son Crepuscule a ma veue est si cher,
> Que d'aultre chose elle n'à ores cure.
> Ià son venir a eschauffer procure
> Le mortel froit, qui tout me congeloit.
> Voyez, mes yeulx, le bien que vous celoit
> Sa longue absence en presence tournée:
> Repaissez donc, comme le Cœur souloit,
> Vous loing priuez d'vne telle iournée.

The aesthetic and psychological movement described by the poet in these three poems, as in D7, is pure *metanoia* – reversal of direction of the mind. These poems as psychological turning points are also pure *diaphoria* required of and resulting in triumphant, difficult poetic beauty. For our love poet, there is life in death, hope in despair, light in dark, in a word (and image), the positive in the negative. This diaphoric process of the *via negativa* is what makes the poet's recovery and triumph over obscurity and despair possible, and what we as readers feel is, to however small a degree, the higher power of mind, emotion, and art to transcend and transform life. *Délie*'s poetic tension is more often than not the source of life, not of derangement or death. Scève's poems which satisfy most are not those which present an easy portrayal of resolution and order, but those we have been looking at which present a new life and light (insight) as the result of and reward for conflict and struggle. This tension is always necessary to an aesthetic of *difficulté vaincue*; it is what makes Scève's most triumphant poems possible and meaningful. Scève's love poetry thrives and survives on revelation, not rationalization. Tension or conflict is always the source of this revelation as the poet persists in coming to terms with the ineffable Délie.

As a model poem of Scève's diaphorically transcendent art, D7 does acknowledge and affirm the existence and even necessity of light and dark in the poet's world. The impact of this poem does indeed come from the poet's knowledge of the power of darkness; he does feel the direct pressure of passion and despair. Otherwise, Scève could not have written so movingly about them. But his faith and his poetic art resist the ultimate influence of this pressure by working together towards the greater possibility of aesthetic sublimation. Still, this does not mean that there is no darkness. Doubt and darkness cannot be dismissed too easily or too quickly. They are the starting points and tensive elements necessary for the ultimate triumph of D7 and the others we have looked at. Scève's poetic faith and art are precarious, constantly being renewed yet always in jeopardy, and it is this precariousness which gives the *Délie* its intense excitement and appeal. The issue of higher love and transcendent art is always in doubt. It is always being measured against concrete experience and is constantly being put to the test. For both Scève's poetic vision and meaning, faith must be seen against doubt as light against dark and as clarity against obscurity. The real achievement of Scève as a great love poet lies in his remarkable ability to acknowledge these contradictory concepts and to hold them in such balanced tension that a greater synthesis is created wherein the positive element emerges victorious. We do not ordinarily live in the realization that light comes from dark or that life comes out of death, and to portray in poetic imagery the dark dissolution that is the prelude to new life, and to continue to struggle for this new life, is the true task and test of the poet who lives much above the common level of feeling and understanding. This is why Scève's "deaths" are always bearable and even exciting for this reader: because their poetic meaning is most often being developed in a positive and even paradisal direction. Scève's statements on death are emblematic of the poles of his emotional life and are the boundary markers of his world – both the world he perceived around him and the higher world he believed in and struggled to create in his love lyrics. It is tempting to see in Scève no more than a poet of strained and unresolved antitheses. The illuminating, paradisal beauty of one side of him and the disturbing, obscure doubt of the other side are evidence of extreme shifts in outlook, the wavering between life and death, hope and despair, between the heights and the depths. Scève is a master at creating interdependent tensions: the darkness of an image that needs the little circle of light to give it meaning; the joy of the same image that consoles only in light of the possibility of sorrow. But the tension of joy and sorrow (and thus light and dark) as two halves of a circle, as reversed images of one another in those supreme moments I call Scève's poetic paradises, is always relieved or resolved in a higher awareness and creation wherein light is victorious, wherein joy triumphs over sorrow, conviction over doubt, "entendement" over "vexation" – moments during which the poet comes to understand the light in the dark as a sign of Délie's presence. This is the higher synthesis and supreme vision of the "centre heureux" and "sainct lieu" the poet depicts in D330. These poetic possibilities can only be reached through the conscious use of the controlling image of light to bestow a positive meaning upon the anguished struggle with darkness.[5]

In this exquisite poem as well, the very existence of the "clarté" of Délie and the poet, to say nothing of his highlighting it through the light-in-dark composition of chiaroscuro as a condensed metaphor, insures the ultimate sublimation of the "desirs funebres" of the poet's passion. Just as there is being described in D330 a projection from the dark existence of our ordinary lives to the higher vision of a more luminous and satisfying existence and reality, so there is taking place a sublimation in the fullest sense of the term. Of this process, the shining object is Délie who represents a principle of spiritual enlightenment and recovery for the poet. She thus performs the primary role of guiding the poet towards paradise. Emblem 37, "La Lune en tenebres," with its motto, "Ma clarté tousiours en tenebre," and this accompanying D330 bring together all the psychological and aesthetic elements I have been trying to elucidate in this chapter. The symbolism, again based on the chiaroscuro and diaphoria of transcendent art, is simple and central:

> Au centre heureux, au cœur impenetrable
> A cest enfant sur tous les Dieux puissant,
> Ma vie entra en tel heur miserable,
> Que pour iamais, de moy se bannissant,
> Sur son Printemps librement fleurissant
> Constitua en ce sainct lieu de viure,
> Sans aultrement sa liberté poursuyure
> Ou se nourrit de pensementz funebres:

Et plus ne veult le iour, mais la nuict suyure.
Car sa lumiere est tousiours en tenebres.

There is no finer poem in all the *Délie* than this one which demonstrates a poetic-psychological triumph over difficulty. The light–dark polarity in this poem and its adjacent emblem operates on all levels – literal, metaphoric, symbolic. It is also being used to signal the main issue of Scève's poetry: the question of whether the poet can behold and embrace an ineffable reality. The interplay of light–dark thus becomes the interplay of faith and doubt, of life and death, of the spiritual and the physical. Scève's pull towards the dark, his predilection for the *via negativa*, does indeed spring from his knowledge of sensual despair (of "pensementz funebres"), yet there is simultaneously, in this diaphoric portrayal based on contiguity and paradox, a higher vision of love and of art at work, of the light in the dark pointing the poet towards that "centre heureux" and "sainct lieu" of a more perfect and more satisfying understanding of love. The poet again is demonstrating his ultimate desire to opt for the light provided him by Délie which is to be found, if looked hard enough for, in the dark ("Car sa lumiere est tousiours en tenebres"). This poem's presentation of the transcendent metaphor of life-in-death ("Ma vie . . . / Que pour iamais, de moy se bannissant") symbolizes the full paradisal state of sublimated and restructured consciousness in which the poet has clearly *chosen* to go beyond a former life defined by the "pensementz funebres" of passion, beyond a life of "liberty" freely flourishing in its "Springtime." ("Liberté" is always a problem for the poet which he is forced to overcome if he is to progress in his love experience. The reader will recall that in D442 the poet's "viure tant amer" and his "erreur" were being caused by, or at least being experienced in, a life of "liberté" – "Ou nous viuons *librement* pour aymer.")[6] Like so many of his other poems, D330 portrays the firm resolve – the verb "constitua" in line 6 carries the very strong and conscious meaning of "to decide" – of the poet's desire to progress through a life of sense, his day of darkness, to reach a higher spiritual reality and significance. The poet is giving up his former day of freedom, his former life seen to be flourishing in its Springtime but one which actually was being nourished with dark thoughts. This is why the poet in his new life no longer wishes to follow day but prefers to follow night: because, as he sees it, in the night is to be found light, the Moon, Délie. In his diaphoric awareness, the poet is substituting or exchanging the day of darkness for the night of light, thereby acquiring a higher understanding of love and life. Paradise, the word-images of "centre heureux" and "sainct lieu," is a consciously *created* state of mind – the higher feeling and reality afforded by *difficulté vaincue*, just as it is in the triumphant word-image of D7: "En la *clarté* de mes desirs funebres," whose purpose and direction also reveal the intense desire and determination of the poet through the light of language and image, through the luminous matter of poetry, to make all clear and right. While light and dark are both present in D330 and its emblem, the psychological as well as the aesthetic weight is clearly on the side of the light. In this poem, as in the others we have been looking at, the reader's eye yields easily to the drama of light and dark: to the brilliant and privileged place-ment of the "centre heureux" and "sainct lieu" within the large and always threatening structure of poetic darkness. However, the definitional presence and orienting power of the light in the dark – of "la Lune," of "ma clarté," of "sa lumiere" – are what most are revealed, stand out, and become the focal point directing the poet towards love's "centre heureux" and "sainct lieu." The power of subjective creativity is being used to transform, transfigure, and illuminate a dark and even misguided objective world. In opting for the inner "sainct lieu" of love, whose "centre heureux" also not only burns but transmutes, the poet is endowing the objective world of "liberté" and "pensementz funebres" with form capable of being perceived in a higher and more expansive way. This diaphoric trans-mutation of poetic matter is, after all, the goal or purpose the poet sets for himself in *Délie*'s introductory poem. The "deaths" that are continually being renewed in the poet ("les mortz, qu'en moy tu renouelles") – his finding new life in death, a new day in night, light in dark – and whose meaning he wishes to explore and to depict are not in the end the result of Venus and Cupid (sensual love), but of his struggling commitment to Amour (spiritual love) who "les [the poet's 'durs Epygrammes'] passa par ses *flammes*." In other words, poetic subject or matter is being illuminated with spirit. The spiri-tual life is being triumphantly depicted. Scève obscured poetic meaning not until it became strained or hermetic, but until it seemed essential, essential to serve a purpose: spiritual recovery and renewal, the illumination of experience, clarity through obscur-ity. This diaphorically obscured poetic art-form is always luciferous by definition and in execution. As Jean Starobinski has so brilliantly shown in his seminal essay on "L'Encre de la mélancolie," this kind of luminous art is what also enabled Shakespeare to triumph over the obscurity and anguish this writer too had to come to terms with in his own love lyrics. For Starobinski, Shakespeare's own black ink of melancholy expressing "les désordres de l'esprit" was also capable, in the end, of reflecting through these very unhappy verses a paradisal psychology and radiance of great human worth and value. Here is how Starobinksi defines Shakespeare's diaphoric art which he sees reflecting this writer's poetic triumphs:

Le fond ténébreux comporte la chance de l'éclat, si on lui superpose une matière lisse. Shakespeare le devine, en évoquant le miracle d'un amour qui resplendit, sauvé des ravages universels du Temps, dans l'encre noire du poème. . . . Mais dans cette ultime transformation métaphorique, la mélancolie devenue encre devient enfin le tain grâce auquel l'image rayonne. L'obscurité la plus dense oppose à la lumière une surface d'où elle rejaillit, luciférienne, comme d'une seconde source.[7]

Whether in Shakespeare or in Scève, diaphoric art is always lucifer-ous: it is what brings light and insight and new life. It exists and is used solely by a poet to illuminate and to transform obscurity and darkness.

The images of "Lune, clarté, lumiere" in D330 and the com-panion emblem function metaphorically in a positive and creative way, just as the very same diaphoric portrayal does in D59 where an even more explicit reference is made to the enlightening and redeeming role of Délie, like that of the moon, to guide the poet through the dark: "Car ie te cele en ce surnom louable, / Pource qu'en moy tu *luys* la nuict obscure" (cf. Psalm 18:28: "The Lord my God lightens my darkness"). The same illuminating portrayal is enacted in yet another companion piece helpful for a better understanding and appreciation of D330, in D365, where the same positive analogy between Délie and the moon is made and where they function aesthetically to lead and conduct the poet towards a higher awareness of the beauty and contentment that can be found in love. Through its own dramatic enactment, in terms of chiar-oscuro, of the struggle between the forces of light and those of dark for control of love, D365, parts of which we have already seen, is another excellent example which celebrates the successful over-coming of textual and psychological difficulty and obscurity. The poetic and aesthetic process of *difficulté vaincue* highlighted throughout this poem is what prepares the way for the full vision and enjoyment of the poet's paradisal experience in love, which is defined by the poet in D330 as the opting for the "centre heureux" and "sainct lieu" of light as opposed to the "pensementz funebres" of passion. In short, the poet's triumph in D365, which also culminates in his rest and repose in love's "joyeux serain," is the same psychological and aesthetic sublimation of mind and art we saw at work in D330 and its adjacent Emblem 37, "La Lune en tenebres":

> La Lune au plein par sa clarté puissante
> Rompt l'espaisseur de l'obscurité trouble,
> Qui de la nuict, & l'horreur herissante,
> Et la paour pasle ensemble nous redouble:
> Les desuoyez alors met hors de trouble,
> Ou l'incertain des tenebres les guide.
> De celle ainsi, qui sur mon cœur preside,
> Le doulx regard a mon mal souuerain
> De mes douleurs resoult la nue humide,
> Me conduisant en son ioyeux serain.

The images of "Lune," "Aulbe," "clarté," "lumiere" found in so many of Scève's poems are turning points for the poet, psychologically and artistically. They are like beacons shining in the dark, showing the way to transcendence and paradise, to love's "sainct lieu," to a higher state of "ioyeux serain." They are part of a whole network of controlling and ordering images of light scattered throughout this love sequence and providing the poet direction and definition: the chiaroscurmatic indwelling and higher potential of light seen above in D365: "La Lune au plein par sa clarté puissante / Rompt l'espaisseur de l'obscurité trouble"; in D59: "Pource qu'en moy tu luys la nuict obscure"; in D7: "En la clarté de mes desirs funebres"; in D446: "Quand sur la nuict le iour vient a mourir, / Le soir d'icy est Aulbe a l'Antipode"; and in D24: "Mais moy conduict dessoubs la sauuegarde / De ceste tienne, & vnique lumiere, / . . . / Ne me pers plus en veue coustumiere." In Scève's love experience and his portrayal of that experience, the poet often feels a crisis of descriptive language because there do not seem to be words and concepts in the ordinary language adequate to convey his experience. This obscurity which is juxtaposed in the *Délie* with flashes of blinding light has, however, profound literary consequences. The poet's double vision permits him to reject the customary way of seeing and to become more and more absorbed in the ineffable. And now ordinary language can no longer express what he sees; he must use a special language in order to reproduce his visions of the ideal. This psychological straining of linguistic resources leads to the art of chiaroscuro and its tensive, diaphoric employment of transcendent metaphor, of renewal phrases and images like "the brightness of my dark desires," "light . . . in shadows," and "When, at night, day comes to die, / Evening here is Dawn in the Antipodes." Scève's initial failure in using a descriptive / analytic language leads him to the highly aesthetic language of chiaroscuro, a very important and powerful technique of all diaphoric art whose primary purpose is always one of difficult "showing" through presenting and asserting rather than describing through explaining. For this poet, love and its higher meaning can best thrive in the light of diaphoric revelation, never in reason which would blight them forever. In Scève's marvelous diaphoric creations, the poet sees everything through the chiaroscuro of transfiguration and transillumination (his only means of coming to terms with Délie's "vnique lumiere") and never relies on the "veue coustumiere" of reason for his poetic discoveries. Boileau's artistic precept later on – "Aimez donc la raison: que toujours vos écrits / Empruntent d'elle seule et leur lustre et leur prix" – would have been to Scève the greatest of all blasphemies against higher love and transcendent art.[8] The "luster" and life of Scève's love lyrics of the ineffable are not beholden to reason. These lyrics are hard-won affirmations of the luminous night of poetry, not the quick and inadequate and impersonal clarities of reason.

Surely the role played by the light in these powerful chiaroscurmatic images on the interaction of light and dark within the love psychology must be viewed as bestowing a higher direction, significance, meaning. Although in our current everyday vocabulary, light metaphors such as "clarté," "Aulbe," "lune," "lumiere" have largely ceased to function as active metaphors and have lost virtually all tensive character, there is no reason to believe that this was true during Scève's time. Indeed, I believe these light metaphors were the body and soul of the metaphoric life Scève was so intent on relating in the love poems of the *Délie*. Interpretation of these poems depends on the recognition by the reader not that clarity is being obscured by darkness but, on the contrary, that clarity can be found in darkness, indeed that there is a special kind of poetic understanding or clarity that can only be discovered and enjoyed in darkness. That is, the light in these images serves to indicate to the poet (and to the reader) the way beyond the problematics and obscurity of passion and poetic discourse to the higher destination of the "sainct lieu" of love by ultimately providing the poet a clear sense of the white radiance of the sacred and the ineffable. These highly metaphoric representations of Délie as the light in the dark *are* Scève's and *Délie*'s poetic beacons, safely conducting the poet towards a higher love and contentment:

Ces tiens, non yeulx, mais *estoilles celestes*,
Ont influence & sur l'Ame, & le Corps:
Combien qu'au Corps ne me soient trop molestes
En l'Ame, las, causent mille discordz,
Mille debatz, puis soubdain mille accordz,
Selon que m'est ma pensée agitée.
Parquoy vaguant en Mer tant irritée
De mes pensers, tumultueux tourment,
Ie suy ta face, ou ma Nef incitée
Trouue son feu, qui son Port ne luy ment. (D243)

In the final analysis, it is the difficult pursuit of beauty and content-
ment through sensation (through sensuous matter or love's
"desirs/pensementz funebres"), a pursuit that must be poetically
raised to the level of sacred passion (i.e., given an exchange value
with idea, be directed towards insight into love's "sainct lieu"),
which D330 and the other companion poems on the light and dark
of love so confidently celebrate. They reflect the struggle of the
human spirit to come to meaningful terms with and to rest in *diffi-
culté vaincue*. Embodying a hermeneutics of recovery for both poet
and reader, these poems do translate a vision of light and life in an
otherwise dark world. This diaphoric vision (D330: "Car sa *lumiere*
est tousiours *en tenebres*") is the same difficult understanding of the
ineffable whose light is always to be found in the darkness which
Blake too will depict later on: "God appears and God is *Light* /
To those poor Souls who dwell *in Night*"; and whose triumphant
portrayal can also be found in poets much closer to Scève, such as
Nicolas Denisot, who quotes John 1:15, "Et la *lumiere* reluist *en
tenebres*, & les tenebres ne l'ont point comprise."[9]

These poems on the light and dark of the love consciousness can
tell us even more about Scève's character and desire as a love poet.
Relying on light as a controlling metaphor through the showing of
this light is preferable, for a love poet like Scève, to trying to explain
it. Scève's art is much more oriented towards aesthetics than it is
towards moralization or poetic didacticism. However, there is a
"message" to be retrieved just the same. I argued in the last chapter
that in the end it is the poet's higher *self*-awareness and *self*-reali-
zation which primarily will benefit from the love experience. I
referred to this statement in D271 to support my claim:

Ie quiers en toy ce, qu'en moy i'ay plus cher.
Et bien qu'espoir de l'attente me frustre,
Point ne m'est grief en aultruy me chercher.

131

This brings us to the message of D330 and the other poems discussed above. Scève's motives or intentions in poetically portraying love, which he sets forth for the reader in the introductory poem of his sequence, are from the beginning clearly placed on the side of Amour (spiritual love) rather than on the side of Venus and Cupid (sensual love). This poetic choice represents much more than mere mythological allegiance. The poet is always forced to go where the dark and the light come together and to choose the one with which to define and affirm the true essence of his love experience. The poet resolves ("constitua" in D330) to progress through human love, which at its highest level leads him, through death and a restructuring and renewal of self, to a vision of sacred love. Scève's transcendent vision transforms human love, but does not destroy it. Though certainly not a religious poet in the formal sense of the word, Scève does form his own spiritual conceptions and turns them into textual realities in his love lyrics. It is only natural, therefore, that Scève's understanding of the sacred and ineffable should come from the faculties most strongly influenced by feeling: that is, from heart and soul (imagination), which are merely a love poet's means of demonstrating a higher ideal and which create and alter objects in accordance with the poet's understanding of that ideal. This very process of defining a higher love does have the potential for both light and darkness in that it brings out whatever qualities or motives are in the beholder to begin with. It activates whatever darkness or light is latent in the lover. Stated purely and simply, if these motives are good, the lover will be positively affected. Scève's light in night, his light in the dark, is always Délie, and since she is the product of the poet's creative imagination, this light is also very much the poet, as we saw in the last chapter. For Scève, love is always a test, bringing out whatever qualities of light or dark, joy or sorrow, life or death may be present in the poet-lover contemplating it. And in D330 and the others discussed in this chapter, the opting for and highlighting of the "centre heureux" and "sainct lieu" by the poet is a sure psychological index of spiritual intention, motive, and struggle – of ever-desired receptivity to light. Scève's light is always the diaphoric light of struggle and triumph. Each time the poet is able to enjoy it, it is a light that is earned and not freely given.

The poet's *clarté* – that metaphysical spark or flash in the darkness symbolizing greatness of spirit and mind and art which has the potential of surfacing at any moment in Scève's poems – is a moving plea for greatness of spirit in literature and poetry. The poetic representations of this refined, higher experience in love become

Scève's poetic paradises and have been central to this present study. If, in its presentation of the poet's complex and often precarious poise between the world he knows and the ineffable world he desires to know, my discussion is viewed as overemphasizing the latter, this book will have achieved its purpose. If great love poetry really is that miraculous and luminous moment when measured, dark strokes on a page suddenly leap into something sacred and eternal (Mallarmé's "black-on-white" metaphor for poetic writing, which we shall discuss in the Epilogue), then the critical effort to capture that poetic epiphany is well worth the risk. In its search for an understanding of the two sides of Scève, this study accepted the difficult interpretive challenge of advancing the aesthetic intelligibility of a higher poetic meaning in the *Délie*, which is to be found in the poet's struggle to know and to experience love's "sainct lieu." This challenge and the potential dangers to be found within it have been fully recognized by Scève's readers:

Il reste pourtant une façon de comprendre Scève et de l'apprécier justement: ce serait de retenter en sa compagnie l'aventure de l'amour; de refaire avec lui *le saut du profane au sacré*. Mais le danger est si grand, la discipline quasiment monastique, l'attention non pas seulement mécanique et cérébrale, mais de l'être tout entier, qu'il n'y a rien d'étonnant à ce qu'il ne se trouve que peu de lecteurs pour s'y risquer.

Hopefully, my own reader will agree that we have already made together this "leap" at this stage of the present study.[10]

To Scève's dark side we must, of course, give sympathetic understanding, but only in order to see better how it blends into his poetry of paradisal life whose ultimate message is illuminating beauty and intense satisfaction. Scève worked in both modes, finally passing through a deathly period to visions of essential life. This life is the paradise of the love consciousness, alight with a sacred joy. The whole notion of what constitutes poetic beauty and paradise rests, of course, in the eye of the beholder. However, there are common characteristics and depths of feeling and meaning to be found in a few masterpieces of poetic love whose very success we might all agree resides in the understanding of a higher poetic experience of beauty and contentment. Diotima's speech in Plato's *Symposium* which we quoted earlier points to the aesthetically ascending journey to be attempted later by such great love poets as Dante and Petrarch. Scève, too, pursues this very same tradition of paradisal poetry. All three strive in their poetic endeavors to understand and to capture that perfected and totally satisfying state of beauty and

love through the intermediary of the human objects of their con-
templation:

When a man has been thus far tutored in the lore of love, passing from
view to view of beautiful things, in the right and regular ascent, suddenly
he will have revealed to him, as he draws to the close of his dealings in
love, *a wondrous vision*, beautiful in its nature; and this, Socrates, is the
final object of all those previous toils.[11]

Dante begins to experience this kind of enraptured and difficult
ascent occasioned by a transcending beauty when he comes under
the dazzling influence of the power of Beatrice's gaze. Her radi-
ance, perceived as a reflection of the divine, leads the poet by
degrees higher and higher:

> Poscia rivolsi alla mia donna il viso,
> a quinci e quindi stupefatto fui;
> ché dentro alli occhi suoi ardea un riso
> tal, ch'io pensai co' miei toccar lo fondo
> della mia grazia e del *mio paradiso*. (*Paradiso*, XV, 32–36)[12]

Petrarch experiences this same wondrous and soul-consuming
vision of beauty and light in the person of Laura. Her beauty is also
perceived by this love poet as illuminated by the divine and as the
worldly means through which he may attain paradise:

> Gentil mia donna, i' veggio
> nel mover de' vostr'occhi *un dolce lume*
> *che mi mostra la via ch'al ciel conduce*;
> et per lungo costume
> dentro là dove sol con Amor seggio,
> quasi visibilmente il cor traluce.   (R72)[13]

And as we have seen, Scève too very often embodies in his love
lyrics this profound poetic longing for paradisal perfection and bliss
in his intense, enlightened, and transcending contemplation of the
beauty and deity of Délie. She not only illuminates this dark world,
but provides a glimpse of divine beauty. As with Dante and
Petrarch, such privileged moments of harmony and ecstasy felt by
the heart and soul in contemplation of the beauty of the beloved
are also for Scève's love poet the way to paradise: "*Mon Paradis
elle ouure*, & lors m'appaise, / Pour non donner aux enuieux esbat:
/ Parquoy ie cele en mon *cœur* si grand aise" (D314). All these poetic
encounters involving personal experiences of human love and
beauty have at least one thing in common: they celebrate and
attempt to capture the sudden and marvelous way in which love

takes hold of the poet's imagination (his heart and soul) and trans-
ports it into higher spheres, into love's "sainct lieu" and "centre
heureux," into the very "shining center" of contemplation and cre-
ation. As Scève describes aesthetically this access to the "wondrous
vision," the transcending power of love "renaist soubdain en moy
celle autre Lune / *Luisante au centre*, ou l'*Ame* à son seiour"
(D106).

The most beautiful and most significant dizains in the *Délie*
describe this aesthetic perception of higher, deeper levels of mean-
ing generated by self-completion and self-advancement, poetic and
psychological, in the beauty and love of Délie – "obiect de plus
haulte vertu" – the intensely studied and illuminated object or rep-
resentative of a higher reality and goal. Thanks to Délie and love,
the poet is led by degrees higher and higher in the act of composing
his paradisal poetry. Leaving the world of anguish, destruction, and
death behind, the poet seeks out meanings and images of a higher,
more glorious, more essential reality which he always strives to
capture in his poems. This chapter has highlighted those poetic
moments when he succeeds. Some of Scève's poems, of course, do
remain on the level of anguish and agitation. This can only be
expected. The kind of intensity and illumination he sought cannot
be sustained in every poem of his sequence. But his best ones, the
most fully achieved ones, seem suddenly to separate themselves
from the others and to reach, however briefly, a spiritual and
psychological point of rest – their desired destination of "clarté,"
"Soleil," "Lune," "centre heureux," "sainct lieu," "ioyeux
serain," "Port," or simply "hault *Paradis*" itself. The poet thus
transcends an initial, dark condition of uncertainty, contradiction,
and torment by casting the celebration of love and beauty in paradi-
sal terms, as he does for us again in D58, where the poet does
succeed in internalizing his individual paradise. And he also shows
us in this poem again that such feelings of paradise can be external-
ized in love lyrics:

> Quand i'apperceu au serain de ses yeulx
> L'air esclarcy de si longue tempeste,
> Ià tout empeinct au prouffit de mon mieulx,
> Comme vn vainqueur d'honnorable conqueste,
> Ie commençay a esleuer la teste:
> Et lors le Lac de mes nouelles ioyes
> Restangna tout, voire dehors ses voyes
> Asses plus loing, qu'oncques ne feit iadis.
> Dont mes pensers guidez par leurs Montioyes,

135

Se paonnoient tous en leur hault *Paradis.*

Whether in older lyric poets such as Dante, Petrarch, and Scève or in our modern poets such as Baudelaire, Valéry, and Mallarmé, this transcendent psychology in contemplation, acquired after much difficulty, is always what produces and enables a poet to enjoy "un tout autre monde" as we have seen Valéry call it. This poetic possibility is also what Hans Robert Jauss has argued so convincingly to be the real achievement of all (both old and modern) great lyric poetry: the fortunate fact that this poetry prepares in the reader (and ultimately must fulfill in him) the "expectation that another, more essential world opens up to us in and through the lyric experience."[14] This other, more essential world in Scève is the new light and new life of love's "sainct lieu" found and confirmed, that is, created, by the poet in the dark.

6

"DE MES TRAUAULX ME BIENHEURANTZ MA PEINE": LOVE POETRY AS THERAPY

The illumination and malleability of mind and matter and art in the *Délie* as I have been exploring them in the preceding chapters have profound therapeutic significance for the poet. Whenever the mind and body of poetic contemplation (i.e., *esprit* and *sens* as Baudelaire called them, or else *idée* and *forme sensible* to use Valéry's terms) are viewed apart, antagonistic, warring, the perspective and poetics of anguish, obscurity, hell assert themselves. However, with the union and unity of mind and matter come the opposite perspective and poetics: that of paradise. Scève's vision and art were, finally, pliant enough and constructive enough to accommodate such a paradise. The psychological and artistic health of the latter is what Scève truly strives towards, a therapeutic process which is a creative response to and progression through the state of disorder of the former poetic possibility. Most great poets and writers and especially love poets have recognized this process and gone, some much farther than others, in the aesthetic direction I have been describing in this book. The distance covered in this enlightened progress of love and art can be quite far – it can range from hell to paradise – but it almost always begins in hell. Antonin Artaud puts it this way: "No one has ever written, painted, sculpted, modelled, constructed, or invented anything, except in order to extricate himself from hell."[1] The distance traveled depends on each writer's success at coming to terms with the unitive-luminous principle of psyche and art and its therapeutic reward. The regaining of this principle and the resultant health it is capable of bestowing upon a work of literature have always been the essence of serious literary art. Augustine, as well as our more modern writers such as Baudelaire, Valéry, and Artaud, knew this principle very well. Higher love and art – what Scève calls "l'ordre illustre" (D271) – are also for Augustine the ultimate condition of right order, which must always be won out of intense struggle with a lesser form of order in the world. Here is Augustine's recognition of this higher unitive principle of love, art, and life: "When I shall once attain to be united unto thee in every part of me, then shall I no more feel either sorrow or labour; yea, then shall my life truly be alive, every way full of thee."[2]

If this unitive-luminous principle so much desired by Augustine and Scève cannot be attained in life, it can at least be had in the accomplishment and life of art. But to have it in art, and in the creation of a work of art, means the necessity of struggle and even of suffering. For Scève, obscurity, anguish, and struggle were inseparable from poetic production. But this obscurity and this suffering were never wasted, even at their darkest moments. Suffering in Scève is not suffering for suffering's sake; rather it serves a productive and positive purpose. It is, finally, a poet's suffering – the suffering brought about, as François Rigolot has so aptly described it, by "le mouvement sans cesse renouvelé d'un Sisyphe de l'écriture."[3] Or, as Scève himself describes it in unmistakable Orphic terms in D177 and again in D384, among many other poems, his suffering is for the sake of Délie, of the ineffable, for the sake of self and art: "Et toutesfoys telz accomplissementz [the poet's 'struggles' – his 'trauaulx' – to come to terms with Délie's ineffability, his central dilemma so well depicted again at the beginning of this D177] / Rendent tousiours ma peine *glorieuse*"; "De mes trauaulx *me bienheurantz* ma peine, / Ie m'extermine . . ." (D384). Pain and struggle in Scève always posit two meanings above and beyond the literal and the ordinary. Rather than simply being the definition or frustrating and unfortunate consequences of love, they are actually, diaphorically speaking, the very means through which a poet like Scève transforms and re-creates this love. Suffering and struggle are always directed towards the poet coming to terms with, that is, contemplating and understanding and portraying, the meaning of transcendent ineffable love. They serve, in other words, a very real therapeutic and creative purpose in the *Délie*. This is why the poet is able to acknowledge in D177 and D384 that his "pain" is being made "happy," is "always" being made "glorious." Scève's poet in love indeed survives and thrives as a Renaissance Sisyphus, as the French Renaissance Orpheus.

From the beginning of recorded time, writers and subsequently critics have expressed the view that all art springs from conflict and suffering, as we saw Artaud suggesting above. For many students of literature today, the very definition of great literature is still the turning of this state of disorder into that of order through the insight and therapy provided by art. We all know the importance given to this notion of literature as therapy by Dr. François Rabelais – of the cleansing and purifying and perfecting principle of art, of the interplay of sickness and health that reveals the restorative properties of his book.[4] Scève was genuinely committed to a similar view as Rabelais of the therapeutically and reconstructively ordering power of literary art. (And thus I believe the criticism leveled against Scève by his contemporary Charles Fontaine which de Rocher cites in his article, "The Curing Text: Maurice Scève's Délie as the *Délie*," p. 23, as justification for a Lacanian reading of the *Délie* is a bit severe: "Brief, ilz [Scève's dizains] ne quierent un lecteur. / Mais la commune autorité / Dit qu'ilz requierent un docteur.") In his diaphoric poems of transcendence, we have already seen Scève actually creating his own poetic therapy and special kind of reconstructive psychology in love, his own version of *discordia concors*. Far from ultimately leading nowhere, the conflicting forces in Scève's poetic expression of his love do in fact lead to a sense of equilibrium and to a transcendent paradisal state. *Délie*'s imagery of conflict (light and dark, night and day, heaven and hell, and so forth), far from resulting in an epistemological and artistic impasse, does end in a sense of stability and harmony, of *discordia concors*, which reaches a harmonious resolution of opposing tensions by producing "a sweet consent of sounds."[5] This poetically therapeutic process is both passive and active, both contemplative and creative. It must first have been tested and validated in the portrayed object of love in order to have been seen and felt through self-portrayal by the subject of love:

> Tes doigtz tirantz non le doulx son des cordes,
> Mais des haultz cieulx l'Angelique *harmonie*,
> Tiennent encor en telle symphonie,
> Et tellement les oreilles concordes,
> Que paix, & guerre ensemble tu accordes
> En ce *concent, que lors ie conceuoys.*   (D196)

We do not really have to turn to Artaud or even to our modern symbolist writers to find support or clarification of this great unitive and healing theme of poetry as therapy, though it is at times useful and interesting to do so, as I have tried to show by frequently turning to these more modern writers. The Greeks were actually the first to recognize the healing and remedial power of poetry.

They worshiped Apollo (also appearing as Phoebus in the *Délie*) as the God of Poetry, Light, and Medicine. The role of poetry to reveal and analyze the human condition has existed from the beginning of time. The discovery and illumination of the unconscious have always been the great work of poets. This theme, so important to the symbolists and to their views on poetic art, is a most important one also in Scève, and in the works of other Renaissance poets. Modern psychological theories have even gone so far as to view the successful poet or artist as a self-cured neurotic, poetry being, on the one hand, a manifestation of psychological disorder and, on the other hand, a therapeutic process by which the poet-patient heals himself of his affliction (this is the thesis of Leedy's work mentioned in Note 4). Without assigning to suffering and illness the preeminent place accorded them by such newer theories, we may acknowledge that Scève's poetic venture is very much a therapeutic process whereby disharmonies are quite often resolved and conflicting elements reconciled in the formal working out and creation of vision. Scève does practice the concept of poetry as an ultimate resolution of his deepest disquiet. Along the way, the poet does view this process as providing a compensation and a remedy, as well as the restoration of order to a fragmented and anguished world. Though one can perhaps see a greater intensity at work in Scève's own version of this reconstructive aesthetic, other Renaissance writers are also perfecting the same aesthetic. The portrayal of the healthy integrity of psyche and art, again the poetic process of turning disorder into order, is a primary concern of *La Concorde des deux langages* by Jean Lemaire de Belges. As love is also portrayed in this work, one kind of order, the disorder of Venus and Mars that thrives on "division" and "discord" ("Laquelle amistié ne fëaulté ne se pourra trouver ou temple de Venus . . . lequel ne quiert si non semer *division et zizanie* entre loyaulx amans"), is shown to lead beyond the anguish and obscurity of this initial condition and state to another kind of order, to the vision of "paix et concorde," to the "grand clarté" of love which can only be enjoyed in the "temple de Minerve":

> En ce lieu noble et saint, propice et desirable,
> Jamais ame ne vit la nuyt obscure et brune
> N'oncques n'y eclipsa la triste et froide lune
> Ainçois ung *luisant* jour eternal y adjourne,
> Du quel la grand *clarté* sans fin dedens sejourne.[6]

This "temple de Minerve" – which can be interpreted symbolically

as Lemaire's own pursuit of "plus haulte vertu," as the final desti-
nation and place of rest for a higher state of mind and art – situated
high atop the "Mont de Vertu" replaces the "temple de Venus" of
the first part of Lemaire's work. This is another fine illustration of
the aesthetic preoccupation with and ultimate triumph of illumina-
ting art to surmount the problematics of sensuality, anguish, and
obscurity as the sustaining principle in life.

Du Bellay will proclaim the therapeutically illuminating and
uplifting value of poetry even more directly and passionately. This
is a major theme of his *Regrets*. The poet concludes his Sonnet 11
in this collection by stating: "Si ne veulx-je pourtant délaisser de
chanter, / Puis que *le seul chant* peult mes ennuys *enchanter*." And
in Sonnet 13, he will develop further his notion of the healing power
and higher purpose of poetry:

> S'ils [les vers] furent ma folie, ils seront ma raison,
> S'ils furent ma blessure, ils seront mon Achille,
> S'ils furent mon venim, le scorpion utile,
> Qui sera de mon mal *la seule guerison*.[7]

And these Renaissance writers make it clear that the purpose of
this therapeutic value of art's healing power is intended for the
reader as well as the poet. They viewed literature as a vehicle of
therapeutic value providing a means of human worth and enjoy-
ment. To appreciate this point, one only needs to reread the pro-
logue of Rabelais's *Quart Livre*, or turn to other poets writing in
Lyons at the same time as Scève and with whom Scève was definitely
familiar, such as Guillaume Guéroult:

> Petit il [mon livre] est, mais il ha bien puissance
> De vous donner quelque resjouyssance,
> Quand vostre esprit de tout soucy deliure.[8]

Scève too believed that the only remedy against the dark side of
love was song, or poetry. Like Du Bellay, he even viewed it as a
cure for the disorder of love, rather than as simply remaining one
of its symptoms. And for Scève, it is not any kind of song or poetry
that will do, but only that particular kind which brings the poet-
singer to unified self-awareness and self-realization. Only then does
the enlightening and remedial character of poetry become truly
fulfilled. Only in creating and enjoying an enlightened perfection
of psyche and form is Scève in his poetry able to control the darker
side of love. Scève's poetic determination and resourcefulness, like
those displayed by the God of Love in D94, a poem I have referred

to so often in this study, are a good indication of the therapeutic value he placed in the positive, life-affirming, and life-defining activity of poetry to minimize the darker, anguished side of love ("vexation"), and to console, to lead to "entendement," that is, to a state of enhanced understanding acquired through the long and aduous efforts of mobilizing his will and creative temper. This recovery from a state of anguish and obscurity and its cure through poetry, so desperately sought, and finally achieved, by Scève in his love lyrics cannot be underestimated or viewed as beyond his purpose or reach:

> Par long prier lon mitigue les Dieux:
> Par l'oraison la fureur de Mars cesse:
> Par long sermon tout courage odieux
> Se pacifie: & *par chansons tristesse*
> *Se tourne a ioye: & par vers lon oppresse,*
> *Comme enchantez, les venimeux Serpentz.*   (D239)

The remedial power of poetic thought and creativity is even presented by Scève as the very antidote and solace for the darker, tormented side of love, as we are told again in D313:

> Grace, & Vertu en mon cœur enflammerent
> Si haultz desirs, & si pudiquement,
> Qu'en vn sainct feu ensemble ilz s'allumerent,
> Pour estre veu de tous publiquement,
> Duquel l'ardeur si moins iniquement
> Et Cœur, & Corps iusqu'aux mouelles gaste,
> *D'vn penser chaste en sorte ie l'appaste*
> *Pour antidote, & qui peult secourir.*

For one who certainly experienced and yet struggled against such feelings of great despair and anguish caused by love, Scève discovered in the therapeutic value of poetic art a means of escape and consolation. Through the poet's struggle with the stylized and especially metaphoric reality of art, he was able to transcend the anguished confines of his existential dilemma and to relieve, or at least lessen, his feelings of rejection and despair. In this way, the poetic reality of the *Délie* may be viewed as a palliative one, helping to reduce love's negative effects:

> Vouldrois ie bien par mon dire attrapper,
> Ou a mes vœutz forcer ma Maistresse?
> Ie ne le fais sinon pour eschapper
> De ceste mienne angoisseuse destresse.   (D329)

And for Scève, to illuminate and experience love poetically, which is finally what the *Délie* is all about, can never really be an escape from love itself, but a confrontation with love, the creative struggle to find release from its anguish and obscurity, from its "angoisseuse détresse." Unlike the wounded Stag portrayed in D352, which actually brings its own end closer in trying to flee from death, the poet's response to love can never be in trying to escape from love:

> Or si ie suis le vulgaire suyuant,
> Pour en guerir, fuyr la me fauldroit.
> Le Cerf blessé par l'archier bien adroit
> Plus fuyt la mort, & plus sa fin approche.
> Donc ce remede a mon mal ne vauldroit.
> Sinon, moy mort, desesperé reproche.

The poet must always confront love head on in order to understand it and enjoy its benefits, for there is a therapeutic reward to be had in coming to terms with it, and going beyond it. The poet's labors will alleviate his pain and even lead him to the perfection and contentment of a special order of love. The poet must go headlong into love's anguish and obscurity in order to experience, newly healed, the "merueille d'vn si hault bien," both within the consciousness and without – in his art. Scève's struggle is an invitation for both poet and reader to read and understand patterns of affirmation and renewed spiritual health:

> Me desaymant par la seuerité
> De mon estrange, & propre iugement,
> Qui me fait veoir, & estre en verité
> Non meritant si doulx soulagement,
> Comme celluy, dont pend l'abregement,
> *De mes trauaulx me bienheurantz ma peine*,
> Ie m'extermine, & en si [grande] hayne
> De mes deffaultz i'aspire a la *merueille*
> *D'vn si hault bien*, que d'vne mesme alaine
> A mon labeur le iour, & la nuict veille.   (D384)

One of the major and certainly most noble purposes of the *Délie* is to show the poet becoming aware of the higher nature of love and of himself. Poetry enables him to discover, and most important, to modify and accept, the self, to realize his higher motives and desires. As such, the *Délie* educates the poetic self; it is the means to the poet's own self-advancement and self-enlightenment. This higher understanding of love and of self coming into meaning in poetry is what gives "souffle a la vie, vertu au sens, & vigueur aux espritz," as the poet tells us at the end of D413. The purpose of Scève's love poetry is to bring tensions and conflicts into the open and to develop in the poet the capacity for creative synthesis and resolution. This synthetic process and the importance of its metaphoric expression have been the subjects of this book. Délie as metaphoric, therapeutic object is this poet's "Cedre encontre le venim / De ce Serpent en moy continuel" (D372). As conceived by the poet in his imagination, that is, felt by him in his heart, Délie as the object of love's contemplation and creation provides this poet "sweet medicines":

> Violenté de ma longue misere
> Suis succumbé aux repentins effortz,
> Qu'Amour au sort de mes malheurs insere,
> Affoiblissant mes esperitz plus forts.
> Mais les Vertus passementantz les bords,
> Non des habitz, mais de ses mœurs diuines,
> Me seruiront de *doulces medecines*,
> Qui mon espoir me fortifieront:
> Et lors ie croy, que *ses graces benignes*
> *Dedans mon cœur la deifieront.*   (D398)

Scève's kind of poetry was written to fulfill wishes in the heart or imagination, which often required bringing seemingly irreconcilable opposites together: body and soul, mind and matter. In this difficult metaphoric unity of Délie/*Délie*, the poet is able to establish a permanent organic relationship and unity of the spiritual and the physical. Metaphor or image was extremely important to Scève for its quality to synthesize and unify a love relationship. Through metaphoric insight, a new universe – one of Order and Beauty and Paradise – was revealed to him. The figurative, transformative process of poetry and metaphor made this linguistic, psychological, and aesthetic world (Valéry's "un tout autre monde") possible. Scève struggled through poetry and metaphor for adequate expression of the true unitive nature of his love. He desired a love which was not mere physical attraction, nor purely spiritual elevation, but one which had its human basis in a harmony of body, intellect, emotion, and spirit. Poetry increasingly becomes for Scève a means of modifying love without destroying it, the only means for him to blend soma and psyche into a syncretically rational and emotive whole and thereby effect harmony between conflicting principles both within himself and without – in his art, his love portrayal of Délie:

"De mes trauaulx me bienheurantz ma peine"

Nature au Ciel, non Peripatetique,
Mais trop plus digne a si doulce folie,
Crea Amour sainctement phrenetique,
Pour me remplir d'vne *melencolie*
Si plaisamment, que ceste qui me lye
A la Vertu me pouuant consommer,
Pour dignement par Raison renommer
Le bien, du bien qui sans comparaison
La monstre seule, ou ie puisse estimer
Nature, Amour, & Vertu, & Raison.   (D444)

It is the poet's very condition of "melancholy" – the despair and anguish and obscurity that come with not seeing clearly and not possessing completely – which has truly been the state of disorder he has had to extricate himself from. Scève too had to compose through the black "ink of despair" in order to reach a higher illumination and meaning of love, which becomes the triumphant radiance of the poetic work itself:

Voy ce papier de tous costez noircy
Du mortel dueil de mes iustes querelles;
Et, comme moy, en ses marges transy,
Craingnant tes mains piteusement cruelles.   (D188)[9]

For Scève too, the illumination and health of mind and psyche and art had to emerge from and be created through the obscurity and disorder of melancholy. Scève's *Délie* is great love poetry because it is, finally, a triumph of therapeutic discernment informed by a radiant intelligence. Scève's cure from melancholy, from love's anguish and obscurity, is to be found in the poet's receptiveness to Apollo or Phoebus, in his own practice of the art of Light, Poetry, and Medicine:

Lors que Phebus de Thetys se depart,
Apparoissant dessus nostre Orizon,
Aux patientz apporte vne grand' part,
Si non le tout, d'entiere guerison:
Et amoindrit, aumoins, la languison,
Et les douleurs, que la nuict leur augmente.
Tout en ce point ma peine vehemente
Se diminue au cler de sa presence:
Et de mes maulx s'appaise la tourmente,
Que me causoit l'obscur de son absence.   (D368)

In the final analysis, the poetic world constructed by Scève is far from being anguished, obscure, dark. The *Délie* has never lost its luster, thanks to the illuminations provided by the poet's art, the only world with which Scève ultimately reckoned, or at least as far as the reader can have knowledge of. Only as artist did Scève have the special privilege of seeing his personal vision of perfection and paradise take tangible and meaningful shape. He exploited imaginatively the thematics and aesthetics of love's paradise to further a feeling of reconciliation, union, and unity. In his love lyrics, Scève envisioned the symbol and the substance of his art, his ideal and its human, concrete representation. There, the lover, the sensualist, the idealist, the poet in him united and found fulfillment of their complex and at times different claims. Out of the very negativity and darkness viewed by many of Scève's readers to be the essence of the *Délie* emerges a radiance which is that of the poetic imagination and the poems themselves. As we have seen, the *Délie* as poetic construct is a setting in which the questions raised by disorder and melancholy may be answered, ultimately leading to release and recovery and new-found unity. Scève's mythology of melancholy is at once a mythology of the self and a mythology of art: *Délie* is the celebration of life, the fragmentation of the self and its reconstruction through art, the achievement of a reconstruction and healing of self through the construction of the poem wherein the finding of living, unified form coincides with the defeat of anguish and melancholy and obscurity. This is the joyful and intelligent and redemptive illumination and value that only a great Orphic love poet can retrieve from his dark poems:

> Ainsi qu'Amour en la face au plus beau,
> Propice obiect a noz yeulx agreable,
> Hault colloqua le reluysant flambeau
> Qui nous esclaire a tout bien desirable,
> Affin qu'a tous son feu soit admirable,
> Sans a l'honneur faire aulcun preiudice:
> Ainsi veult il par plus louable indice,
> Que mon Orphée haultement anobly,
> Maulgré la Mort, tire son Euridice
> Hors des Enfers de l'eternel obly.   (D445)

Unlike the mythical Orpheus, Scève as the new Orpheus, in and through his love poetry, does extricate himself and Délie the beloved/*Délie* the love text from the dark oblivion of hell, from death. Going beyond the Hermetic poetic mode, the *Délie* as Orphic construct, uniting and embodying the sacred and the profane, is a love symbol of the eternal life that art makes possible. That Scève does pull his two Délies (his love object and love text) from hell can only be fully and finally assessed by considering his last love poem, D449. Scève is a complex poet whose love vision is difficult to define once and for all with absolute and reassuring certainty, for any argument stressing one point of view over another, for example Scève's paradisal, Orphic side over his dark, Hermetic side, can seemingly be countered with textual evidence that supports the opposite point of view. At times, Scève was a double love poet: he did experience both anguish and paradise and conveyed them simultaneously in his poetry. The objection could be stated that in those poems I have chosen in this study to highlight his Orphic side, I am presenting only half the picture, that in other poems and even in other parts of the very poems I have discussed the poet can sometimes be seen expressing the opposite outlook. To this I will simply say that a negatively dark, self-defining poetic vision, such as a poet's Hermetic outlook of melancholy, anguish, and obscurity, gains nothing or very little in being juxtaposed with a radiant paradisal perspective and poetic; the latter gains everything when it is juxtaposed with the former, and especially when the poet also gives it the most privileged place of all as his *last* statement on love, as is the case presented in D449. Before considering this final love poem of Scève, I wish to turn one more time to another modern symbolist poet, to Gérard de Nerval, whose own dark poetics of melancholy can shed light on the resplendent presence and power of illumination of so many of Scève's poems, and especially his last, D449. I wish to refer to Nerval's famous love sonnet "El Desdichado" considered by many to express this poet's most intense and intimate view of love:

> Je suis le ténébreux – le veuf – l'inconsolé,
> Le prince d'Aquitaine à la tour abolie:
> Ma seule *étoile* est morte – et mon luth constellé
> Porte le *soleil noir* de la *Mélancolie*.
>
> Dans la nuit du tombeau, toi qui m'as consolé,
> Rends-moi le Pausilippe et la mer d'Italie,
> La *Fleur* qui plaisait tant à mon cœur désolé,
> Et la treille où le pampre à la rose s'allie.
>
> Suis-je Amour ou Phébus? . . . Lusignan ou Biron?
> Mon front est rouge encor du baiser de la reine:
> J'ai rêvé dans la grotte où nage la sirène . . .
>
> Et j'ai deux fois vainqueur traversé l'Achéron:
> Modulant tour à tour sur la lyre d'Orphée
> Les soupirs de la sainte et les cris de la fée.[10]

This is the Hermetic poetic mode at its best, and we are dark-years away from Scève's view and treatment of love. It was impossible for Nerval's love vision and love art to rise above the darkness, death, and hell of his *created* world. Nerval does not extricate himself from hell. The very title of Nerval's sonnet, which translates from the Spanish as "the disconsolate, the unfortunate one," announces the familiar theme and poetic condition of melancholy and establishes in the reader at least the anticipation that the poet will come to successful terms with it, as most love poets attempt to do. Nerval's sonnet develops the same theme we have seen in Scève of the relation between suffering and art. However, in Nerval's poem, there are no signs or indications of any remedial or thera-peutic role of art to triumph over suffering. Nerval seems to be more interested in lamenting love's fate than in exploring the higher meaning of that love. Nerval's portrayal remains the Hermetic depiction of the tragic poet. Nerval's sonnet is, to be sure, a beauti-ful and moving singing of sorrow in poetic art, but one is left with the impression the poet is not truly able to find in it any consolation. Nerval's expression of suffering through song does give a definite value to pain, in that he makes us acutely aware that pain is very much a part of the human condition; Nerval's response to suffering is important because of the poetry of anguish it engenders. Many a love poem and even whole love sequence have been composed for the same reasons and effects. But Nerval's picture is a statically dark one: it fulfills no higher purpose and provides no insight into love. Nerval's poet as Orpheus is the failed Orpheus. The final picture the reader is left with of the poet's lute in "El Desdichado" does present it as becoming "starred," just as the lyre is portrayed in the mythic account of the legendary Orpheus. However, unlike the mythic account, there is something very wrong with Nerval's symbolism, if one looks to it for higher meaning. Nerval's *starred* instrument can only bear the *black* light of Melancholy. It is incapable, like the dark art on which it is modeled – Dürer's "Melancholia" – of shining in the heavens and illuminating this poet's dark world: "Ma seule *étoile* est morte – et mon luth constellé / Porte le *soleil noir* de la *Mélancolie.*"

Here is Scève's final, lustrously starred version of Orphic love and meaning as the poet portrays them in his last love poem, D449:

> *Flamme* si saincte en son *cler* durera,
> Tousiours *luysante* en publique apparence,
> Tant que ce Monde en soy demeurera,

> Et qu'on aura Amour en reuerence.
> Aussi ie voy bien peu de differenċe
> Entre l'ardeur, qui noz cœurs poursuyura,
> Et la vertu, qui viue nous suyura
> Oultre le Ciel amplement long, & large.
> Nostre Geneure ainsi doncques viura
> Non offensé d'aulcun mortel Letharge.

Contrary to Nerval, poetic language, metaphor, and meaning as portrayed by Scève the true Renaissance Orphic love poet are not in the end dark and abysmal. For Scève, there is little difference between *ardeur* and *vertu* – body and soul, heart and art – as long as they are united as one in the service of higher love and its enlightened and everlasting expression. Ardor's emotive form ("flamme") and virtue's spiritual idea ("si saincte en son cler") brought together at the very beginning of this poem comprise Scève's unified and glorious final poetic vision. This unitive-luminous principle of vision and art is what enables our love poet to give an ultimate denial to the anguish and obscurity of melancholy, to the death and oblivion and darkness of Lethe, from having any lasting place and value in a higher kind of poetic love. The love radiance of "another, more essential *world*" (Jauss), of "un tout autre *monde*" (Valéry) that shines through Scève's dark lyrics – this "Flamme si saincte en son cler" which emerges from the poet's "papier de tous costez noircy" (D188) – is what this Renaissance poet prefers ultimately to see and to create in his love poems. This diaphorically transcendent vision of light in an otherwise dark world is clearly Scève's and can even possibly become his reader's paradise, that is, as long as this very special Love World and its meaning will last and can be held in reverence by its readers: "Tant que ce *Monde* en soy demeurera, / Et qu'on aura *Amour* en reuerence."

Epilogue
SCEVE, MALLARME, AND THE ART OF TRANSCENDENCE

Throughout the chapters of this book, I have been suggesting that there exists a very real aesthetic connection between Scève and Mallarmé. A more precise analysis of this literary affinity shall serve as a fitting conclusion to this book. What Valéry saw in Mallarmé's magical power of poetic incantation can be seen in Scève. We now know the formula by which Valéry defined it. His definition of Art and its supreme principle of spiritually transfigured objects applies to Scève and his love words. Délie as the beloved, sensuous object (Valéry's "forme sensible" providing a "séduction immédiate") becomes the paradisally portrayed image (Valéry's "idée" or "substance précieuse de pensée") through which the sacred is apprehended, just like Délie as love text is the poetic medium through which the poet communicates to us the same ineffable experience of combining emotive form with higher meaning. What is intriguing in Scève, and can be very revealing and helpful in reading him, is the degree to which he anticipates our more modern symbolist concern with sacralizing the secular. The constant use to which he puts poetry is not simply as a means of recording and relating experience, as other Renaissance poets seem to use it, but as a continuous series of creative acts intent on revelation, as the epistemological means of truly discovering and creating experience. Scève is forever concerned with capturing the sacred within the profane, the eternal within the temporal, the spiritual within the physical, in a word, with acquiring an understanding and knowledge of metaphysical light and life within physical darkness. So too is Mallarmé. Mallarmé's poetic world and Scève's are not, in reality, as far apart as they may appear. Their poetry posits a belief in the transcendence of the creative act, which is precisely the meaning of Valéry's definition of the art of poetry. They both practiced and perfected, in spite of some real and significant differences, a transcendent aesthetic which, in the end, gives an ontological value to poetic activity. The central aesthetic and artistic problem posed by Mallarmé in his notion of the "black on white" principle of poetic discourse is in many respects the same diaphoric one we have been looking at in Scève: the intense and difficult struggle to transform the ordinary meanings of words into higher connotations, to redeem and refashion the inadequate nature of descriptive language so as to express and to reveal, literally to create *through* human words, the sacred and ineffable.[1]

To accomplish their ineffable ideal, both Scève and Mallarmé had to free language from a purely rational, limiting linguistic and reality-depicting mode of understanding and writing in order that it might become malleable enough to express the luminosity of a higher conceived essence and form. Like Scève, Mallarmé too was consumed with the notion of poetry as a kind of "obiect de plus haulte vertu," as an expression of an ineffable state. Mallarmé shares with Scève the notion of poetry as a sacred and consecrating venture. For Mallarmé, this higher perception is also achieved through an art which diaphorically transfigures the objects of this world to become the image of "une rose dans les ténèbres," of *Le Livre: instrument spirituel*, or of the poetic text as a "CONSTELLA-TION" surviving and thriving and radiant in its transcendent beauty.[2] For Scève, they become images of the mirror reflecting a brightness greater than it is supposed to reflect (Délie as "l'oultrepasse"), of Délie as the night-light, of the celestial whiteness of Délie's hands and skin, or simply of the brilliant radiance of Délie's face. The spiritual truth of these images in both poets is a human emotional truth. Though these object-images are specifically different, they are aesthetically the same. They all enact the mirroring of the ineffable. They point in the same direction and require the same difficult means of getting there: a critical response to poetic tension and to the inherent obscurity of poetic creation in which the poet, like the reader, is challenged to find order, to understand and concretize a "black on white" art-form finally revealing the sacred and ineffable. These concrete words and earthly images do embody and reflect a positive, transcendent aesthetic as well as a paradisal epistemology of the poetic human imagination.

Both Scève and Mallarmé believed in the transcendent world only to the extent that it could be revealed and made meaningful here and now. Neither Scève nor Mallarmé really starts, in good Platonic fashion, with a description of the purely ideal and then proceeds to show the reader how this ideal reflects reality. Instead, the reader (like the poet) first encounters vibrant and living words and forms and images which hold out the possibility of reaching, *through them*, the enlightenment and illumination so necessary to discover and define the ideal world in a human context. The ineffable or transcendent only exists, in the *Délie* as in Mallarmé's poems, in the illumination provided by imagining, which is creation. For Mallarmé and Scève, the distance between the poet's creative contemplation and the achievement of higher meaning is bridged in the act of diaphoric decipherment and transfiguration, in the malleability of ordinary language to become poetic language, in not only the writing of black marks *on* white paper but in the very transformation of these black marks *into* white, into Idea. The poet is the privileged interpreter of the world and its objects, whose natural obscurity must forever be the starting point and foundation of creation, but whose obscurity is only relative to the capacity of the poet's imagination to penetrate this world, to illuminate these objects and artistically and diaphorically to turn black into white. This process of mind and art at work is a kind of poetic deformation for the better, a bestowing upon the world and its objects a higher meaning and permanence. The poet must always begin "soubz le carré d'vn *noir* tailloir," but he ends with "si haulte Architecture," with a Column's "doulx traictz *viuement angeliques*" (D418). In a word, the sacredly transcendent poem must always exhibit a diaphoric unity under tension, a creative striving through the natural obscurity and darkness of worldly form or image for an ineffable dimension which so many of Scève's and Mallarmé's best poems translate.[3]

For this reader, the poetic art of the imagination as practiced by Scève and Mallarmé is seductively diaphoric, that is, seductively "elemental" (Staudt) in its intense constructs of black and white and in the consciousness itself creating these constructs. Their emphasis on the chiaroscurmatic origin and operation of image or metaphor, on its intimate relationship with light and darkness, so clearly depicted above in D418, points to the problematic and always risky and precarious poetic business of transcendence – naming the unnamable and describing the indescribable, in a word, the continual struggle to obtain clarity through obscurity. Scève and Mallarmé both practiced what I see to be the art of diaphoric juxtaposition, a "white-through-black" aesthetic: the black is the struggle with emotive form; the white, its exchange value in higher idea. The products of this intense kind of art are diaphoric constructs of light and whiteness: a Poet-Painter's view of a "CONSTELLATION" and of "White bouquets of perfumed stars snowing down"

("Neiger de blancs bouquets d'étoiles parfumées") found in "Apparition" (p. 30); or of "la blancheur telle, a peu près qu'on peult veoir" (D291) such as is found in D377: "Ce cler luisant sur la couleur de paille / . . . / Et ce neigeant flocquant parmy ces fentes." Understood literally, such statements as "And this snow-color puffing out from amongst dark crannies" and "White bouquets of perfumed stars snowing down" make little sense, but as a system of words and images with suggestive connotations, they evoke a world in its deepest reality. They embody that marvelous combination, praised so much by Valéry, of emotive form (delight of the senses) and ineffable or spiritual idea (connotations of purity, the ideal, the sacred).

Scève and Mallarmé as phenomenological symbolist poets of the ineffable were painfully aware of the difficulty and struggle involved in contemplating and creating such an ineffable ideal. In their poetry, the recognition of this difficulty and struggle is just as important as the final attainment itself. But the point really is that neither the struggle nor the actual achievement should be denied or underestimated in these poets. Délie as a symbol of light and whiteness always connotes for Scève both poetic impotency-failure-struggle (darkness) as well as the purity of the ideal sought (light, whiteness). Mallarmé came to know very well and to experience this same "white agony" later on: "Tout son col secouera cette *blanche agonie* / Par l'espace infligée à l'oiseau qui le nie, / Mais non l'horreur du vol où le plumage est pris" ("Le vierge, le vivace et le bel aujourd'hui," p. 68). Mallarmé presents again this dilemma of his poet coming to terms with a sacred and ineffable dimension in "Brise marine" with the haunting image of "le vide papier que la blancheur défend" (p. 38). Again, white (the ineffable) can be terrifying, forbidding. But for Mallarmé as for Scève, the sacred and ineffable can be, and finally must be, seen and experienced, though if perhaps only through a "windowpane," which is art, through black marks on white paper, the elements of vision: "Est-il moyen, ô Moi qui connais l'amertume, / D'enfoncer le *crystal* par le monstre insulté / Et de m'enfuir . . ." ("Les Fenêtres," p. 33).

Scève too was just as obsessed, as we have seen in this study, with being able to see through opaque matter (i.e., words and objects and images). He conveys this obsession very poignantly in D229 with the extremely reflexive presentation of self-as-matter as the medium for capturing and reflecting the ineffable object of contemplation. In this highly specular poem, the love poet *is* Délie's / *Délie*'s "*cristal* opaque" who registers the ineffable object "completely" ("Te reçoit *toute*": both Délie's physical body and spiritual being, her "forme" and her "vertu"), and then whose own "lustre vacque / A [la] monstrer en sa reflexion." Scève too is always concerned with penetrating opaque matter and worldly objects to get at the ideal they enclose, to grasp their higher connotations: "Si *transparent* m'estoit son chaste *cloistre* [Délie's body enclosing her spirit] / Pour reuerer si grand' diuinité, / Ie verrois . . ." (D127). The diaphoric aesthetic of clarity (the ineffable vision and its expression, light, whiteness) through obscurity (the material, the concrete, black ink) is the ideal that both Mallarmé and Scève struggled for, and achieved. As Scève also puts it, substituting this time the image of "bruyne" for Mallarmé's "crystal," to see clearly through the gloom and darkness and deformation of "mist" and thus to prosper one radiant day in the attainment of the ideal are the ends of contemplation and art: "Vysse ie au moins *esclercir ma bruyne* / Pour vn *cler iour* prosperer" (D70; cf. also D51: "esclercir mes pensées funebres" and D7, perhaps Scève's best expression of clarity through obscurity: "En la clarté de mes desirs funebres"). This "if only I were able" ("Vysse ie au moins . . .") is what kept both Scève and Mallarmé writing. It also signals in both poets the "black on white" principle of writing as a metaphor of the struggle to find an aesthetic which will translate a higher, purer, more essential reality. (Sometimes Mallarmé, like Scève, appears to give up in his quest of the ineffable. In "L'Azur," he calls upon images like "fog," "mud," and "smoke" and uses them in a most poignant – but of course out-of-desperation and unsuccessful – attempt to blot out the ideal.) For Scève, "mist," like lines of poetry, like dark marks on white paper, is what threatens to obscure essential reality (and thus it is always a question of "la blancheur *telle, a peu près* qu'on peult veoir" – D291: Scève's diaphoric recognition of his own "white agony," of his own uncertainty over art and where its opposing principles of darkness and brightness will lead). It is the poet's supreme duty "to see clearly through" ("esclercir") this mist in order to get at the reality behind it and beyond it.

As we have seen, Mallarmé presents this dilemma of transcendent contemplation and writing in "Les Fenêtres" with the image of poetic vision necessarily operating through a windowpane, and in the toast poem "Salut," which anticipates *Un Coup de dés*, he presents the same dilemma with images of a sea voyage which also pertain to the poetic potential and struggle of art. In this poem, the reader is presented the diaphoric juxtaposition of poetry with "nothing," poetry with "foam" ("Rien, cette écume, vierge vers")

– which is another fine illustration of Mallarmé's concern with a "white-through-black" aesthetic, of his own recognition of the struggle involved in obtaining clarity through obscurity. Scève is conveying this same diaphoric awareness, as we just saw above, when he connects the activity of poetry, the creative act of consciousness itself, with "mist." From a negative point of view, these image-concepts for Mallarmé are what threaten to overturn the "blanc souci de notre toile" (p. 27), to thwart the "white concern" of the poetic voyage. In their positive meaning, however, they posit the continual struggle to achieve the impossible, the capturing of what remains after struggle, crisis, or catastrophe – the ineffable object of consciousness finally manifested and shining in words. Diaphorically put, these opaque elements (champagne foam/sea foam/poetry foam/poetry mist), through which a higher, more enduring reality must somehow be reached and necessarily created, are what potentially jeopardize the success of the poetically transcendent imagination in its efforts to create out of the inherent chaos of consciousness and the world meaningful and lasting constructs of clarity and contentment, that is, as far as black lines of poetry will allow.

For Mallarmé as toaster-navigator-poet, however, the white-through-black obsession does become finally a shining Constellation in the center of the page and in the center of consciousness. For Scève also, as navigator-poet, it becomes the similar image of a shining Moon enjoying the same privileged placement and meaning: Délie as the poet's Moon or focal point for mind and art in which struggle and crisis are resolved and human worth and salvation asserted:

> La Lune au plein par sa clarté puissante
> Rompt l'espaisseur de l'obscurité trouble,
> Qui de la nuict, & l'horreur herissante,
> Et la paour pasle ensemble nous redouble:
> Les desuoyez alors met hors de trouble,
> Ou l'incertain des tenebres les guide.   (D365)

As Scève too so often depicts the problem and final triumph of his own poetic voyage or struggle (his own "blanche agonie" or "blanc souci de notre toile") in pursuit of the ineffable ideal, he provides the reader numerous textual affirmations and manifestations of this ideal through his own receptivity to and creation of Constellations. Such Constellations are always those – *"luisante[s] au centre"*

155

(D106) – radiating at the creative center of this love poet's con-
sciousness and aesthetic understanding:

> Parquoy vaguant en Mer tant irritée
> De mes pensers, tumultueux tourment,
> Ie suys ta *face* [Délie's *"estoilles celestes"*] ou ma nef incité
> Trouue son *feu*, qui son Port ne luy ment.   (D243)

> Car ie te cele en ce surnom louable ["la *Lune*"],
> Pource qu'en moy tu luys la nuict obscure.   (D59)

> De toute Mer tout long, & large espace,
> . . .
> Surmonteras la haulteur des *Estoilles*
> Par ton sainct nom, qui vif en ma langueur
> Pourra par tout nager a plaines voiles.   (D259)

From potentially chaotic elements within consciousness which
threaten its desire for fulfillment in creation, from such chaotic
"elements" symbolized by "mist" in Scève and by "foam" in Mal-
larmé standing in the way of and obscuring higher vision, emotive
forms (word-images, thought) are born and progress towards their
culmination and final resting place in Idea, in a Constellation or a
Moon and Stars around which clarity and order and beauty and
contentment can prevail. This diaphorically precarious progression
of mind and art whose end is clarity (white) through obscurity
(black: Mallarmé's "souci" and Scève's "langueur") always begins
by putting black marks on white paper. That Mallarmé in *Un Coup
de dés* even tried to transform a page of black marks to the ineffable
power of the starry sky was, in itself, enough of an accomplishment
for Valéry: "Il a essayé, pensai-je, d'élever enfin une page à la
puissance du ciel étoilé."[4] This is also enough of an accomplishment
for this reader of the *Délie*: Scève's same marvelous fulfillment of
the poetic voyage. As we discussed specifically in Chapter 5, this is
the same kind of aesthetic triumph that Starobinski saw in Shake-
speare's art ("le miracle d'un amour qui *resplendit*, sauvé des
ravages universels du Temps, dans l'encre noire du poème," and
so forth) and that this study has been attempting to understand and
appreciate in Scève. Mallarmé's "shipwreck" and Scève's "deaths"
("les mortz qu'en moy tu renouelles") are one and the same thing:
ontological death(s) necessary for liberating mind and art in their
struggle for a transcendent paradisal state.

Mallarmé's *Livre, instrument spirituel* is another attempt at repre-
senting this transcendent paradisal state. Like *Délie, obiect de plus
haulte vertu*, it seeks to capture a higher meaning in the life of art

through the aesthetically transformational power of its words and imagery. For Mallarmé, the "foldings" of the poet's "book," when unfolded or separated by the reader in the act of reading, can become a source of enchantment and spiritual renewal. Poetry as conceived by both Scève and Mallarmé moves beyond the mere naming of objects (Délie or Livre) to create the higher potential and syntheses suggested by these objects ("instrument spirituel" and "obiect de plus haulte vertu"). Again, the symbolism and meaning in both poets are profoundly and diaphorically simple: achieving the sacred through the profane, the eternal through the material, higher idea through sensuous form, vision through words – the diaphoric art and malleability of ordinary language pointing to a higher spiritual reality, such as a Moon or a Constellation, such as a rose or light in darkness. For Mallarmé, the requirement or principle of Art is that all earthly experience must ultimately be contained in a book. ("Une proposition qui émane de moi . . . tout, au monde, existe pour aboutir à un livre.") What kind of book will it be and who will read it? It will be a hymn of harmony and joy, an immaculate blend of relationships working together in cele-bration of some miraculous and joyous occasion. And that occasion is the divine insight acquired by the reader through the pages of the open book. ("Quel est-il: l'hymne, harmonie et joie, comme pur ensemble groupé dans quelque circonstance fulgurante, des relations entre tout. L'homme chargé de voir divinement, en raison que le lien, à volonté, limpide, n'a d'expression qu'au parallélisme, devant son regard, de feuillets.") The foldings of this book before the author-reader (for the reader is also the writer of this book, as Mallarmé insists in good phenomenological fashion) have an almost religious significance. They embody in the form of a *tombeau poétique* the place of rest and renewal for our souls. ("Le pliage est . . . un indice, quasi religieux: qui ne frappe pas autant que son tassement, en épaisseur, offrant le minuscule tombeau, certes, de l'âme.") In reading this book, we are reading the meaning of Self and of Transcendence. Our mind and spirit will be united and rarefied in reading this Body of Poetry, imbued with Idea, which becomes perfect Music. ("Un solitaire tacite concert se donne, par la lecture, à l'esprit qui regagne, sur une sonorité moindre, la sig-nification; aucun moyen mental exaltant la symphonie, ne man-quera, raréfié et c'est tout – du fait de la pensée. La Poésie, proche l'idée, est Musique, par excellence – ne consent pas d'infériorité" – *Le Livre*, pp. 378–82.) This same Music is being created by the poet and can be heard from Scève's own "spiritual instrument," the diaphorically transfigured poem of the *Délie*, as we have seen in this study:

> Tes doigtz tirantz non le doulx son des cordes,
> Mais des haultz cieulx l'Angelique harmonie,
> Tiennent encor en telle symphonie,
> Et tellement les oreilles concordes,
> Que paix, & guerre ensemble tu accordes
> En ce concent, que lors *ie conceuoys*. (D196)

It is the same celestial Music which always accompanies the creation of a kind of mythology where the reader is invited to hear, taste, touch, or see intense living forms of light and whiteness created out of darkness and obscurity, out of consciousness and its expression in art. Here is the final image Mallarmé uses to close *Le Livre*, with its emphasis on seeing and showing the ineffable: "Attribuons à des songes, avant la lecture, dans un parterre, l'attention que sollicite quelque *papillon blanc*, celui-ci à la fois partout, nulle part, il s'évanouit; pas sans qu'un rien d'aigu et d'ingénu, où je réduisais le sujet, tout à l'heure ait passé et repassé, avec insistance, devant l'étonnement." Mallarmé, as metaphysical poet, creates a world of potent symbol and living metaphor. So does an earlier metaphysical love poet back in the Renaissance – Maurice Scève. This luminous accomplishment in Scève as in Mallarmé of transforming black into living forms of white or light is the apogee of the sacredly human art of poetic transcendence.

If some of Scève's and Mallarmé's readers and critics today have lost the living sense of their poetic words, images, and metaphors – their works' transcendent, allusive significance – this is the critical legacy of a literalism which equates poetic truth with historical and biographical truth.[5] As Soskice has shown, these kinds of literal readings are bound by a poet's exact words; they often approach a body of poetry as simply a book of biographical fact, as a poet's seemingly reality-depicting statements on obscurity and anguish. As I have tried to show, Scève's *Délie*, like Mallarmé's *Livre*, is not really a book, but a religion of the book whose love words are not to be taken finally and literally at face value. These words are used ultimately to illuminate and transform an otherwise dark world, to re-create this world, not to leave it fragmented and obscure. They are vehicles of revelation for a distinguished interpretive tradition, from the perspectives of both the writer and the reader. The role of the reader in both poets is crucial for understanding and appreciating their triumphs of *difficulté/résistance vaincues*. The real tradition to which Scève's and Mallarmé's poetry belongs and through which this poetry challenges us to read it is phenomenology. In its readerly implication, such reception-theory (i.e., that advocated by, among others, especially Wolfgang Iser and Roman Ingarden) would have us understand that Scève's *Délie*, like Mallarmé's poetic texts, indeed contains many elements which are potential and indeterminate and which require the reader, along with the poet, to actualize the texts' meanings, to "fill out" the texts' "gaps" (Iser) and thus to "concretize" these texts (Ingarden).[6] The objective of all this phenomenological activity (by both reader and poet) is always the acquired *consciousness* of an actualized *aesthetic object* invested with values (Délie as "obiect de plus haulte vertu"), a consciousness focused not on any reality that exists independently of the work, but on an increasingly meaning-acquiring literary reality, the poeticized fictional world of *Délie* as "beaulté esmerueillable Idée."

In *Crise de vers*, Mallarmé advocates and demonstrates, just as Scève does in the *Délie*, the writerly implications of this phenomenological theory and perspective. His own aesthetic object here, which he too invests with values (with "idée même et suave"), is "a flower," an *imaginary* flower existing only in consciousness as "the pure notion." In other words, in Mallarmé's poetry, just as we have seen in Scève's, the vision of an ineffable and purer potential is always just beneath, or else just beyond, the actual one, and readers and critics of these works belonging to a powerful transcendant literary tradition are wrong to deny or underestimate this central and most compelling aspect and beauty of their poetry:

> A quoi bon la merveille de transposer un fait de nature en sa presque disparition vibratoire selon le jeu de la parole, cependant; si ce n'est pour qu'en émane, sans la gêne d'un proche ou concret rappel, *la notion pure*.
> Je dis : une fleur! et, hors de l'oubli où ma voix relègue aucun contour, en tant que quelque chose d'autre que les calices sus, musicalement se lève, *idée même et suave, l'absente de tous bouquets*. (Mallarmé, p. 368)

Mallarmé's aesthetic obsession with creating "the pure notion," with conveying "idea itself and sweet" through "une fleur" which is "l'absente de tous bouquets," reflects the very same intense preoccupation of Scève with composing a love aesthetic of presence-in-absence, as we first suggested and discussed briefly in Scève at the end of Chapter 2. For this reader, the ultimate message to be understood in both Scève and Mallarmé is that the real world – one whose potential for obscurity and anguish is infinite – this world can never be idea; the ineffable world created in art can. Perhaps this helps to explain why phenomenological poets like Scève and Mallarmé rely so fundamentally on the thematics and art of absence. For Mallarmé, the created vision of a flower absented is idea; for Scève, the same created vision of Délie absented is also idea. Both of these "visions" and "creations" come, as we saw earlier in this chapter, from "nothing/nothingness," from the darkness and obscurity of mind and consciousness struggling to come to terms with a higher meaning. Ironically, such visions and creations also become "nothing" in their largely non-referential, non-relational status to ordinary life, to worldly vision and logic, to the real world. But this nothing (i.e., understanding and portrayal of idea) that is the ineffable is in reality everything that is unique and ultimately meaningful for poets like Scève and Mallarmé. Like Mallarmé's "absent flower," the "absent Délie" as an "object" for higher/highest virtue is Délie turned into aesthetic image and object, Délie as construct of mind/art or the poet's *virtus imaginativa*, Délie made Idea. In other words, she is "celle image" of the poet's sense of "beaulté esmerueillable *Idée*" (D275) – the product of his desire that Délie become *Délie*. Quite often for Scève, as for Mallarmé and his understanding of objects and their potential of becoming "idée même et suave," for Délie to really exist and be present, she must necessarily be absent. Only then – "Et sans du iour m'apperceuoir encore" as the poet says in D232 – only in these privileged moments of contemplating and creating presence-in-absence in anticipation of presence can he truly enjoy "si *doulce pensée*," that is, this other "World" of "form and color" of the ineffable Délie:

> Tout le repos, ô nuict, que tu me doibs,
> Auec le temps mon *penser* le deuore:
> Et l'Horologe est compter sur mes doigtz
> Depuis le soir iusqu'a la blanche Aurore.
> Et sans du iour m'apperceuoir encore,
> Ie me pers tout en si *doulce pensée*,
> Que du veiller l'Ame non offensée,
> Ne souffre au Corps sentir celle douleur
> De vain espoir tousiours recompensée
> Tant que ce *Monde* aura *forme, & couleur.*

Not even Délie's disdain and coldness in love, the ultimate form of "death" or absence, can deny the poet his sense of the higher presence and meaning which Délie occupies in his thought:

Tes fiers desdaingz, toute ta froide essence,
Ne feront point, me nyant ta presence,
Qu'en mon *penser audacieux ne viue*,
Qui, maulgré Mort, & maulgré toute absence,
Te represente a moy trop plus, que viue.   (D264)

Délie's absence can never really harm the poet, for she is always with him, that is, she is always in his thought. She *is* his thought:

Parquoy de rien ne me nuyt son absence,
Veu qu'en tous lieux, maulgré moy, ie la suys.   (D141)

What Mallarmé produces through absence, that is, through a presence of mind and art, and what Valéry saw in Mallarmé's creations of absence can be seen in Scève. Scève too transposes worldly "facts" and "forms" and "objects" into "ideas," into palpable and potent living symbols. As we have seen, Scève, like Mallarmé, often absents the real world and its objects in order to transpose and re-create them anew:

Ainsi absent la memoyre posée,
Et plus tranquille, & apte a conceuoir,
Par la raison estant interposée,
Comme clarté a l'obiect, qu'on veult veoir . . .   (D434)

There is no doubt that the reason which motivates Scève and Mallarmé to absent the world is somewhat different for each poet. The latter wishes to stress the uniqueness or unreality of consciousness and creation; Scève is also very much interested in this purpose, as we discussed earlier in Chapter 1 (cf. our discussion, pp. 10–12, of his rejection in D24 of the "veue coustumiere" in love and its expression). But as he also tells us in D165, he is quite often forced by his tears to close his eyes to his object of contemplation in order better to contemplate it. Whatever their reasons, however, the end result and accomplishment by both poets are the same: poetic triumphs of the creative imagination working its way through absence to find the presence of a more complete reality or "purer" meaning. Textual absenting or deformation of reality, by both Scève and Mallarmé in the sense of their poets going beyond the unsatisfying and lacking and "bitter" reality perceived around them (Mallarmé's "amertume" and Scève's "langueur"), is reconstructive in execution, not something finally deconstructive and negative. Poetry in their hands and vision serves a positive and productive end: to transform the obscurity, anguish, and imperfection of ordinary life and logic into a more meaningful and understandable and unique world, a world of new-found order and beauty as only art and mind harmoniously working together can produce. It is nothing less in both poets than the triumphant affirmation of Mind-Idea-Art over reality. What is fascinating for this reader in Mallarmé and in Scève is that they share Valéry's phenomenological notion of consciousness (creative imagination) as a liberating transformation of our ordinary sense of reality and that they demonstrate this notion textually by showing the supreme power of mind and art to create what Valéry calls "un tout autre monde":

> Mes pleurs clouantz au front ses tristes yeulx,
> A la memoire ouurent *la veue instante*,
> Pour admirer, & contempler trop mieulx
> Et sa vertu, & sa forme elegante.   (D165)

This "presence" perceived by the poet of Délie's "vertu, & sa forme elegante" is the same marvelously perceived presence-in-absence which the poet also acknowledges above at the end of D434: "Ainsi absent la memoyre posée, / . . . / Gouste trop mieulx sa vertu, & sa grace." Absenting (closing one's eyes to or negating) the world (i.e., performing the phenomenological act of *epoché*: "bracketing" or suspending and detaching consciousness from the "fact-world" so as to capture the aesthetic object of contemplation as directly perceived by the mind) can accomplish the higher constructive task of conceiving and presenting this world re-created, of re-presenting it each time as a unique and original creation. The transcendent world is always a new and unique construct each time and for whatever reason it is created. It is as if it never has really existed, except, of course, until each time it is newly seen and created. The represented and re-presented world of higher consciousness through art and its forms, not life, is Scève's obsession, as it is Mallarmé's. This imaginary world conceived and composed through language and image often has little connection with the fact-world and thrives without concern for a reality-depicting purpose.

The "purpose" ("A quoi bon . . ." as Mallarmé says in his famous passage above) in both Scève and Mallarmé of transposing objects of the fact-world or real world into their almost complete and vibratory disappearance with the poetic play of words (i.e., through the workings of the imagination) is indeed to bring forth from this operation, each time it is performed, the pure(r) notion. This is creation, and re-creation: the workings of a phenomenological poetic of the ineffable. This is what has been taking place in so many of Scève's transfigured and transilluminated poems we have been looking at in this study. To quote again one of the best of them: the image in D230 of Délie being reflected in a clear mirror and from which is revealed not likeness, as the poet insists, but an intensely transposed image reflecting an even more radiant face which is that of the *ineffable* Délie ("l'oultrepasse"), whose "diuin, & immortel visage" becomes this love poet's "notion pure." With the word being used as image to translate idea (i.e., the art of metaphoric presence-in-absence), something more real and lasting and absolute is created in these kinds of poetic "imaginings" than can ever be found in the real objects of the world. For both Scève and Mallarmé, the transcendence provided by the creative act is the real and only source of knowledge. Such aesthetic imaginings and understandings have the unique power to give light and life to the invisible and ineffable, whether it is a question of outer object or self as object coming into being. In their struggle with creation, both Scève and Mallarmé had the desire and the determination to recover clarity from obscurity, to create idea out of nothingness, to call into being a new, unique, more meaningful existence. They both do this by understanding poetry as creative act, poetry as the transcendent operation of "délier." Here are Valéry's thoughts on this operation of art in Mallarmé, observations which I believe are of great importance for understanding Scève and his struggle with Délie and *Délie* as "obiect de plus haulte vertu":

Mallarmé se justifia devant ses pensées en osant jouer tout son être sur la plus haute et la plus hardie d'entre elles toutes. Le passage du songe à la parole occupa cette vie infiniment simple de toutes les combinaisons d'une intelligence étrangement *déliée*. Il vécut pour effectuer en soi des trans-formations admirables.   (I, 622)

Thanks to Scève's love ,poet's own marvelous transcendent imaginings, the *Délie* is informed by a similar "intelligence étrange-ment déliée." Scève and Mallarmé are indeed poets who effect a passage from the world of dream or desire into the world of words and images and ideas, a world as Valéry says of "transformations admirables." These transformations are always seen in the actual capturing of an aesthetic object or in the difficult recognition of self coming to terms with capturing this object. In both poets, there is a "freeing" ("délier") of the imagination to create higher, purer vision. This diaphorically liberated intelligence that is Mallarmé's and Scève's is what insures the triumph of a phenomenological kind of poetic consciousness and writing going beyond the contingent, and all too limiting and inadequate, "real" world or fact-world to translate the ineffable in the more permanent world of art. From the "imagining" (Valéry's "songe") of Mallarmé's poet emerges the vision of a "pur vase," that is, the *idea* of "une rose dans les ténèbres," which fills the vase's "empty neck" like a "baiser des plus funèbres" ("Surgi de la croupe et du bond," p. 74). From Scève's own "funereal" contemplation, from always-threatening darkness and nothingness, something real and fertile (*idea*) is also born: the same clarity as in Mallarmé of mind and art flowering in the darkness – as Scève puts it in D7, the rebirth of poetic conscious-ness itself "en la clarté de [ses] desirs funebres" (self-affirming consciousness) or, as he depicts the same idea in D59, the image of Délie as the Moon or Night-Light who lights up the poet's "nuict obscure" (object-affirming consciousness). Both of these recog-nitions and creations are diaphoric triumphs of mind and art in clarity. Scève constructs out of the chaos and nothingness of con-templation and experience "beauté esmerueillable Idée," which is the same thing as Mallarmé's "idée même et suave." For Scève as for Mallarmé, the real objects of contemplation are the contents of consciousness itself and not objects in the so-called "real world," that is, objects as *constituted* by consciousness and not objects exist-ing outside consciousness. This higher world of mind and idea is, finally, the ineffable one Scève is really talking about in D330, that seminal and glorious poem we spent a lot of time considering in Chapter 5. There, the poet "*constitua* en ce *sainct lieu* de vivre," that is, to live in this "holy place" that is the ineffable captured in art.

To conclude this whole discussion of Scève and Mallarmé in the form of an aesthetic equation, we can say that Scève's "oultrepasse" or "clarté" or "Lune" as embodiment of this love poet's aesthetics of "beauté esmerueillable Idée" is a prefiguration of Mallarmé's "absente de tous bouquets" or "rose" or "CONSTELLATION" as embodiment of this poet's aesthetics of "idée même et suave." And both of these imagistic sets of creative understandings or poetic "marvels" are illustrations of Valéry's "la forme sensible d'un dis-cours et sa valeur d'échange en *idées*" thanks to which both poet and reader are truly able to participate "d'un tout autre monde que le monde où les paroles et les actes se répondent" (I, 647). This other world of "idea itself and sweet," as Mallarmé himself calls it, is the end of all transposed, transcendent art: the revelation (seeing) and creation (showing) in an imperfect world of illuminating and sweet image, of "si doulce pensée" (D232), as we have also seen Scève call it. Such sweet thought in Scève is always the image of the ineffable Délie or the personal recognition of poetic self success-fully contemplating and creating this ineffable image. Through his diaphoric insights highlighting the aesthetic principle of clarity through obscurity does Scève, like Mallarmé, triumph in his quest for pure consciousness.[7]

NOTES

1. The problem of the dark side of a love poet: an introduction and reassessment

1 *Recherches de la France* (Paris: Louys Billaine, 1665), p. 344. All italics in this book are mine, unless otherwise indicated.

2 "Les Editions originales," *Revue des Deux Mondes*, 1 March 1888, p. 217.

3 *Histoire de la littérature française* (Paris: Hachette, 1894), p. 276.

4 "Reading *Délie*: Dialectic and Sequence," *Symposium*, 34 (1980), 155. See also Joseph Pivato, "Maurice Scève's *Délie*: Unpetrarchan and Hermetic," *Studi Francesi*, 27 (1983), 14–28.

5 *The Romanic Review*, 78 (1987), 10–24. Here, for de Rocher, is how Scève's generation of meaning works:

> The point is that the poet's powers of textual generation spring from a pathological condition to be sought less in Scève than in the "buried" discourses revealing the repressed conflicts of the poet's psyche. The unattainable desire for textual wholeness must be cast in terms of a powerfully reductive intertext whose nature can be represented as Ficinian Neoplatonism and the *Rime sparse* in league with its epigonous confections. The poet-subject is forced into endless microcosmic rehearsals – suggested by the actual number 449 – of the macrocosmic antonymy: language, endlessly driven by desire to "subdue" reality, must constantly miss the mark, so to speak, or else *reduce to chaos* an order inherently dependent upon signifiers that are constantly in flux. This closed system might be called the *Délie*'s hypochondriacal syndrome and the copious fount of its repetition. (p. 16)

I view Scève's situation to be just the opposite. The purpose of Scève's sustained poetic activity and struggle is not at all to reduce order to chaos, but to reconstruct and thus create order out of chaos, as I shall argue in this book.

6 Randolph Runyon, "Scève's 'Aultre Troye': Placement and Other Tie(r)s in *Délie*," *Modern Language Notes*, 90 (1975), 535–47.

7 Pascal Quignard, *La Parole de la Délie* (Paris: Mercure de France, 1974), especially Chapter VI: "Le baratin d'amour"; p. 175 for the quotation.

8 "The Poetic Sensibility of Scève," in Jerry C. Nash, ed. *Pre-Pléiade Poetry* (Lexington, KY: French Forum, Publishers, 1985), p. 131.

9 See Odette de Mourgues, "An Early Metaphysical Poet – Maurice

Scève," in her *Metaphysical, Baroque and Précieux Poetry* (Oxford: Clarendon Press, 1953), pp. 6–25.

10 E. Caldarini, ed., *L'Olive*, "Préface de 1549" (Genève: Librairie Droz, 1974), p. 169.

11 Quotations from the *Délie* are taken from the critical edition of I. D. McFarlane (Cambridge: Cambridge University Press, 1966). Emendations of this text will always be indicated by brackets.

12 Trans. Charles G. Osgood (New York: The Liberal Arts Press, 1956), pp. 58–60. For the humanist tradition to which Boccaccio's *Genealogia* and poetic theory belong and for their great influence in the Renaissance, see Jean Seznec, *La Survivance des dieux antiques* (Paris: Flammarion, 1980).

13 The above passage from Valéry is taken from his extremely insightful essay on the art of poetry entitled "Je disais quelquefois à Stéphane Mallarmé . . .". I shall be returning to this powerful and critically rewarding essay throughout this book. Paul Valéry, *Œuvres*, ed. Jean Hytier (Paris: Gallimard, 1957), I, 644–45. I do wish to make a couple of acknowledgements for critical and theoretical terms I shall be using in this book. My understanding of the metaphoric and structural process of the *via negativa* based on a "diaphoric" mode of consciousness, which I shall be discussing in Scève and secondarily in other French writers of the more modern period whose use of it can be helpful for an understanding of Scève's, stems from a reading of the critical theory on metaphor, phenomenological in nature, elaborated especially by Philip Wheelwright, *Metaphor and Reality* (Bloomington: Indiana University Press, 1962) and *The Burning Fountain: A Study in the Language of Symbolism* (Bloomington: Indiana University Press, 1968). A good assessment of both of these works is provided by Frank B. Brown, *Transfiguration: Poetic Metaphor and the Languages of Religious Belief* (Chapel Hill: University of North Carolina Press, 1983). To a lesser extent, I am also indebted to Paul Ricœur, *The Rule of Metaphor* (Toronto: University of Toronto Press, 1977). For Wheelwright (cf. *Metaphor and Reality*: "Tensive Language," pp. 45–69, and "Two Ways of Metaphor," pp. 70–91), there are two kinds of metaphor, the "epiphoric" and the "diaphoric." The use of the latter is an illustration of both Samuel Johnson's celebrated definition of the metaphysical conceit as the striking combination and interaction of dissimilar images or concepts producing a sense of stability and harmony in things apparently unlike, and Mallarmé's proposition that poems are made with words and the sharp juxtaposition of words, and that only then are "ideas" possible. Diaphoria is fundamentally the dialectical art of *discordia concors* – that is, the often paradoxical merging or juxtaposing of dissimilar and even contradictory elements giving the impression of totally new meaning or synthesis. (Examples discussed by Wheelwright: Eliot's line "Garlic and sapphires in the mud" and Mallarmé's "Tonnerre et rubis aux moyeux.") In a diaphoric construct, some form of physicality is often being used to reveal spirituality; there is

an association or merger of something abstract or spiritual and something concrete or material (with human objects as well as natural objects being used in this "merger"). In addition to having this metaphoric value, all diaphoric art, including Scève's, also has a structural value. This value proposes that movement or progression towards poetic insight and renewal must emanate from a *via negativa*, from what Wheelwright defines as "tensive language." Both the metaphoric and the structural implications of diaphoric art, as Wheelwright so very convincingly argues, work always to highlight a poet's sense of struggle to underscore the difficult poetic process itself of obtaining clarity *through* obscurity (which is also, as we shall see, precisely the writerly and the readerly meaning of what Valéry calls "résistances vaincues"). We will be continually concerned with and will explore further this diaphoric theory of image-making and meaning-making in our study of Scève's transcendent art and his efforts to come to terms with the poetic ineffable.

14 See Malcolm Bowie, *Mallarmé and the Art of Being Difficult* (Cambridge: Cambridge University Press, 1978); and also John Porter Houston, *French Symbolism and the Modernist Movement* (Baton Rouge: Louisiana State University Press, 1980). It has been very convincingly argued that the obscurity and difficulty of modern poetry represent a negative response to cultural and social change, a critical understanding which I do not at all see as applicable to Scève. Many modern critics and poets have interpreted the obscure vision and style as the poets' way of implying a negative judgment on the complexities and contradictions of modern life, on the multiple beliefs they are asked to assimilate and to come to terms with. This kind of poetic obscurity as cultural-social crisis translates the modern poets' sense of isolation and alienation in a world they can no longer relate to. Modern obscurity has brought about what is commonly called, thanks to T. S. Eliot, a "dissociation of sensibility" – when the intellect or reason and the imagination do not function in unison in the service of advancing any higher, preestablished ideal. Among others, the poet Delmore Schwartz has expressed the above ideas in his excellent critical piece, "The Isolation of Modern Poetry," *Kenyon Review*, 3 (1941), 209–20. Scève's obscurity, as I see it, has little to do with any such notion of cultural crisis. It is, artistically, an important prerequisite state for coming to *poetic* terms with the higher meaning and ideal that Délie incarnates. As we shall see in subsequent chapters, there is indeed in Scève a kind of dissociation of sensibility, but one which is *reconstructed* aesthetically and which permits this love poet ultimately to accept and even take delight in his world.

15 "L'homme de la Renaissance recherche une stabilité au milieu de l'instabilité prévalente, et la certitude dans le labyrinthe de l'irrésolution . . . cette réalisation définit également la situation scévienne." Marcel Tetel, *Lectures scéviennes* (Paris: Klincksieck, 1983), pp. 15–16.

16 Obviously, Boccaccio is more interested in the readerly implication of *difficulté vaincue* than he is in its writerly implication. Scève and sub-

sequent writers will highlight especially its artistic import, placing before the reader dramatic portrayals of the struggle and progression from a state of *vexation* to that of *entendement*. In his correspondence with Louise Colet, here is how Flaubert will later affirm the artistic value of *difficulté vaincue* for literary creativity:

Si vous voulez à la fois chercher le Bonheur et le Beau, vous n'atteindrez ni à l'un ni à l'autre, car le second n'arrive que par le sacrifice. L'Art, comme le Dieu des Juifs, se repaît d'holocaustes. Allons! déchire-toi, roule-toi dans la cendre, avilis la matière, crache sur ton corps, arrache ton cœur! . . . Et tu rouleras, perdue dans l'ouragan, avec cette petite lueur à l'horizon. Mais elle grandira, comme un *soleil* . . . tu seras éclairée du dedans, tu te sentiras légère et tout esprit, et après chaque saignée la chair pèsera moins.

Gustave Flaubert, *Correspondance*, ed. Louis Conard (Paris: Louis Conard, 1926), III, 306. Proust will likewise praise and make very much a part of his own work the interdependent aesthetic notions of obscurity and *difficulté vaincue*. He will provide the reader a particular image of man, of the "Poet," that is as intensely and consistently dramatic as Scève's in his love lyrics. Like Scève, Proust's difficult diaphoric portrayal reflects the optimistic art of the possible whose dramatic form highlights human action, struggle and triumph. Both of these intriguing writers do provide the reader a wisdom on life and on art – that of an individual's (and a Poet's) response to chaos and his attempts to make some sense out of that chaos. As Proust wrote: "On ne reçoit pas la sagesse, il faut la découvrir soi-même après un trajet que personne ne peut faire pour nous, ne peut nous épargner, car elle est un point de vue sur les choses. Les vies que vous admirez, les attitudes que vous trouvez nobles . . . représentent un *combat* et une *victoire*." Marcel Proust, *A la recherche du temps perdu*, ed. Pierre Clarac and André Ferré (Paris: Gallimard, 1954), I, 864. Valéry's aesthetic outlook and assessment of the art of poetry are identical. The struggle and triumph over obscurity, anguish, chaos are for him the real achievements of a great poet:

Mais un homme qui se mesure à soi-même et se refait selon ses *clartés* me semble une œuvre supérieure qui me touche plus que toute autre. Le plus bel effort des humains est *de changer leur désordre en ordre* et la chance en pouvoir; c'est là la véritable *merveille*.   (I, 654)

Scève too was firmly convinced of the ultimate value and greater reward to come from poetic struggle:

> De mes *trauaulx* me bienheurantz ma peine,
> Ie m'extermine, & en si [grande] hayne
> De mes deffaultz i'aspire a la *merueille*
> D'vn si hault bien, que d'vne mesme alaine
> A mon *labeur* le iour, & la nuict veille.   (D384)

For the large number of references Scève makes to the poetic struggle and ordeal in coming to terms with this "si hault bien" (i.e., the concepts of "trauail," "labeur," "bataille," "combat," and so forth), see my *Maurice*

Scève: Concordance de la Délie (Chapel Hill: North Carolina Studies in the Romance Languages and Literatures, 1976), 2 vols.

17 The poems we have been considering thus far which are definitely oriented towards indeterminacy and irresolution make it tempting for the reader to interpret Scève's textuality in the modern Derridean sense of *différance* (i.e., *différer*): poems which deny and defer meaning, the "putting off of meaning" as Raymond C. La Charité has so convincingly argued recently for the textuality of Rabelais. See his introductory essay "Rabelais, 'sans pair, incomparable et sans parragon' " in his edited volume *Rabelais's Incomparable Book: Essays on His Art* (Lexington, KY: French Forum, Publishers, 1986), pp. 9–12. But in Scève, I do not believe it is the poet who obfuscates meaning but rather it is this meaning which eludes the poet, for a while anyway. Meaning in Scève is almost always denied and deferred because the poet has not *yet* found a means of coming to terms with it, not because the poet wishes to make it even more obscure. *Délie*'s textual resistance will ultimately serve a productive purpose, that of generating meaning, as we shall see in the remaining chapters of this book. Scève's dialectic of "adversity" as he presents the picture in many of his anguished and (for some readers) unsatisfying poems has as its purpose to direct the poet towards "chose plus haultaine," "mieulx," "plus seconde chose," and so forth which are actually the same metaphorical direction implied in the sequence's sub-title: "obiect de *plus haulte vertu.*" This dialectic is not, ultimately, intended by the poet to thwart higher meaning, and certainly not to exhibit any impasse or crisis of psyche and art. On the contrary, it is what guarantees the poet's continued progression to a higher insight, meaning, and order. On this important and meaning-acquiring purpose of "dialectical turning points," as Marshall Brown has called them, see this critic's "'Errours Endless Traine': On Turning Points and the Dialectical Imagination," *PMLA*, 99 (1984), 9–25. For a different and complementary study concerned with order in the *Délie*, and especially in regard to patterns of sequential linking and structuring devices in contrast to my more overall interest in aesthetic order, see Doranne Fenoaltea, *"Si haulte Architecture": The Design of Scève's Délie* (Lexington, KY: French Forum, Publishers, 1982). Since Scève seems to dwell so much on and to take such delight in his "doulce bataille" (D78), in whose resistance and irresolution the poet sees himself so "pleasantly suspended," one might still have the impression that Scève is creating his own obscurity in love rather than being confronted by it, and thus that he may be playing games with the reader as well as with himself. This rhetorical strategy of love games in the neo-Petrarchan tradition which presents layer upon layer of antithesis and oxymoron was, of course, popular during Scève's time. Love was often viewed as a pretext for bringing language and poetry into being in a "sweet battle" and holding the reader in "suspense" by throwing before him one obstacle after another for the purpose of impressing and titillating him. This all had been the goal before of many a good love poet

(cf. also D84: "Ie ris en moy ces fictions friuoles"). I have called attention to this ironic and playful perspective on love as it is portrayed in Louise Labé's sonnets: "Louise Labé and Learned Levity," *Romance Notes*, 21 (1980), 227–33. For other love poets sharing this perspective, see Leonard Forster, *The Icy Fire: Five Studies in European Petrarchism* (Cambridge: Cambridge University Press, 1969); Jérôme Peignot, *Les Jeux de l'amour et du langage* (Paris: Union Générale d'Editions, 1974); and also Roland Barthes, *Fragments d'un discours amoureux* (Paris: Seuil, 1977). Tempting as this playful possibility is also for interpreting the obscurity and anguish of Scève's love lyrics, I believe it must, in the final analysis, be rejected. (In the above D84, the poet is not laughing at the "frivolous fictions" that are his poetry, but at the "lies" that had been told about Délie and his association with her.) The poet's "sweet battle" and "suspense" are a necessary and integral and serious part of his struggle to get at the kind of higher love ("chose plus haultaine") he is attempting to understand and portray. In any event, there can be little doubt that Scève's intention in portraying higher love is to demonstrate and to make the reader feel and appreciate the ordeal itself involved in expressing such a love. As Boccaccio put it, this ordeal is what makes the reader "value" even more the love experience being portrayed (p. 61).

18 *Stultifera navis* (London: John Cawood, 1570), p. 246. This quotation from Barclay and the one below from Giarda, whose transcriptions I have verified for accuracy, are from Robert J. Clements, *Picta Poesis: Literary and Humanistic Theory in Renaissance Emblem Books* (Rome: Edizioni di Storia e Letteratura, 1960), pp. 106 and 107. In an earlier piece of mine on Scève, I began exploration of the artistic implication of the *vertu*- concept in the *Délie*, views which I am greatly expanding in this book. See "The Notion and Meaning of Art in the *Délie*," *The Romanic Review*, 71 (1980), 28–46.

19 "Pour deviner l'âme du poète, ou du moins sa principale préoccupation, cherchons dans ses œuvres quel est le mot ou quels sont les mots qui s'y représentent avec le plus de fréquence. Le mot traduira l'obsession." Charles Baudelaire, *Journaux Intimes*, ed. Jacques Crépet and Georges Blin (Paris: José Corti, 1949), p. 231. For word frequencies in the *Délie*, see again my *Maurice Scève: Concordance de la Délie*.

20 Dizains where *vertu* appears simply to connote the ethical principle exemplifying the morally good life are 210, 225, 254, 413. Ruth Mulhauser treats *vertu* in this way in her "The Poetic Function of the Emblems in the *Délie*," *L'Esprit Créateur*, 5 (1965), 80–89. There *vertu*, virtuous love, ultimately wins out over *ardeur*, earthly love. Neoplatonic *vertu*, the poet's intellectual apprehension of ideal Beauty and Perfection in the person of Délie, may be found in 2, 15, 23, 66, 149, 165, 182, 208, 281, 283, 424, 436, 444. For a discussion of Scève's Neoplatonism, see Jean Festugière, *La Philosophie de l'Amour de Marcile Ficin* (Paris: Vrin, 1941), pp. 97ff.; Leo Spitzer, "The Poetic Treatment of a Platonic-Christian Theme," *Compara-*

tive Literature, 6 (1954), 193–217; and Robert V. Merrill and Robert J. Clements, *Platonism in French Renaissance Poetry* (New York: New York University Press, 1957), pp. 59–78.

21 See Lionello Sozzi, "La 'dignitas hominis' dans la littérature française de la Renaissance," in *Humanism in France*, ed. A. H. T. Levi (Manchester: Manchester University Press, 1970), pp. 176–98. In his very suggestive chapter on *Délie* in his book *Le Curieux Désir: Scève et Peletier du Mans poètes de la connaissance* (Geneva: Droz, 1967), Hans Staub was the first to give prominence in Scève to the poetic quest of a kind of "connaissance de soi," of the poet-lover's *humanitas* realizing itself in the love object: "Dans *Délie*, évidemment, le domaine de l'expansion reste celui de l'amour même. C'est l'aimée qui apparaît comme le complément exact de l'amant. Mais elle est plus que cela, elle est le monde où l'amant se réalise dans son *humanitas*" (p. 49). Thus, Staub sees an incarnational impulse in Scève through which "le progrès de la connaissance" is translated "par le mouvement poétique même" (p. 7). Staub reads the *Délie* and the *Microcosme* as "poésie scientifique" and "poésie savante" in the philosophical context of Nicolas of Cusa's *De conjecturis*. The present study will go in the opposite direction for notions on a transcendent aesthetic in the *Délie*; we will be turning to the views and practice of poetry by such writers as Baudelaire, Mallarmé, and especially Valéry. For I. D. McFarlane is absolutely right when he says of Scève's love poetry: "Behind the poems lie not only emotions, but mind; and sometimes his writing reminds us of Mallarmé and Valéry. These are all poets whose verse gives the impression of powerful emotional forces held in balance by equally powerful aesthetic and intellectual controls" (*Renaissance France 1470–1589* [London: Ernest Benn Limited, 1974], p. 160). Furthermore, *Délie*'s imposing theme of poetic struggle will always be one of the primary concerns of this book. This major theme in Scève can also be better understood and appreciated by turning to the more modern French writers. Again, my purpose in doing this is not to turn Scève into a "modernist," into a Mallarmé *avant la lettre*, and certainly not to ally him, as some critics have, with what they consider to be the modernist tendency for artistic and psychological crisis. On the contrary, I wish to suggest that the notion and practice of poetic struggle and paradise, of the difficult attainment of an artistic *vertu* through a diaphorically transcendent poetic of paradise, belong to a long and diverse and distinguished literary tradition and can surface in any period of intense literature.

22 Ed. Enzo Giudici (Paris: Vrin, 1976). The literal antecedent of "ce tems perdu" is the first line of this introductory sonnet: "Le vain travail de voir divers païs." Metaphorically, this image reminiscent of Proust refers to that self-questioning, sustained, vital poetic activity which Scève also associates in the *Délie* with the *vertu*-concept.

23 "La vraie vie, la vie enfin *découverte et éclaircie*, la seule vie par conséquent réellement *vécue*, c'est la littérature, cette vie qui, en un sens,

habite à chaque instant chez tous les hommes aussi bien que chez l'artiste."
Proust, ed. Clarac and Ferré, III, 895.

24 A. R. Chisholm describes the artistic process as "a series of creative
acts, corresponding to the incessant Creation which furnishes the starting-
point of poetic activity, namely the external phenomena out of which ideas
and images are made." "Mallarmé 'Victorieusement fui le suicide
beau . . .' ", *French Studies*, 14 (1960), 156.

25 Terence Cave describes the kind of process and development I
shall be exploring more fully in Scève in this way: "Self-evidence is stasis:
a premature arrival at an empty place. It is only through the awareness of
not-having, of not-seeing, that the movement towards possession and
insight (true evidence) may be released." *The Cornucopian Text: Problems
of Writing in the French Renaissance* (Oxford: Oxford University Press,
1979), p. 102. My thesis on Scève will carry this process one step further
by showing that Scève does indeed often reach the ultimate destination of
what he considers to be true, paradisal insight.

26 See his two studies: *Maurice Scève, Pernette Du Guillet, Louise Labé:
l'Amour à Lyon au temps de la Renaissance* (Paris: Nizet, 1981); *Maurice
Scève, prince des lumières, virtuose du regard, fils de l'aurore* (Paris: Expan-
sion, 1976). This critic's interpretation of the *Délie* (along with Staub's
above in *Le Curieux Désir*) forms a critical counterpoint to those surveyed
in this chapter which stress Scève's anguish, obscurity, and so forth as
primary and final features of his poetic accomplishment.

27 Flaubert's metaphoric demonstration of this principle of artistic *vertu*
is also worth quoting again:

Si vous voulez à la fois chercher le Bonheur et le Beau, vous n'atteindrez ni à l'un
ni à l'autre, car le second n'arrive que par le sacrifice. L'Art, comme le Dieu des
Juifs, se repaît d'holocaustes. Allons! déchire-toi, roule-toi dans la cendre, avilis la
matière, crache sur ton corps, arrache ton cœur! . . . Et tu rouleras, perdue dans
l'ouragan, avec cette petite *lueur* à l'horizon. Mais elle grandira, comme un
soleil . . . tu seras éclairée du dedans, tu te sentiras légère et tout esprit, et après
chaque saignée la chair pèsera moins.   (Conard, III, 306)

For many Renaissance symbolist writers too, including Scève, the sun or
any form of light triumphant was poetic virtue, whose depiction rep-
resented a powerful means of achieving *difficulté vaincue*. This is why
Christophorus Giarda placed the seal of the sun on his allegorical figure of
Poesy: because "the sun so truly fills by its rays the world with virtue, that
virtue, like poetry itself, unmindful of death, keeps growing daily" (*Icones
symbolicae* [Milan: I. B. Bidellinin, 1628], p. 93). The love poetry of Scève
also reveals a progressively radiant virtue – "celle *vertu*, qui tant la faict
reluire," as the poet describes his "eternelle amytié" in D66 – an intense
and intensifying light and illumination which rescue his text from darkness
and obscurity and his poetic vision from torment and suffering. One of the
purposes of the present study is to demonstrate this point.

2. In search of love's epistemology: affirming the role of the creative imagination

1 "The Conflict of Interpretations and the Limits of Pluralism," *PMLA*, 98 (1983), 341.

2 *Confessions*, I, vi. This quotation from Augustine is used as a point of departure by Peter S. Hawkins and Anne Howland Schotter, editors, in their Introduction (p. 1) to a provocative collection of essays on the problems involved in expressing the inexpressible in a wide range of literary texts concerned with the ineffable: *Ineffability: Naming the Unnamable from Dante to Beckett* (New York: AMS Press, 1984).

3 For more discussion of *Délie*'s twists and turns in these "oui–non" poems comprising the structural principle of anti-closural closure, see my essay "Logic and Lyric: Poetic Closure in Scève's *Délie*," *French Studies*, 38 (1984), 385–98. Scève's impasse, often depicted structurally and thematically in his poems as well as psychologically, his struggle or "conflict" which forces him "a constamment pour *si hault bien* périr" (D189), certainly mirrors what Jacques Maritain has called the basic conflict to be found in all artists and writers who rely on "la raison" to accomplish aesthetic portrayal. This conflict is always the same one "entre la transcendance de la beauté et l'étroitesse matérielle de l'œuvre à faire." See his *Art et scolastique* (Paris: Louise Rouart et Fils, 1927), p. 74.

4 *Enneads*, VI, ix, 10, *The Essence of Plotinus*, ed. Grace H. Turnbull (New York: Oxford University Press, 1934), p. 221.

5 Scève's epistemological treatment of the poet's failure to come to terms with higher meaning through rational conceptualization certainly supports modern linguistic theories on language and its use, or rather its limits of use. See the linguistic principle of "limitation theory" as developed especially by Noam Chomsky in *Language and Mind* (New York: Harcourt Brace, 1968). For the importance of epistemology in Renaissance literature, see the classic study by Rosalie L. Colie, *Paradoxia Epidemica: The Renaissance Tradition of Paradox* (Princeton: Princeton University Press, 1966).

6 It is here, I believe, that Scève diverges from Mallarmé and other symbolist poets. To leave the inexpressible literally unexpressed means either not to write a poem or, as sometimes is the case of Mallarmé, to write it spatially through the blank space and its configuration. Although Scève's handling of the inexpressibility topos suggests a sacred immensity too great to be contained in human words, he ultimately relies on these very words to communicate with and to convey it, and thus to find a means of renewal in it through them. The limitation strategy of "O vain desir, ô folie euidente, / A qui de faict espere y paruenir" (D97) becomes finally the new perspective of confident sacred portrayal, of the poet's ability to communicate Délie's (and *Délie*'s) "*Parolle saincte* en toute esiouissance" (D278). In a word, or better still in an aesthetic image, Scève's poetic "I cannot" becomes the artistic "I can." This is what Scève intends Délie and

us to understand above in D393 when the poet, being bombarded by doubt and uncertainty, says that being able to do no more, he does more than he can: "Parquoy durant si longue phrenesie, / Ne pouant plus, ie fais plus que ne puis." He does keep on composing, and not through the aesthetic of the blank space but through the aesthetic of the ineffable word, the ineffable image, which is this love poet's only means of turning disorder of psyche and art into order:

> Par long prier lon mitigue les Dieux:
> Par l'oraison la fureur de Mars cesse:
> Par long sermon tout courage odieux
> Se pacifie: *& par chansons tristesse*
> *Se tourne a ioye: & par vers lon opresse,*
> *Comme enchantez, les venimeux serpentz.*   (D239)

For Mallarmé's "esthetic of space," see the intriguing study by Virginia A. La Charité, *The Dynamics of Space: Mallarmé's Un Coup de dés jamais n'abolira le hasard* (Lexington, KY: French Forum, Publishers, 1987). For a poetic of the ineffable in Mallarmé that is defined by absence, negation, and silence, see Thomas A. Williams, *Mallarmé and the Language of Mysticism* (Athens: University of Georgia Press, 1970). And for another and excellent study of French Renaissance literature and the ineffable, of the "unspoken" in Marguerite de Navarre, see Robert D. Cottrell, *The Grammar of Silence: A Reading of Marguerite de Navarre's Poetry* (Washington: Catholic University of America Press, 1986). In spite of the critically acclaimed importance of silence in the *Délie*, as studied by Pascal Quignard (*La Parole de la Délie*) and others, my own experience with Scève leads me to believe he was much less inclined towards it than was Marguerite or even Mallarmé. Perhaps the reason for this lies in the difference between metaphysical and mystical poetry, the latter having had a long tradition of a poetics of silence which was missing in the former. In any event, Cottrell's perceptive analysis of silence conveying the ineffable in Marguerite is a good demonstration of what Hawkins and Schotter have termed the "negative ineffable" (*Ineffability*, p. 2), as opposed to the "positive ineffable" which I see Scève developing in his love aesthetics and which the present study will be concerned with.

7 The importance of sight as the "aggressive eye topos" in Scève has been studied by Lance K. Donaldson-Evans. See his *Love's Fatal Glance: A Study of Eye Imagery in the Poets of the Ecole lyonnaise* (University, MS: Romance Monographs, Inc., 1980), especially pp. 94–144. For a good presentation of the Renaissance view of the perceptual limitations of the senses, including sight which commands the others and by which explanations of mental and rational operations were attempted, see Walter Ong, "System, Space, and Intellect in Renaissance Symbolism," *Bibliothèque d'Humanisme et Renaissance*, 17 (1956), 231–57.

8 Leo Spitzer has called the writerly testing or search for a language of transcendence – that is, the formulation in due time by a poet's creative

imagination of a "sense-beyond-sense" – the poet's true task. This poetic purpose also has serious readerly implications:

Thus, by means of words of our daily life, there is given the possibility of a logic beyond our human logic. . . . Poetry consists of *words*, with their meaning *preserved*, which, through the magic of the poet who works with a prosodic whole, arrive at a sense-beyond-sense; and . . . it is the task of the philologist to point out the manner in which the transfiguration just mentioned has been achieved. . . . The irrationality of the poem need not lose anything at the hands of a descreet linguistic critic . . . insofar as he will patiently and analytically retrace the way from the rational to the irrational: a distance which the poet's imagination may have covered in one bold leap.

Spitzer's italics. "Three Poems on Ecstasy: John Donne, St. John of the Cross, Richard Wagner," in his *Essays on English and American Literature* (Princeton: Princeton University Press, 1962), pp. 141–42.

9 *The Délie of Maurice Scève*, p. 391. On p. 156, where McFarlane presents this poem and its accompanying emblem and motto, he does make this important reservation: "The picture of a woman with spindle and distaff ["La Femme qui desuuyde"] might well induce the association with Fate and Death; but the motto ["Apres long trauail vne fin"], which is worked into the final line of the following dizain, is used for a very different purpose." As I shall shortly argue, McFarlane's initial suggestion for interpreting this poem is worth pursuing. This poem very much concerns death, but a special kind of Death.

10 *An Illustrated Love 'Canzoniere': The Délie of Maurice Scève* (Geneva: Slatkine, 1981), pp. 19–21.

11 The poet's struggle with Délie's tyrannical beauty, her "beauté amère," reflects the greater aesthetic experience he is undergoing more than any amorous experience. In a very seductive study, Jean-Michel Rabaté has shown this same encounter to be the real subject of other great poets and writers concerned with aesthetic and ineffable meaning. See his discussion of the violent aesthetic of Beauty-that-kills in *La Beauté amère: fragments d'esthétiques* (Seyssel: Editons du Champs Vallon, 1986), especially the chapter on "La beauté tragique et la 'seconde mort' " (pp. 123–52). See also Alain Michel, *La Parole et la Beauté* (Paris: Les Belles Lettres, 1982) whose thesis is this: "La beauté véritable, celle qui tue, celle qui exprime la transcendance, porte en elle les caractères de l'inhumain" (p. 21).

12 See Josiane Rieu, "La 'Beauté qui tue' dans les *Amours* de Ronsard," *Revue d'Histoire Littéraire de la France*, 4 (1986), 693–708. I agree entirely with Rieu's splendid interpretation of Ronsard and with her critical notions, which I too share and have tried to incorporate into this book on Scève. Here is what she has to say on the notion of poetic paradise, a purely artistic concept as opposed to literal and biographical interpretation: "Ce qui nous touche, aujourd'hui encore, c'est ce *'paradis' littéraire* – la fiction n'est fausse que par rapport à une réalité biographique, mais n'exclut pas

une *réalité vécue par le poète* . . . témoignant d'un travail sur la langue, et qui joue avec les limites de la langue" (p. 693; cf. my turning to Proust in this matter of art and life in Chapter 1, Note 23: "La vraie vie . . . la seule vie par conséquent réellement *vécue*, c'est la littérature").

13 I am fully aware that this suggestion of a higher meaning associated with death in the *Délie* contradicts much previous critical thinking on the subject. For one of the darkest treatments of death in the *Délie*, in spite of its aspirations to the contrary, see Jean-Pierre Attal, "Dix propositions emblématiques pour *Délie*," in his *L'Image métaphysique* (Paris: Gallimard, 1969), pp. 135–56. These few quotations from there will provide a good idea of Attal's position: "Quelles sont ces morts, sinon les effets d'une guerre incessante où les victoires portent le masque de la défaite: toujours vaincu, toujours détruit" (p. 137); "Sous le signe de l'amour, la vie de Scève prend un caractère tragique: il était libre, il devient prisonnier; il était heureux, insouciant, il devient sombre, triste . . . son seul espoir de délivrance: *La Mort, seul bien des tristes affligez*" (p. 147; Attal's italics); "Mais l'art de Scève, malgré les rapprochements qui ont été tentés, demeure étranger à celui de Mallarmé ou de Valéry" (p. 153 – an observation which I hope this book will show not to be entirely well founded); "Pourtant, en gardant les yeux ouverts, en maintenant le passé dans un éternel présent, Scève se condamnait à la souffrance, à l'angoisse et à un labeur incessant" (Attal's final words on Scève on p. 156 of his essay).

14 "Ronsard: de la femme à l'Idée," in *From Marot to Montaigne: Essays on French Renaissance Literature*, ed. Raymond C. La Charité, *Kentucky Romance Quarterly*, 19, Supplement No. 1 (1972), 106.

15 "The Beauty of Woman: Problems in the Rhetoric of Renaissance Portraiture," in *Rewriting the Renaissance: The Discourses of Sexual Difference in Early Modern Europe*, ed. Margaret W. Ferguson, Maureen Quilligan, and Nancy J. Vickers (Chicago: University of Chicago Press, 1986), p. 189. This stimulating essay by Cropper on the interrelations of Renaissance art and poetry, which often stresses their aesthetic differences in outlook and method, is invaluable for anyone working on this subject.

16 Kristeva, *Histoires d'amours* (Paris: Denoël, 1983), pp. 268ff.; and Frank Kermode, *Forms of Attention* (Chicago: University of Chicago Press, 1985). In his conclusion to his discussion of *Hamlet*, Kermode summarizes the inherently specular nature of literary forms of attention, of how the creative imagination must inform and illuminate them: "The play is a fiction, a dream of passion, in which there are dreams within dreams, and *mirror on mirror mirrored is all the show*. Moreover, the conversations of interpreters are shadows or images, fat or thin, and not matters of substance, except that where there is shadow there must be substance, and a light on it; so the end of all this shadowy talk is after all to keep a real and valued object in being" (p. 63). See also Gisèle Mathieu-Castellani, "Poésie et specularité: la représentation de l'écriture dans les *Amours* de Ronsard," *Revue d'Histoire Littéraire de la France*, 4 (1986),

659–66. For a different approach to the notion of specularity in Scève, see the chapter on "Poésie et spécularité" (pp. 101–27) in Marcel Tetel's *Lectures scéviennes*. Tetel is not concerned with the above mirroring images of absence–presence which I consider very significant examples of specular expression in the *Délie*. His concern is with Scève's "langage anagrammatique," his "valorisation du dire poétique aux dépens d'un taire affectif," and finally with "le métier du poète et les difficultés de cette entreprise" (p. 101). For a general overview of the mirror theme in early poetry, see Jean Frappier, "Variations sur le thème du miroir de Bernard de Ventadour à Maurice Scève," *Cahiers de l'Association Internationale des Etudes Françaises*, 2 (1959), 134–59.

17 Paris: Presses Universitaires de France, 1985. Dubois is especially strong when he discusses the poetic process of self-awareness, the discovery and affirmation of the creative imagination by Renaissance writers (and not all of these are poets – he considers Montaigne at some length). In this chapter, we too have seen Scève affirm the importance and the crucial role of this higher faculty of the imagination. Scève does succeed in finding a means of coming to terms with Délie as ineffable object of poetic contemplation and writing – the answer to the central question we posed at the beginning of this chapter. In the next one, we will see this imaginative faculty at work creating the actual love forms of our poet's vision.

18 Though Scève carries, I believe, this theme and process of *poetic* love, of love and its representation in art – his poet's real concern with acquiring an ability to *concevoir les choses* as opposed to lamenting some pretended unrequited love – farther than any other poet of the French Renaissance, other love poets of the period were also very much concerned with this same "projet littéraire." Yvonne Bellenger also argues this interpretation for the love poetry of Ronsard and Du Bellay in her highly rewarding book *La Pléiade: La Poésie en France autour de Ronsard* (Paris: Nizet, 1988). Bellenger even reminds us of the critical mistakes and errors committed at the beginning of this century by those who pursued meaning in Ronsard's love poetry along purely biographical lines. The "Marie" of *Sur la mort de Marie* published in 1578 has turned out to be someone very different than previously thought and written about by these earlier critics. The real Marie "ne fut jamais bergère mais princesse . . . la jeune morte en était la maîtresse" (i.e., of Henry III; p. 39). As Bellenger points out, the real interest in these love poems, as Ronsard's contemporaries such as Belleau recognized, lies "guère sur la demoiselle prétendument aimée; tout, en revanche, sur le projet littéraire" (p. 39). In other words, we should read these love lyrics as the poet's attempt to come to terms with a literary reality rather than some biographical reality. From her own readings of Ronsard and Du Bellay, Bellenger is able to conclude, and very convincingly so, for Renaissance love poetry in general: "Le poète du XVIe siècle entend représenter pour ses lecteurs une certaine façon de *concevoir les choses*. . . . L'imagerie amoureuse . . . n'est souvent que la description

quasi clinique du *triomphe de l'amour* tel qu'on *l'imaginait* au XVIe siècle"
(pp. 39–40). As we have already begun to see in this chapter, this kind of
"imagining" also constitutes the central love theme of Scève's *Délie*.

3. Embodying the sacred and ineffable: poetic forms of transcendence and paradise

1 Of the many writings by Eliade on the subject, see especially these
two: *Images et symboles* (Paris: Gallimard, 1952) and *Traité d'historie des
religions* (Paris: Payot, 1953). In the latter, his initial chapter on "Approxi-
mations: Structure et la morphologie du sacré" (pp. 15–46) contains his
best discussion of this dialectic of hierophanies, of the difficult passage
from profane to sacred art. Eliade's views form the basis of another splen-
did book on the subject by Vincent Buckley, *Poetry and the Sacred*
(London: Chatto & Windus, 1968), which is concerned with exploring the
"religious impulse" in literature, and in particular, with poetry viewed as
"an act both sacred and sacralising" by certain writers (Wyatt, Donne,
Blake, Melville, Yeats, and Eliot) in whose works "it is not to ideas of
'sacred' or 'divine' poetry that they are resorting, but to conceptions of the
poetic venture as such" (pp. 8–9). Obviously, I believe that Scève in his
own poetic venture would fit nicely in the above list.

2 D443's metaphysical denial of death coming after a rational confir-
mation of death, the poet's insight ("Mon ame ainsi de son obiect pour-
ueue") replacing his sight ("De tous mes sens me rend abandonné"), also
forms the basis of John Donne's transcendent rhetoric of "paradoxical
epistemology." For his soul too, "Death must usher, and unlocke the
door" (*Second Anniversary*). See Rosalie Colie, *Paradoxia Epidemica*,
especially Chapter 13, "The Rhetoric of Transcendent Knowledge"; p. 422
for the above quotation from Donne.

3 *Plato*, ed. W. R. M. Lamb (Cambridge, MA: Harvard University
Press, 1961), V, 205.

4 Claude-Gilbert Dubois, *L'Imaginaire de la Renaissance*, p. 254. This
aesthetically shaping, ordering, and unifying power of the creative mind
or imagination in its transcendent art is what enabled the Renaissance poet
to see inner relationships, such as the identification of truth with beauty,
and paradisal relationships, that of heaven and earth, as Dubois shows us
in Ronsard's love poetry written to Hélène:

> Tes mœurs et ta vertu, ta prudence et ta vie,
> Tesmoignent que l'esprit tient de la Deité:
> Tes raisons de Platon, et ta Philosophie,
> Que le vieil Promethée est une vérité
> Et qu'en ayant la flame à Jupiter ravie,
> *Il maria la Terre à la Divinité*   (pp. 236–37).

5 *Marot, Rabelais, Montaigne: l'écriture comme présence* (Paris-
Geneva: Champion/Slatkine, 1987).

6 Blake, *Complete Writings*, ed. Geoffrey Keynes (London: Oxford University Press, 1969), pp. 431 and 434. The other half of the Blake quote (whose entirety I gave at the beginning of this book) we will save for discussion in Chapter 5. Indeed, it will become the very subject of that chapter.

7 "For the law of the *Spirit of life in Christ Jesus* has set me free from the law of sin and death." I also refer the reader once again to Valéry and his recognition of this transcendent principle of immanence, of spirit being perceived and portrayed as living in human form, which saves poetry from excessive idealization not connected to reality and life. To embody spirit in some earthly form (which Valéry unfortunately calls "pagan" – unfortunate because this principle is the essence of Christian art as well) is the requirement of a great poet: "Mais la Poésie est toute païenne: elle exige impérieusement qu'il n'y ait point d'*âme* sans *corps*, – point de *sens*, point d'*idée* qui ne soit l'*acte* de quelque *figure remarquable*, construite de timbres, de durées et d'intensités" (Valéry's italics, p. 656). For some of Mallarmé's modern readers who have shared Valéry's assessment of him, this diaphoric principle and portrayal of spirit-in-matter is the essence of Mallarmé's aesthetics, as I have been trying to show it is of Scève's. For Guy Delfel, Mallarmé's poetic images and metaphors succeed in capturing and portraying the sacred and ineffable precisely because they resolve the problem, inherent in all transcendent art-forms, of "ne pas pouvoir exprimer l'éternel que par la *matière*, l'extra-terrestre que par l'*image* et la *figure*" (*L'Esthétique de Stéphane Mallarmé* [Paris: Flammarion, 1951], p. 58). Scève's poetic art succeeds along the same diaphorically transcendent lines. For a good discussion of a Christian poetics in literature which thrives on the principle of immanence, see Michael Edwards, *Towards A Christian Poetics* (Grand Rapids, MI: William B. Eerdmans Publishing Company, 1984) and G. Wilson Knight, *The Christian Renaissance* (New York: W. W. Norton, 1963).

8 Once again, I refer the reader to a passage from Valéry on this crucial point: "Celui qui est à l'excès pour soi est en extrême danger de l'être pour le public. Qui se consume, par exemple, à composer dans une même œuvre les qualités de *séduction immédiate* qui sont essentielles à la poésie, avec une *substance précieuse de pensée* sur quoi l'esprit puisse revenir et s'arrêter quelque peu sans regret, décime ses chances d'en finir avec son travail, non moins que celles d'être lu" (p. 652). Valéry's famous quotation has also been used by Dorothy Gabe Coleman in her very suggestive essay "Lire Scève et entendre Scève," in *Lire Maurice Scève*, ed. Françoise Charpentier and Simone Perrier, *Textuel*, No. 3 (1987), 9–14. Coleman does recognize (though for a different emphasis) in the "creation" of the *Délie* the importance of what I have been exploring at length in this chapter and have been calling Scève's diaphorically transcendent art of *discordia concors*:

Mais c'est spécifiquement la manière dont il allie deux mots qui sont totalement en désaccord l'un avec l'autre qu'il force le lecteur à accepter l'incompatibilité qui existe dans deux êtres humains et à l'intérieur de chacun d'eux [i.e., through the union of the abstract and the concrete as in 'celestement humaine']. . . . *Délie* est une analyse de tous les éléments contradictories dont se compose l'amour affectant et le corps et l'esprit, et l'un de ces éléments c'est l'effort pour retrouver la complexité de la passion et de redonner au lecteur une vision transcendentale qui est l'essence de l'amour humain. (pp. 11–12)

For me, this artistic process is concerned less with the poet's effort to "[faire] accepter l'incompatibilité qui existe dans deux êtres humains" and to "retrouver la complexité de la passion" than it is with his determination to control love's passion and to reverse its incompatibility by creating unity and order and harmony within his own love consciousness. The achievement of *Scève's* vision of transcendence provided by the diaphoric act is what always defines his poetic paradises. The possibility then is opened up for the reader to share in these poetic triumphs, as I have tried to show especially in this chapter. These triumphs of Scève – his magnificent and captivating art of incarnation energized and highlighted always by such diaphoric expressions as "celestement humaine" (D372) or "humainement haultaine" (D105) – reflect the same preoccupation – and truly the obsession – of other Renaissance "love" poets composing within the same dual aesthetic orientation of immanence/transcendence. In his Canto XI, Nicolas Denisot will express diaphoric insight into Christ as Scève does above into Délie in using these similarly juxtaposed terms: "Diuin en humanité/Humain en diuinité." For Denisot too, as for Scève and Valéry and their fascination with *discordia concors*, with the blending of the abstract (spiritual) and the concrete (physical), the attainment of the poetic ineffable is always one of seeing and composing the immanent and transcendent meaning and unity of incarnational art: "Et *voir* ce que nous *voyons*: / Ces trois en IESVCHRIST: / Dieu, la chair, & l'esprit! / O *ineffable* nature! / Que mesme en sa creature / *Createur* a *forme* pris." *Cantiques du premier aduenement de Jesus-Christ* (Paris: La Veuve Maurice de la Porte, 1553), pp. 87–88. For more discussion of Denisot and this poet's art of incarnation, see my essay "The Devotional Aesthetics of a Humanist: Nicolas Denisot's *Cantiques*," in *Essays in Early French Literature Presented to Barbara M. Craig*, ed. Norris J. Lacy and Jerry C. Nash (York, SC: French Literature Publications Company, 1982), pp. 129–46.

4. Becoming what one sees: the unity and identity of poetic self

1 Charles Baudelaire, *Œuvres complètes*, ed. Yves Le Dantec and Claude Pichois (Paris: Gallimard, 1961), pp. 347–48.
2 Cambridge University Press, 1985. Ebreo published a syncretic work, the *Dialoghi d'Amore* (Rome, 1535), which became a primary source of ideas about love for the Renaissance theorists regardless of philosophical position. Scève's close friend, Pontus de Tyard, translated Ebreo's dialogues into French and they were published by Scève's own Lyonese pub-

lisher, Jean de Tournes. As Ebreo points out, the two schools of thought, the Aristotelians and the Platonists, differed precisely in the degree of importance they assigned to the body in love. Ebreo leaves little doubt about his position in this debate. His naturalism proposes that just as man in reality is soul and body together, the actions of soul and body are therefore indivisible in love and its contemplation as in everything else: "Love is of soul and body, and the operations of the soul depend upon the body . . . the one ministers to the other in voluptuousness, and to delight the one without the other is impossible" (Smith, p. 203). For additional testimony from the period in support of the Aristotelian point of view, see Smith's section on "Aristotelian theorists of love" (pp. 195–204). Also helpful for the historical ramifications of this debate on love is Irving Singer, *The Nature of Love*, 2 vols. (Chicago: University of Chicago Press, 1984), and especially his second volume on *Courtly and Romantic* ("Neoplatonism and the Renaissance," pp. 165–208).

3 Even though Scève at times disavows being influenced by the Aristotelian philosophy of love and art ("Nature au Ciel, *non Peripatetique*," D444), he continues in this same poem and in others to acknowledge and construct the very kind of unity of reason and desire or mind and matter which the Aristotelian theorists of love were advocating:

> Pour dignement par Raison renommer
> Le bien, du bien qui sans comparaison
> La monstre seule, ou ie puisse estimer
> Nature, Amour, & Vertu, & Raison.

In his chapter quoted from above, Smith talks about the tendency among Renaissance poets, including Speroni and to a lesser extent even Ebreo, not to wish to align themselves too openly with Aristotelian views which were struggling for acceptance in the still Neoplatonically dominated literary milieu. Perhaps this helps to explain Scève's disclaimer in D444. In any case, Scève certainly subscribes to the view, formulated by Thomas Aquinas long before this Renaissance debate on love, that all knowledge, whether of outer object or inner self, takes its rise from sensation, and that a spiritual reality, to have meaning, must be metaphorically, that is, diaphorically, embodied in the physicality of this world: "Holy Scripture fittingly delivers divine and spiritual realities *under bodily guises*. . . . Now we are of the kind *to reach the world of intelligence through the world of sense*, since all our knowledge takes its rise from sensation. Congenially, then, holy Scripture delivers spiritual things to us *beneath metaphors taken from bodily things*. The divine *rays* cannot enlighten us except wrapped up in many *sacred veils*." *Summa theologica*, I. a. 1, 9. Ed. and trans. Herbert McCabe (London: Blackfriars, 1964), I, 33–35. This passage from Aquinas, which expresses views on the poetic art of contemplation later to be developed by Baudelaire and Valéry as we just saw above, could have served as a preamble to the present book on Scève's own kind of "sacred" love poetry and diaphoric aesthetics, for it contains most of the major points the chapters of this study have been developing.

4 Plotinus, *Enneads*, VI, ix, 10, ed. Turnbull, pp. 220–21.

5 V, i, 12–17. *The Complete Works of Shakespeare*, ed. Hardin Craig, (Chicago: Scott, Foresman and Company, 1961), p. 201.

6 Scève's metaphysical faith in love is the same that Pascal will acquire later on: a triumph of fideism over reason. Plotinus, Scève, and Pascal all believed that it is man's *heart*, not his reason, that is capable of helping him in his struggle to come to terms with and to know the ineffable, whether this ineffable be (Self-)Unity, Délie, or God. Moreover, for these writers, coming to know the ineffable object of one's contemplation (Pascal's "Dieu" or "être universel") always means coming to know and to love the self ("soi-même"): "Nous connaissons la vérité non seulement par la raison mais encore par le *cœur*. C'est de cette dernière sorte que nous connaissons les premiers principes et c'est en vain que le raisonnement, qui n'y a point de part, essaie de les combattre. . . . C'est sur ces connaissances du cœur et de l'instinct qu'il faut que la raison s'appuie et qu'elle y fonde tout son discours" (*Pensées*, 110); "Le cœur a ses raisons que la raison ne connaît point; on le sait en mille choses. Je dis que le cœur aime l'être universel naturellement et soi-même naturellement, selon qu'il s'y adonne. . . . C'est le cœur qui sent Dieu et non la raison. Voilà ce que c'est que la foi. Dieu sensible au cœur, non à la raison" (*Pensées*, 423–24). Pascal, *Œuvres complètes*, ed. Louis Lafuma (Paris: Seuil, 1963), pp. 512, 552.

7 For more general discussion of object-relations theory in love poetry which aims at producing deeper levels of unity through its development of object-defining and subject-defining techniques, see Mariann Sanders Regan, *Love Words: The Self and the Text in Medieval and Renaissance Poetry* (Ithaca: Cornell University Press, 1982).

5.   Struggle, light, and love's "sainct lieu"

1 Stéphane Mallarmé, *Œuvres complètes*, ed. Henri Mondor and G. Jean-Aubry (Paris: Gallimard, 1945), p. 74. Scève's so-called obscurity, like that of Mallarmé, is certainly to a large degree the diaphoric art of doubt and tension, an art based upon a predilection for resistance that challenges the reader through this very resistance. However, both writers strove for a kind of clarity or "purity" of poetic expression (hence the imagistic preference for "light" and "rose") and were fully aware that this kind of poetry constituted an arduous exercise for the mind of the reader. The "rose" which Mallarmé sees in the darkness, in nothingness, and Scève's own vision of the light operating in the same darkness have much more in common than what at first meets the eye. Indeed, Scève also connects the floral image of the rose to the recovery and triumph of light over darkness:

La blanche Aurore a peine finyssoit

D'orner son chef d'or luisant, & de roses,
Quand mon esprit, qui de tout perissoit
Au fons confus de tant diuerses choses,
Reuint a moy soubz les Custodes closes
Pour plus me rendre enuers Mort inuincible.   (D378)

Scève's affinity with Mallarmé and other symbolist poets lies more in his overall artistic belief in the difficult yet marvelous transformational, transcendent power and purpose of poetry than in any particular technical application of it, as we shall begin to see in this chapter and will see more fully in the Epilogue.

2 *Maurice Scève, Poet of Love: Tradition and Originality* (Cambridge: Cambridge University Press, 1975), p. 128.

3 *La Création poétique au XVIe siècle en France* (Paris: Nizet, 1955), p. 182.

4 Maud Bodkin, quoting the psychologist A. Carver on the significance of the idea of death, in her seminal *Archetypal Patterns in Poetry* (London: Oxford University Press, 1951), p. 66. My own understanding of the psychology of a death-and-rebirth poetic pattern in Scève owes much, spiritually as well as critically, to this monument of poetic criticism.

5 For one of the best discussions of tension in poetry as psychological obscurity and darkness, see the early piece by W. K. Wimsatt, Jr., "Poetic Tension: A Summary," *New Scholasticism*, 32 (1958), 73–88. See also Wheelwright, *Metaphor and Reality*, "Tensive Language," pp. 45–69.

6 In this chapter, I am more interested in the aesthetics and psychology of poetic sublimation, and especially in sublimation as a higher, perfecting principle and process of art – Valéry's notion already quoted of "changing disorder into order" – than in ethics or moral outlook which we more normally associate with the idea of sublimation in literature. Admittedly, the two areas of aesthetics and ethics work together in most portrayed operations of sublimation and are not always easy to separate for sake of analysis. However, I have already considered the ethical side of Scève's love vision in a previous study, and it can provide the reader additional material and discussion of the sensual implication of "liberté" contained in many of Scève's poems (as well as in the works of Rabelais, Jean Lemaire de Belges, and Marguerite de Navarre). See my "Stoicism and the Stoic Theme of *Honestum* in Early French Renaissance Literature," *Studies in Philology*, 76 (1979), 203–17.

7 *La Nouvelle Revue Française*, 123 (1963), 423.

8 *L'Art poétique*, ed. René d'Hermies (Paris: Librairie Larousse, n.d.), p. 66.

9 Blake, ed. Keynes, p. 434; Denisot, *Cantiques*, p. 33, Canto III, his magnificent apostrophe to Night whose introductory "Argument" heralds this diaphoric principle and image and insight which Denisot, like Scève quite probably, found in John 1:15 ("The *light* shines *in the darkness*, and the darkness has not overcome it"). For a very different interpretation of

D330 and Emblem 37, see Dorothy Gabe Coleman, *An Illustrated Love 'Canzoniere'. The Délie of Maurice Scève*, pp. 63–64, where she views Scève's treatment of the light imagery here as further evidence of the continual dark side of this love poet:

The analogy is between the moon and Délie. The dizain is a description of the poet's state. It depicts the complete withdrawal of the poet from himself into the being of Délie, the loss of his own life, the alienation from himself and the living in someone else. His nourishment is *pensementz funebres* and the analogy between the moon and Délie, his light, enters at the end. The moon in darkness would awaken for the sixteenth-century reader associations of the obscuring of mental faculties, the state of depression or melancholy, and these are precisely the harmonics which are appropriate to this dizain. (p. 64)

In her analysis, Coleman does not mention what I consider to be the all-important images of the "centre heureux" and "sainct lieu" which the poet has *decided* to concentrate and focus on as opposed to the "pensementz funebres" of his "Liberty" and "Springtime." Indeed, had his vision in this poem remained tied to the latter, then the dark harmonics "of the obscuring of mental faculties, the state of depression or melancholy" would have been the final poetic perspective and message. But the poet does not stop there, as I have tried to argue and show. For another very recent discussion of the meaning of light and dark in the *Délie*, see Françoise Charpentier, ". . . En moi tu luis la nuit obscure," *Europe*, Nos. 691–92 (1986), whose interpretation supports the ideas I have been developing in this chapter: "Une représentation majeure, à la fois métaphore, identification, personnification, domine le recueil, supportée par le nom même de Délie: la déesse venue de Délos, jumelle d'Apollon, Lune, Diane, Cynthie, Hécate. . . . Mais plus encore, l'Amant *est* littéralement orage, ténèbres, fournaise. Délie *est* véritablement celle qui emplit les nuits de sa lumière" (her italics; pp. 89 and 85).

10 Jean-Pierre Attal, "Dix propositions emblématiques pour *Délie*," p. 154. Ironically, Attal does not pursue this transcendent interpretive path in his reading of the *Délie*, which he correctly suggests might lead to a better understanding and appreciation of this "tortured" and "obscure" body of love poetry. In fact, Attal's remarks come at the very end of his essay on Scève, one which promises at each step to go beyond the problematics of anguish and obscurity in Scève but fails to do so. For me, one of the most successful attempts to do so is T. Anthony Perry's in his brief section on Scève in his *Erotic Spirituality: The Integrative Tradition from Leone Ebreo to John Donne* (University, AL: The University of Alabama Press, 1980), pp. 35–52.

11 Ed. Lamb, V, 205.

12 *La Divina Commedia*, ed. Natalino Sapegno (Florence: La Nuova Italia Editrice, 1970), III, 87.

13 *Rime e Trionfi*, ed. Raffaello Ramat (Milan: Rizzoli Editore, 1957).

14 *Aesthetic Experience and Literary Hermeneutics*, trans. Michael Shaw (Minneapolis: University of Minnesota Press, 1982), p. 259.

6. "De mes trauaulx me bienheurantz ma peine": love poetry as therapy

1 "Van Gogh, The Suicide Provoked by Society," *Horizon: A Review of Literature and Art*, 17, No. 97 (1948), 48. In spite of the fact that artists and poets must go through "that stage in illumination when thought flows back on itself in disorder," Artaud also firmly believed in the power of the human mind through art to change this disorder into order and even to express the infinite that can be extracted from human existence. And like Scève, Valéry, and Mallarmé, Artaud believed this can be accomplished through the poetically sacred light and life provided by transcendent imagining and art: "And how many . . . luminous currents of the forces which work on reality were necessary to overthrow the barrier [of disorder] before being finally compressed, raised on to the canvass and accepted? . . . One can live for the infinite, only take pleasure in the infinite; there is enough infinite on the earth and in the stars to satiate a thousand great geniuses" (pp. 48–49).

2 *Confessions*, X, xxviii. *Saint Augustine's Confessions*, ed. William Watts (Cambridge, MA: Harvard University Press, 1961), II, 147.

3 *Le Texte de la Renaissance* (Geneva: Droz, 1982), p. 184.

4 See Raymond C. La Charité, "Rabelais: The Book as Therapy," in *Medicine and Literature*, ed. Enid Rhodes Peschel (New York: Neale Watson Academic Publications, Inc., 1980), pp. 11–17. The range of authors and subjects treated in this collection of essays on the therapeutic and medical value to be found in literature is quite impressive: Rabelais, Shakespeare, Baudelaire, Proust, Michaux, Mann, Breton, Whitman, and so on, including several very interesting comparative pieces. For those interested in pursuing more modern theory on the healing power and purpose of poetry and in particular poetry as a response to neurosis, see *Poetry Therapy: The Use of Poetry in the Treatment of Emotional Disorders*, ed. Jack J. Leedy (Philadelphia: J. B. Lippincott Company, 1969) and Molly Harrower, *The Therapy of Poetry* (Springfield, IL: Charles C. Thomas, Publisher, 1972). Three fairly recent studies have considered different aspects of *Délie*'s own kind of therapy and can be read with profit: Jane M. Drake-Brockman, "Scève, the Snake and the Herb," *French Studies*, 33 (1979), 129–36; Joan A. Buhlman, "Philosophical Alchemy as a Mode of Transformation in Scève's *Délie*," *Romance Notes*, 23 (1982), 44–52; and Joan A. Buhlman, "The Three Graces: Cosmic Harmony in Scève's *Délie*," *Bibliothèque d'Humanisme et Renaissance*, 44 (1982), 53–63. Finally, another very recent study has explored the notion of recovery in the *Délie* by tracing Scève's concern with the Narcissus legend: Deborah Lesko Baker, *Narcissus and the Lover: Mythic Recovery and Reinvention*

in Scève's Délie, Stanford French and Italian Studies 46 (Saratoga, CA: Anma Libri & Co., 1986). In spite of the vast critical literature on the subject of poetry and therapy, much of it very theoretical and technical in nature, authors themselves have always been the best and most revealing sources for studying this connection, whether in Boccaccio, Scève, Flaubert, Baudelaire, Valéry, or the other writers I have often turned to in this study, or whether in Yeats, Housman, and other English and American writers to whom John Press often turns in his exciting essay on poetry, *The Fire and the Fountain* (London: Methuen, 1966):

> Whether we hold with Yeats that poetry springs from our quarrel with ourselves, or whether we prefer to say with Housman that it exists to harmonize the sadness of the world, we are recognizing the fact that *it is a way of restoring order to a fragmentary and disquieting universe*, wherein all seems broken and decayed. James Joyce says that the purpose of art is "to try slowly and humbly and constantly to express, to press out again, from the gross earth or what it brings forth, from sound and shape and colour which are the prison gates of our soul, *an image of the beauty we have come to understand*." . . . Whitman also exults in the poet's power to create harmony and to cleanse our perceptions. . . . The task of poetry, says Francis Thompson, is "to see and restore ye divine idea of things, freed from ye disfiguring accidents of their Fall"　　　　　　　　　　　　　　　　(pp. 220–21)

– and so forth, with statements from many other poets and writers on the notion of restoration and therapy provided by literary art.

5 See "harmonie" in Randle Cotgrave, *A Dictionarie of the French and English Tongues* (London: Whitaker, 1611).

6 Ed. Jean Frappier (Paris: Droz, 1947), pp. 6 and 42.

7 Ed. J. Jolliffe and M. A. Screech (Geneva: Droz, 1966), pp. 70 and 72.

8 *Le Premier Livre des emblesmes* (Lyon: Jean de Tournes, 1550), p. 5.

9 Again, for a superb discussion of the diaphoric progression and poetic magic of turning black into white, of the black ink of melancholy reflecting a paradisal radiance of great human worth and value, see Jean Starobinski, "L'Encre de la mélancolie." Starobinski concludes his essay in referring to Shakespeare and his firm belief, found in Sonnet 65, in the therapeutic role of art to assuage the despair, obscurity, and destruction all too often associated with human love. To the question of who or what can save love and give it permanence and higher meaning, Shakespeare answers: "O, none, unless this miracle have might, / That in black ink my love may still shine bright" (ed. Craig, p. 482).

10 Gérard de Nerval, *Œuvres*, ed. Henri Lemaître (Paris: Garnier, 1958), I, 758; Nerval's italics. Granted, Nerval's situation in love and thus the cause of his despair and anguish were different from Scève's. Nerval's beloved had died, and this sonnet grieves that loss. Scève's own despair and anguish, if we are to believe his literal statements on their causes as in fact most of his readers have done, were produced by unrequited love. But is there really that much difference from the point of view of intensity and

depth of feeling between loss caused by love's death and loss caused by unrequited love? Both these situations can have devastating effects. The two situations produce the same acute despair and anguish, the same melancholy. What separates the two poets, however, is that Scève's treatment of despair and anguish leads him in a totally different direction from Nerval. Both poets are presented exactly the same problem – that of coming to terms with "melancholy." In my view, one succeeds; the other does not.

Epilogue. Scève, Mallarmé, and the art of transcendence

1 Mallarmé seems to have intended his "black on white" poetic image-principle quite literally, which of course does not prevent others, such as Valéry and critics working on Mallarmé today, from interpreting it symbolically: "Mais est-ce que l'opération même d'écrire n'est pas de mettre du noir sur du blanc?" This quotation, which originally appeared in the *Figaro* on September 13, 1898, is from Albert Thibaudet, *La Poésie de Stéphane Mallarmé* (Paris: Gallimard, 1926), p. 64. Thibaudet's interesting chapter on Mallarmé's "obscurity" ("Les Sources de l'obscurité," pp. 60–72) will prove helpful to anyone working on obscurity in literature. He carefully moves the reader into the diaphoric nature of the subject, as one can see in his opening sentences: "Sur l'obscurité de Mallarmé, on a porté des regards très divers. D'elle on s'est fait une idée obscure. Il faut, a dit Hegel, comprendre l'inintelligible comme tel: éclaircissons le principe de cette obscurité" (p. 60). For an excellent discussion of Mallarmé and the ineffable, see Kathleen Henderson Staudt, "The Poetics of 'Black on White': Stéphane Mallarmé's *Un Coup de dés*," in *Ineffability*, ed. Hawkins and Schotter, pp. 147–61. As the title of her essay indicates, the idea of "mettre du noir sur du blanc" is precisely what Staudt pursues in Mallarmé: "The poet works in a world of pure darkness and light, the exact negative of the stars against a black sky. Black ink and white paper are his materials, and these represent, for Mallarmé, something as mysterious and elemental as the stars" (p. 149). My own version of that mysterious and marvelous "something" connecting Mallarmé and Scève will become more apparent as we reach the end of this discussion.

2 Ed. Mondor and Jean-Aubry, pp. 74, 378–82, 477, respectively.

3 Baudelaire's ideas on the purpose of diaphoric illumination and transfiguration can also be of help here. In "La Chambre double," Baudelaire will define for us, in clear Scèvian accents, the diaphoric nature of the transcendent poetic imagination and its operation in art. Scève was also struggling with and composing through this same aesthetic principle of clarity through obscurity. In Baudelaire's "chambre véritablement *spirituelle*" (his italics), which he also calls his "chambre paradisiaque," sufficient clarity and delightful obscurity penetrate everything: "Ici, tout a la suffisante clarté et la délicieuse obscurité de l'harmonie" (*Œuvres complètes*, ed. Le Dantec and Pichois, pp. 233–34). And for Baudelaire, as for

Scève and Mallarmé and Valéry, obscurity can be "delightful" only because as a chiaroscurmatic counterpoint to something higher (as a kind of aesthetic "résistance" to use Valéry's term), it demands to be successfully challenged, transfigured, and thus surmounted. In seeking to create a higher spiritual meaning, it is the creative imagination that bestows this higher meaning upon the natural obscurity of the world and its objects of contemplation. Baudelaire is very clear on this point. It is the imagination – "l'*âme*" as he specifically calls it (as so often too did Scève) – "qui jette une *lumière* magique et surnaturelle sur l'obscurité naturelle des choses" (p. 1061). For Baudelaire, Edgar Allen Poe was a great literary artist precisely because he accomplished this kind of intense illumination, because he probed the transcendent potential and meaning of worldly things through the higher synthesizing and luminous power of his own poetic imagination: "Pour lui, l'Imagination est la reine des facultés; mais par ce mot il entend quelque chose de plus grand que ce qui est entendu par le commun des lecteurs. . . . L'Imagination est *une faculté quasi divine qui perçoit tout d'abord*, en dehors des méthodes philosophiques, les rapports intimes et secrets des choses, les correspondances et les analogies." *Nouvelles histoires extraordinaires*, ed. Jacques Crépet (Paris: Louis Conard, 1933), p. xv. In spite of all the stress Baudelaire placed on death and darkness and despair, he too recognized that a higher level of meaning (of clarity through obscurity, *entendement* as Scève often calls it) could be achieved in the diaphoric progression from black to white, from dark to light, from innate, worldly obscurity to an artfully, spiritually translated clarity. This meaning is always a purely creative function of the poet's "soul" or imagination. This is a constant theme and challenge in Baudelaire's poetry, as it is in Scève's.

4 Quoted and discussed in Wallace Fowlie, *Mallarmé* (Chicago: University of Chicago Press, 1962), p. 228.

5 For the same critical development and problem of "literalism" in the Bible and its interpretation, see the very convincing argument made by Janet Martin Soskice, to whom I am indebted for helping me see this problem in Scève and his criticism: *Metaphor and Religious Language* (New York: Oxford University Press, 1985).

6 See Iser's "The Reading Process: A Phenomenological Approach," in *Reader-Response Criticism: From Formalism to Post-Structuralism*, ed. Jane P. Tompkins (Baltimore: Johns Hopkins University Press, 1983), pp. 50–69; and Ingarden's monumental *The Literary Work of Art* (Evanston, IL: Northwestern University Press, 1973).

7 For a good (and different) discussion of the theory and practice of "transcendental phenomenology" in Mallarmé, see Neal Oxenhandler, "The Quest for Pure Consciousness in Husserl and Mallarmé," in *The Quest for Imagination: Essays in Twentieth-Century Criticism*, ed. O. B. Hardison (Cleveland: The Press of Case Western Reserve University, 1971), pp. 149–66. This phenomenological quest in Scève is, finally, what

makes this poet "modern" and so exciting. As we have seen so often in this study of his love aesthetics, it is not only possible but necessary to go beyond the subject of unrequited love and read in the poems of the *Délie* the notion and meaning of transcendent art.

BIBLIOGRAPHY

Ardouin, Paul. *Maurice Scève, prince des lumières, virtuose du regard, fils de l'aurore.* Paris: Expansion, 1976.

Maurice Scève, Pernette Du Guillet, Louise Labé: l'Amour à Lyon au temps de la Renaissance. Paris: Nizet, 1981.

Armstrong, Paul B. "The Conflict of Interpretations and the Limits of Pluralism," *PMLA*, 98 (1983), 341–52.

Artaud, Antonin. "Van Gogh, The Suicide Provoked by Society," *Horizon: A Review of Literature and Art*, 17, No. 97 (1948), 48–49.

Attal, Jean-Pierre. *L'Image métaphysique.* Paris: Gallimard, 1969.

Baker, Deborah Lesko. *Narcissus and the Lover: Mythic Recovery and Reinvention in Scève's Délie*, Stanford French and Italian Studies 46. Saratoga, CA: Anma Libri & Co., 1986.

Barclay, Alexander. *Stultifera navis.* London: John Cawood, 1570.

Barthes, Roland. *Le Plaisir du texte.* Paris: Seuil, 1973.

Fragments d'un discours amoureux. Paris: Seuil, 1977.

Bellenger, Yvonne. *La Pléiade: La Poésie en France autour de Ronsard.* Paris: Nizet, 1988.

Bodkin, Maud. *Archetypal Patterns in Poetry.* London: Oxford University Press, 1951.

Bowie, Malcolm. *Mallarmé and the Art of Being Difficult.* Cambridge: Cambridge University Press, 1978.

Broda, Martine. "Amour platonique," in *Lire Maurice Scève*, ed. Françoise Charpentier and Simone Perrier, pp. 107–13.

Brown, Frank B. *Transfiguration: Poetic Metaphor and the Languages of Religious Belief.* Chapel Hill: University of North Carolina Press, 1983.

Brown, Marshall. " 'Errours Endless Traine': On Turning Points and the Dialectical Imagination," *PMLA*, 99 (1984), 9–25.

Brunetière, Ferdinand. "Les Editions originales," *Revue des Deux Mondes*, 1 March 1888, 216–20.

Buckley, Vincent. *Poetry and the Sacred.* London: Chatto & Windus, 1968.

Buermeyer, Laurence. *The Aesthetic Experience.* Merion, PA: The Barnes Foundation Press, 1975.

Buhlman, Joan A. "Philosophical Alchemy as a Mode of Transformation in Scève's *Délie*," *Romance Notes*, 23 (1982), 44–52.

"The Three Graces: Cosmic Harmony in Scève's *Délie*," *Bibliothèque d'Humanisme et Renaissance*, 44 (1982), 53–63.

Caldarini, Ernesta, ed. Joachim Du Bellay, *L'Olive*. Geneva: Droz, 1974.

Cave, Terence. *The Cornucopian Text: Problems of Writing in the French Renaissance*. Oxford: Oxford University Press, 1979.

"Correcting Petrarch's Errors," in *Pre-Pléiade Poetry*, ed. Jerry C. Nash, pp. 112–24.

Céard, Jean. "Le Temps et la mémoire dans *Délie*," *Europe*, Nos. 691–92 (1986), 104–16.

"Sens, cœur, raison, mémoire dans *Délie*: la psychologie de Scève," in *Lire Maurice Scève*, ed. Françoise Charpentier and Simone Perrier, pp. 15–25.

Charpentier, Françoise. " '. . . En moi tu luis la nuit obscure'," *Europe*, Nos. 691–92 (1986), 83–94.

"De *Délie* à *Microcosme*," in *Lire Maurice Scève*, ed. Françoise Charpentier and Simone Perrier, *Textuel*, No. 3 (1987), pp. 35–42.

ed. *Dix études sur la Délie de Maurice Scève*. Paris: Collection de l'ENSJF, 1987.

Chisholm, A. R. "Mallarmé 'Victorieusement fui le suicide beau . . .'," *French Studies*, 14 (1960), 153–56.

Chomsky, Noam. *Language and Mind*. New York: Harcourt Brace, 1968.

Cirlot, J. E. *A Dictionary of Symbols*. New York: Philosophical Library, Inc., 1962.

Clarac, Pierre and André Ferré, eds. Marcel Proust, *A la recherche du temps perdu*. Paris: Gallimard, 1954.

Clements, Robert J. *Picta Poesis: Literary and Humanistic Theory in Renaissance Emblem Books*. Rome: Edizioni di Storia e Letteratura, 1960.

Cohen, Jean. *Structure du langage poétique*. Paris: Flammarion, 1966.

Coleman, Dorothy Gabe. "Images in Scève's *Délie*," *Modern Language Review*, 59 (1964), 375–86.

Maurice Scève, Poet of Love: Tradition and Originality. Cambridge: Cambridge University Press, 1975.

"Word-Play and Verbal Delight in Scève's *Délie*," *French Studies*, 30 (1976), 257–63.

An Illustrated Love 'Canzoniere': The Délie of Maurice Scève. Geneva: Slatkine, 1981.

"The Poetic Sensibility of Scève," in *Pre-Pléiade Poetry*, ed. Jerry C. Nash, pp. 125–35.

"Lire Scève et entendre Scève," in *Lire Maurice Scève*, ed. Françoise Charpentier and Simone Perrier, pp. 9–14.

Colie, Rosalie L. *Paradoxia Epidemica: The Renaissance Tradition of Paradox*. Princeton: Princeton University Press, 1966.

Conard, Louis, ed. Gustave Flaubert, *Correspondance*. Paris: Louis Conard, 1926.

Cornilliat, François. "Le Discours et les signes," *Europe*, Nos. 691–92 (1986), 116–24.

Cotgrave, Randle. *A Dictionarie of the French and English Tongues*. London: Whitaker, 1611.

Cottrell, Robert D. *"Graphie, phonè*, and the Desiring Subject in Scève's *Délie," L'Esprit Créateur*, 25 (1985), 3–13.

The Grammar of Silence: A Reading of Marguerite de Navarre's Poetry. Washington: Catholic University of America Press, 1986.

Craig, Hardin, ed. *The Complete Works of Shakespeare*. Chicago: Scott, Foresman and Company, 1961.

Crépet, Jacques, ed. Charles Baudelaire, *Nouvelles histoires extraordinaires*. Paris: Louis Conard, 1933.

Crépet, Jacques and Georges Blin, ed. Charles Baudelaire, *Journaux intimes*. Paris: José Corti, 1949.

Cropper, Elizabeth. "The Beauty of Woman: Problems in the Rhetoric of Renaissance Portraiture," in *Rewriting the Renaissance: The Discourses of Sexual Difference in Early Modern Europe*, ed. Margaret W. Ferguson, Maureen Quilligan, and Nancy J. Vickers. Chicago: University of Chicago Press, 1986, pp. 175–90.

Dauvois, Nathalie. "Invention/ réinvention," in *Lire Maurice Scève*, ed. Françoise Charpentier and Simone Perrier, pp. 85–92.

Defaux, Gérard. *Marot, Rabelais, Montaigne: l'écriture comme présence*. Paris/Geneva: Champion/Slatkine, 1987.

Delfel, Guy. *L'Esthétique de Stéphane Mallarmé*. Paris: Flammarion, 1951.

DellaNeva, JoAnn. *Song and Counter-Song: Scève's Délie and Petrarch's Rime*. Lexington, KY: French Forum, Publishers, 1983.

De Man, Paul. "Lyric and Modernity," in *Forms of Lyric*, ed. Reuben A. Brower. New York: Columbia University Press, 1970, pp. 151–76.

de Mourgues, Odette. *Metaphysical, Baroque and Précieux Poetry*. Oxford: Clarendon Press, 1953.

de Rocher, Gregory. "The Curing Text: Maurice Scève's Délie as the *Délie," The Romanic Review*, 78 (1987), 10–24.

Derrida, Jacques. *Marges de la philosophie*. Paris: Minuit, 1972.

d'Hermies, René, ed. Boileau, *L'Art Poétique*. Paris: Librairie Larousse, n.d.

Donaldson-Evans, Lance K. *Love's Fatal Glance: A Study of Eye Imagery in the Poets of the Ecole lyonnaise*. University, MS: Romance Monographs, Inc., 1980.

Drake-Brockman, Jane M. "Scève, the Snake and the Herb," *French Studies*, 33 (1979), 129–36.

Dubois, Claude-Gilbert. *L'Imaginaire de la Renaissance*. Paris: Presses Universitaires de France, 1985.

Duval, Edwin M. " 'Comme Hécate': Mythography and the Macrocosm in an Epigram by Maurice Scève," *Bibliothèque d'Humanisme et Renaissance*, 41 (1979), 7–22.

"Articulation of the *Délie*: Emblems, Numbers, and the Book," *Modern Language Review*, 75 (1980), 65–75.

Edwards, Michael. *Towards A Christian Poetics*. Grand Rapids, MI: William B. Eerdmans Publishing Company, 1984.

Eliade, Mircea. *Images et symboles*. Paris: Gallimard, 1952.

Traité d'histoire des religions. Paris: Payot, 1953.

Eliot, T. S. *The Use of Poetry and the Use of Criticism*. Cambridge: Harvard University Press, 1933.

Fenoaltea, Doranne. "The Polyphonic Quality of Scève's *Délie*," *Symposium*, 29 (1975), 330–44.

"The Final Dizains of Scève's *Délie* and the *Dialogo d'Amore* of Sperone Speroni," *Studi Francesi*, 59 (1976), 201–25.

"Obscurité et clarté – à la recherche de la *Délie* de Maurice Scève," *Œuvres et Critiques*, 5 (1980), 25–40.

'Si haulte Architecture': The Design of Scève's Délie*. Lexington, KY: French Forum, Publishers, 1982.

"La Selve obscure: la signalisation du texte et la démarche du lecteur," in *Lire Maurice Scève*, ed. Françoise Charpentier and Simone Perrier, pp. 69–76.

"Scève's *Délie* and Marot: A Study of Intertextualities," in *Pre-Pléiade Poetry*, ed. Jerry C. Nash, pp. 136–53.

Festugière, Jean. *La Philosophie de l'Amour de Marcile Ficin*. Paris: Vrin, 1941.

Fingarette, Herbert. *The Self in Transformation: Psychoanalysis, Philosophy and the Life of the Spirit*. New York: Harper & Row, 1965.

Fletcher, Jefferson B. *The Religion of Beauty in Woman*. New York: Haskell House, 1966.

Forster, Leonard. *The Icy Fire: Five Studies in European Petrarchism*. Cambridge: Cambridge University Press, 1969.

Fowlie, Wallace. *Love in Literature: Studies in Symbolic Expression*. Bloomington: Indiana University Press, 1965.

Mallarmé. Chicago: University of Chicago Press, 1962.

Frappier, Jean, ed. Jean Lemaire de Belges, *La Concorde des deux langages*. Paris: Droz, 1947.

"Variations sur le thème du miroir de Bernard de Ventadour à Maurice Scève," *Cahiers de l'Association Internationale des Etudes Françaises*, 2 (1959), 134–59.

Garelli, Jacques. "La Vision préréfléchie de 'l'Etre au monde' et le problème de la transcendance." In *La Gravitation poétique*. Paris: Mercure de France, 1966, 21–31.

Bibliography

Giarda, Christophorus. *Icones symbolicae*. Milan: I. B. Bidellinin, 1628.

Giordano, Michael. "Reading *Délie*: Dialectic and Sequence," *Symposium*, 34 (1980), 155–67.

Giudici, Enzo. *Maurice Scève poeta della Délie*. Vol. I: Rome, Ateneo, 1965. Vol. II: Naples, Liguori, 1969.

ed. Maurice Scève, *Microcosme*. Paris: Vrin, 1976.

"In margine ad alcune recenti publicazioni riguardanti Maurice Scève e Louise Labé," *Quaderni di Filologia e Lingue Romanze*, 4 (1982), 39–67.

Glauser, Alfred. *Le Poème-symbole de Scève à Valéry*. Paris: Vrin, 1967.

Greene, Thomas M. "Styles of Experience in Scève's *Délie*," *Yale French Studies*, 47 (1972), 57–75.

The Light in Troy: Imitation and Discovery in Renaissance Poetry. New Haven: Yale University Press, 1982.

Guéroult, Guillaume. *Le Premier Livre des emblesmes*. Lyon: Jean de Tournes, 1550.

Hallett, Ronald A. "Three Analytical Dizains in Scève's *Délie*," *Romance Notes*, 18 (1977), 237–42.

Hallyn, Fernand. "Maurice Scève, poète scientifique," in *Lire Maurice Scève*, ed. Françoise Charpentier and Simone Perrier, pp. 43–50.

Harries, Karsten. "Metaphor and Transcendence," in *On Metaphor*, ed. Sheldon Sacks. Chicago: University of Chicago Press, 1979, pp. 71–88.

Harrower, Molly. *The Therapy of Poetry*. Springfield, IL: Charles C. Thomas, Publisher, 1972.

Hawkins, Peter S. and Schotter, Anne Howland, ed. *Ineffability: Naming the Unnamable from Dante to Beckett*. New York: AMS Press, 1984.

Hertz, Neil. "The Notion of Blockage in the Literature of the Sublime," in *Psychoanalysis and the Question of the Text*, ed. Geoffrey H. Hartman. Baltimore: Johns Hopkins University Press, 1978, pp. 62–85.

Houston, John Porter. *French Symbolism and the Modernist Movement*. Baton Rouge: Louisiana State University Press, 1980.

Hytier, Jean, ed. Paul Valéry, *Œuvres*. Paris: Gallimard, 1957.

Ingarden, Roman. *The Literary Work of Art*. Evanston, IL: Northwestern University Press, 1973.

Iser, Wolfgang. "The Reading Process: A Phenomenological Approach," in *Reader-Response Criticism*, ed. Jane P. Tompkins. Baltimore: Johns Hopkins University Press, 1983, pp. 50–69.

Jauss, Hans Robert. *Aesthetic Experience and Literary Hermeneutics*, trans. Michael Shaw. Minneapolis: University of Minnesota Press, 1982.

Jennings, Elizabeth. *Every Changing Shape*. London: André Deutsch, 1961.

Jolliffe, J. and Screech, M. A., eds. Joachim Du Bellay, *Les Regrets*. Geneva: Droz, 1966.

Jones, Ann Rosalind and von Ohlen, H. Bruce. " 'Si doulx, & attrayant subiect': Scève's *Délie* and Four Modern Critics," *The Romanic Review*, 68 (1977), 85–102.

Kawin, Bruce F. *The Mind of the Novel: Reflexive Fiction and the Ineffable*. Princeton: Princeton University Press, 1982.

Kermode, Frank. *Forms of Attention*. Chicago: University of Chicago Press, 1985.

Keynes, Geoffrey, ed. William Blake, *Complete Writings*. London: Oxford University Press, 1969.

Knight, G. Wilson. *The Christian Renaissance*. New York: W. W. Norton, 1963.

Kristeva, Julia. *Histoires d'amours*. Paris: Denoël, 1983.

La Charité, Raymond C., ed. *From Marot to Montaigne: Essays on French Renaissance Literature*. Kentucky Romance Quarterly, 19, Supplement No. 1, 1972.

"Rabelais: The Book as Therapy," in *Medicine and Literature*, ed. Enid Rhodes Peschel. New York: Neale Watson Academic Publications, Inc., 1980, pp. 11–17.

ed. *Rabelais's Incomparable Book: Essays on His Art*. Lexington, KY: French Forum, Publishers, 1986.

La Charité, Virginia A. *The Dynamics of Space: Mallarmé's Un Coup de dés jamais n'abolira le hasard*. Lexington, KY: French Forum, Publishers, 1987.

Lacy, Norris J. and Nash, Jerry C., ed. *Essays in Early French Literature Presented to Barbara M. Craig*. York, SC: French Literature Publications Company, 1982.

Lamb, W. R. M., ed. *Plato*. Cambridge: Harvard University Press, 1961.

Lanson, Gustave. *Histoire de la littérature française*. Paris: Hachette, 1894.

Le Dantec, Yves and Pichois, Claude, ed. Charles Baudelaire, *Œuvres complètes*. Paris: Gallimard, 1961.

Leedy, Jack J., ed. *Poetry Therapy: The Use of Poetry in the Treatment of Emotional Disorders*. Philadelphia: J. B. Lippincott Company, 1969.

Lemaître, Henri, ed. Gérard de Nerval, *Œuvres*. Paris: Garnier, 1958.

Lotman, Yury. *Analysis of the Poetic Text*. Ann Arbor: Aridis, 1976.

Maritain, Jacques. *Art et scolastique*. Paris: Louise Rouart et Fils, 1927.

Mathieu-Castellani, Gisèle. "Emblèmes de la mort," *Europe*, Nos. 691–92 (1986), 125–35.

"Poésie et spécularité: la représentation de l'écriture dans les *Amours* de Ronsard," *Revue d'Histoire Littéraire de la France*, 4 (1986), 659–66.

"Scève syntaxier," in *Lire Maurice Scève*, ed. Françoise Charpentier and Simone Perrier, pp. 93–106.

McCabe, Herbert, ed. and trans. Thomas Aquinas, *Summa theologica*. London: Blackfriars, 1964.

Bibliography

McFarlane, I. D. "Notes on Maurice Scève's *Délie*," *French Studies*, 13 (1959), 99–112.

——— ed. *The Délie of Maurice Scève*. Cambridge: Cambridge University Press, 1966.

——— *Renaissance France 1470–1589*. London: Ernest Benn Limited, 1974.

Meerhoff, Kees. *Rhétorique et poétique au XVIe siècle en France: Du Bellay, Ramus et les autres*. Leiden: E. J. Brill, 1986.

Merrill, Robert V. and Clements, Robert J. *Platonism in French Renaissance Poetry*. New York: New York University Press, 1957.

Meschonnic, Henri. "Scève dans la modernité," in *Lire Maurice Scève*, ed. Françoise Charpentier and Simone Perrier, pp. 135–46.

Michel, Alain. *La Parole et la beauté*. Paris: Les Belles Lettres, 1982.

Minta, Stephen. *Love Poetry in Sixteenth-Century France*. Manchester: Manchester University Press, 1977.

Mondor, Henri and Jean-Aubry, G., ed. Stéphane Mallarmé, *Œuvres complètes*. Paris: Gallimard, 1945.

Moss, Ann. *Poetry and Fable: Studies in Mythological Narrative in Sixteenth-Century France*. Cambridge: Cambridge University Press, 1984.

Mouchard, Claude. "Liens," in *Lire Maurice Scève*, ed. Françoise Charpentier and Simone Perrier, pp. 115–21.

Mulhauser, Ruth. "The Poetic Function of the Emblems in the *Délie*," *L'Esprit Créateur*, 5 (1965), 80–89.

——— *Maurice Scève*. Boston: Twayne, 1977.

Nash, Jerry C. *Maurice Scève: Concordance de la Délie*. Chapel Hill: North Carolina Studies in the Romance Languages and Literatures, 1976, 2 vols.

——— "Stoicism and the Stoic Theme of *Honestum* in Early French Renaissance Literature," *Studies in Philology*, 76 (1979), 203–17.

——— "Louise Labé and Learned Levity," *Romance Notes*, 21 (1980), 227–33.

——— "The Notion and Meaning of Art in the *Délie*," *The Romanic Review*, 71 (1980), 28–46.

——— "The Devotional Aesthetics of a Humanist: Nicolas Denisot's *Cantiques*," in *Essays in Early French Literature Presented to Barbara M. Craig*, ed. Norris J. Lacy and Jerry C. Nash, pp. 129–46.

——— "Logic and Lyric: Poetic Closure in Scève's *Délie*," *French Studies*, 38 (1984), 385–98.

——— ed. *Pre-Pléiade Poetry*. Lexington, KY: French Forum, Publishers, 1985.

——— "Maurice Scève, poète de l'ineffable," in *Lire Maurice Scève*, ed. Françoise Charpentier and Simone Perrier, pp. 51–59.

——— "Maurice Scève et la poésie paradisiaque," in *Il Rinascimento a Lione*, ed. Giulia Mastrangelo Latini and Antonio Possenti. Rome: Edizioni dell'Ateneo, 1988, pp. 779–94.

——— "La Conquête humaniste de la Fortune dans la *Délie* de Maurice Scève," in *Il Tema della Fortuna nella letteratura francese e italiana del Rinascimento*, ed. Enea Balmas. Florence: Leo S. Olschki Editore,1990, forthcoming.

Ong, Walter. "System, Space, and Intellect in Renaissance Symbolism," *Bibliothèque d'Humanisme et Renaissance*, 17 (1956), 231–57.

Ormerod, Beverly. "Délie and the Hare," *French Studies*, 30 (1976), 385–92.

"Scève's *Délie* and the Mythographers' Diana," *French Studies*, 33 (1979), 86–93.

Ortali, Ray. "Ronsard: de la femme à l'Idée," in *From Marot to Montaigne: Essays on French Renaissance Literature*, ed. Raymond C. La Charité, *Kentucky Romance Quarterly*, 19, Supplement No. 1 (1972), 99–107.

Osgood, Charles G., trans. Boccaccio, *Genealogia deorum gentilium*. New York: The Liberal Arts Press, 1956.

Oxenhandler, Neal. "The Quest for Pure Consciousness in Husserl and Mallarmé," in *The Quest for Imagination*, ed. O. B. Hardison. Cleveland: The Press of Case Western Reserve University, 1971, pp. 149–66.

Pasquier, Estienne. *Recherches de la France*. Paris: Louys Billaine, 1665.

Peignot, Jérôme. *Les Jeux de l'amour et du langage*. Paris: Union Générale d'Editions, 1974.

Perrier, Simone. "Inscription et écriture dans *Délie*," *Europe*, Nos. 691–92 (1986), 139–50.

"A la recherche d'un corps imaginaire," in *Lire Maurice Scève*, ed. Françoise Charpentier and Simone Perrier, pp. 27–33.

Perry, T. Anthony. *Erotic Spirituality: The Integrative Tradition from Leone Ebreo to John Donne*. University, AL: University of Alabama Press, 1980.

Pivato, Joseph. "Maurice Scève's *Délie*: Unpetrarchan and Hermetic," *Studi Francesi*, 27 (1983), 14–28.

Polivanov, Evguéni. "Le Principe phonétique commun à toute technique poétique," *Change*, 6 (1970), 32–50.

Preminger, Alex, ed. *Princeton Encyclopedia of Poetry and Poetics*. Princeton: Princeton University Press, 1974.

Press, John. *The Chequer'd Shade: Reflections on Obscurity in Poetry*. Oxford: Oxford University Press, 1958.

The Fire and the Fountain. London: Methuen, 1966.

Quignard, Pascal. *La Parole de la Délie*. Paris: Mercure de France, 1974.

Rabaté, Jean-Michel. *La Beauté amère: Fragments d'esthétiques*. Seyssel: Editions du Champs Vallon, 1986.

Ramat, Raffaello, ed. Petrarch, *Rime e Trionfi*. Milan: Rizzoli Editore, 1957.

Raybaud, Antoine. "L'Argument poétique (Scève: l'exemple de *Délie*)," in *Lire Maurice Scève*, ed. Françoise Charpentier and Simone Perrier, pp. 127–34.

Read, Herbert. "Obscurity in Poetry," in *In Defense of Shelley and Other Essays*. London: Heinemann, 1936, 147–63.

Regan, Mariann Sanders. *Love Words: The Self and the Text in Medieval and Renaissance Poetry*. Ithaca: Cornell University Press, 1982.

Ricardou, Jean. "La Querelle de la métaphore," *Tel Quel*, 18 (1964), 56–68.

Ricœur, Paul. *The Rule of Metaphor*. Toronto: University of Toronto Press, 1977.

Rieu, Josiane. "La 'Beauté qui tue' dans les *Amours* de Ronsard," *Revue d'Histoire Littéraire de la France*, 4 (1986), 693–708.

Rigolot, François. "Pétrarquisme et onomastique: la signification poétique du nom dans la *Délie* de Maurice Scève," *Studi di Letteratura Francese*, 4 (1975), 85–105.

Poétique et onomastique: l'exemple de la Renaissance. Geneva: Droz, 1977.

"L'Intertexte du dizain scévien: Pétrarque et Marot," *Cahiers de l'Association Internationale des Etudes Françaises*, 32 (1980), 91–106.

"Prosodie et sémantique: une hypothèse sur le sens des dizains atypiques de la *Délie* de Maurice Scève," in *The Equilibrium of Wit: Essays for Odette de Mourgues*. Eds. Peter Bayley and Dorothy Gabe Coleman. Lexington, KY: French Forum, Publishers, 1982, pp. 28–40.

Le Texte de la Renaissance. Geneva: Droz, 1982.

Risset, Jacqueline. *L'Anagramme du désir: Essai sur la Délie de Maurice Scève*. Rome: Bulzoni, 1972.

Runyon, Randolph. "Scève's 'Aultre Troye': Placement and Other Tie(r)s in *Délie*," *Modern Language Notes*, 90 (1975), 535–47.

Sapegno, Natalino, ed. Dante, *La Divina Commedia*. Florence: La Nuova Italia Editrice, 1970.

Saulnier, V.-L. "Maurice Scève et la clarté," *Bulletin de l'Association Guillaume Budé*, 5 (1948), 96–105.

Maurice Scève. Paris: Klincksieck, 1948.

Schwartz, Delmore. "The Isolation of Modern Poetry," *Kenyon Review*, 3 (1941), 209–20.

Seznec, Jean. *La Survivance des dieux antiques*. Paris: Flammarion, 1980.

Singer, Irving. *The Nature of Love*. Chicago: University of Chicago Press, 1984.

Smith, A. J. *The Metaphysics of Love: Studies in Renaissance Love Poetry from Dante to Milton*. Cambridge: Cambridge University Press, 1985.

Soskice, Janet Martin. *Metaphor and Religious Language*. New York: Oxford University Press, 1985.

Sozzi, Lionello. "La 'dignitas hominis' dans la littérature française de la Renaissance," in *Humanism in France*, ed. A. H. T. Levi. Manchester: Manchester University Press, 1970, pp. 176–98.

Bibliography

Spitzer, Leo. "The Poetic Treatment of a Platonic-Christian Theme," *Comparative Literature*, 6 (1954), 193–217.

Essays on English and American Literature. Princeton: Princeton University Press, 1962.

Starobinski, Jean. "L'Encre de la mélancolie," *La Nouvelle Revue Française*, 123 (1963), 410–23.

Staub, Hans. *Le Curieux Désir: Scève et Peletier du Mans poètes de la connaissance*. Geneva: Droz, 1967.

"Le Thème de la lumière chez Maurice Scève," *Cahiers de l'Association Internationale des Etudes Françaises*, 20 (1968), 125–36.

Staudt, Kathleen Henderson. "The Poetics of 'Black on White': Stéphane Mallarmé's *Un Coup de dés*," in *Ineffability*, ed. Peter S. Hawkins and Anne Howland Schotter, pp. 147–61.

Stone, Donald, Jr. "*Délie* 393," *Romance Notes*, 9 (1968), 1–4.

"Scève's Emblems," *The Romanic Review*, 60 (1969), 96–103.

Tetel, Marcel. "Renaissance Aborted and Renascences: Scève's *Délie*," in *Medieval and Renaissance Studies* (Proceedings of the Southeastern Institute of Medieval and Renaissance Studies, Summer 1976). Durham: Duke University Press, 1979, pp. 100–18.

Lectures scéviennes. L'Emblème et les mots. Paris: Klincksieck, 1983.

"*Délie*: du dire entre parenthèses," in *Mélanges sur la littérature de la Renaissance à la mémoire de V.-L. Saulnier*. Geneva: Droz, 1984, pp. 707–17.

"Poétique du dé-," in *Lire Maurice Scève*, ed. Françoise Charpentier and Simone Perrier, pp. 61–68.

The Holy Bible (Revised Standard Version). Cleveland: Meridian Books, 1962.

Thibaudet, Albert. *La Poésie de Stéphane Mallarmé*. Paris: Gallimard, 1926.

Thompson, John. "*La Structure linguistique et le vers*," *Change*, 6 (1970), 22–31.

Tompkins, Jane P., ed. *Reader-Response Criticism*. Baltimore: Johns Hopkins University Press, 1980.

Tournon, André. "Altérations," in *Lire Maurice Scève*, ed. Françoise Charpentier and Simone Perrier, pp. 77–83.

Turnbull, Grace H., ed. *The Essence of Plotinus*. New York: Oxford University Press, 1934.

Vargaftig, Bernard. "L'Image de la chose," in *Lire Maurice Scève*, ed. Françoise Charpentier and Simone Perrier, pp. 123–25.

Watts, William, ed. *Saint Augustine's Confessions*. Cambridge: Harvard University Press, 1961.

Weber, Henri. *La Création poétique au XVIe siècle en France*. Paris: Nizet, 1955.

Wheelwright, Philip. *Metaphor and Reality*. Bloomington: Indiana University Press, 1962.

The Burning Fountain: A Study in the Language of Symbolism. Bloomington: Indiana University Press, 1968.

Bibliography

"Catharsis," "Myth," "Philosophy and Poetry," "Religion and Poetry," "Semantics and Poetry," in *Princeton Encyclopedia of Poetry and Poetics*, ed. Alex Preminger.

Williams, Thomas A. *Mallarmé and the Language of Mysticism*. Athens: University of Georgia Press, 1970.

Wilson, Dudley. "Remarks on Maurice Scève's *Délie*," *Durham University Journal*, 60 (1967–68), 7–12.

Wimsatt, W. K., Jr. "Poetic Tension: A Summary," *New Scholasticism*, 32 (1958), 73–88.

INDEX

Cambridge Studies in French

General editor: MALCOLM BOWIE

Also in the series